P9-ARZ-786

# Great Medical Discoveries

**Other books in the Turning Points series:**

Turning|Points

IN WORLD HISTORY

# Great Medical Discoveries

C.J. Shane, *Book Editor*

Daniel Leone, *President*
Bonnie Szumski, *Publisher*
Scott Barbour, *Managing Editor*

GREENHAVEN
PRESS ®

THOMSON

™

GALE

San Diego • Detroit • New York • San Francisco • Cleveland
New Haven, Conn. • Waterville, Maine • London • Munich

THOMSON

GALE

Cover credit: © J.L. Charmet/Photo Researchers, Inc.
This pencil drawing by Mucha depicts Louis Pasteur (1822–1895) conducting an immunology
experiment in his laboratory. Pasteur made an important contribution to the understanding
of immune response and infection both in man and in animals. This drawing is now in the
Institute Pasteur, Paris.

Library of Congress, 146, 197
National Library of Medicine, 102, 182

| LIBRARY OF CONGRESS CATALOGING-IN-PUBLICATION DATA |
| --- |
| Great medical discoveries / C.J. Shane, book editor. |
| p. cm. — (Turning points in world history) |
| Includes bibliographical references and index. |
| ISBN 0-7377-1438-7 (pbk. : alk. paper) — ISBN 0-7377-1437-9 (lib. : alk. paper) |
| · 1. Medicine—History 2. Medical research—History. I. Shane, C.J. II. Series. |
| R130.5.G743 2004 |
| 610'.9—dc21                                                    2003054005 |

20.96

# Contents

"animalcules" he sees when he looks through a microscope at drops of rainwater. He carefully describes the forms and behaviors of the creatures and, in so doing, provides the first descriptions of bacteria.

## Chapter 3: Medical Procedures

America to be the first credited with using anesthesia to relieve pain in surgery. Physician Crawford Long administers ether to patients, and William Morton publicly demonstrates the technique.

## Chapter 4: Pharmaceuticals

# Chapter 5: Medical Tools

# Chapter 6: The Social Impact of Great Medical Discoveries

plied. Humankind must be vigilant to make sure that genetic information is not used to limit human potential.

# Foreword

Certain past events stand out as pivotal, as having effects and outcomes that change the course of history. These events are often referred to as turning points. Historian Louis L. Snyder provides this useful definition:

> A turning point in history is an event, happening, or stage which thrusts the course of historical development into a different direction. By definition a turning point is a great event, but it is even more—a great event with the explosive impact of altering the trend of man's life on the planet.

History's turning points have taken many forms. Some were single, brief, and shattering events with immediate and obvious impact. The invasion of Britain by William the Conqueror in 1066, for example, swiftly transformed that land's political and social institutions and paved the way for the rise of the modern English nation. By contrast, other single events were deemed of minor significance when they occurred, only later recognized as turning points. The assassination of a little-known European nobleman, Archduke Franz Ferdinand, on June 28, 1914, in the Bosnian town of Sarajevo was such an event; only after it touched off a chain reaction of political-military crises that escalated into the global conflict known as World War I did the murder's true significance become evident.

Other crucial turning points occurred not in terms of a few hours, days, months, or even years, but instead as evolutionary developments spanning decades or even centuries. One of the most pivotal turning points in human history, for instance—the development of agriculture, which replaced nomadic hunter-gatherer societies with more permanent settlements—occurred over the course of many generations. Still other great turning points were neither events nor developments, but rather revolutionary new inventions and innovations that significantly altered social customs and ideas, military tactics, home life, the spread of knowledge, and the human condition in general. The developments of writing, gunpowder, the printing press, antibiotics, the electric light, atomic energy, television, and the computer, the last two of which have recently ushered in the world-altering information age, represent only some of these innovative turning points.

Each anthology in the Greenhaven Turning Points in World History series presents a group of essays chosen for their accessibility. The anthology's structure also enhances this accessibility. First, an introductory essay provides a general overview of the principal events and figures involved, placing the topic in its historical context. The essays that follow explore various aspects in more detail, some targeting political trends and consequences, others social, literary, cultural, and/or technological ramifications, and still others pivotal leaders and other influential figures. To aid the reader in choosing the material of immediate interest or need, each essay is introduced by a concise summary of the contributing writer's main themes and insights.

In addition, each volume contains extensive research tools, including a collection of excerpts from primary source documents pertaining to the historical events and figures under discussion. In the anthology on the French Revolution, for example, readers can examine the works of Rousseau, Voltaire, and other writers and thinkers whose championing of human rights helped fuel the French people's growing desire for liberty; the French *Declaration of the Rights of Man and Citizen*, presented to King Louis XVI by the French National Assembly on October 2, 1789; and eyewitness accounts of the attack on the royal palace and the horrors of the Reign of Terror. To guide students interested in pursuing further research on the subject, each volume features an extensive bibliography, which for easy access has been divided into separate sections by topic. Finally, a comprehensive index allows readers to scan and locate content efficiently. Each of the anthologies in the Greenhaven Turning Points in World History series provides students with a complete, detailed, and enlightening examination of a crucial historical watershed.

# Introduction

People have always sought relief from the suffering of disease and injury. The search for an end to illness and pain has led to many medical discoveries over the centuries. These discoveries have grown into a body of knowledge about human health and illness that scientists draw from when they attempt to solve a health problem or cure a disease. Sometimes a discovery is so important that it becomes a turning point in scientific thought and contributes greatly to human health.

Medical discoveries can be categorized into three general types: problem-solving discoveries, accidental discoveries, and discoveries made while engaged in pure research. This last category is often called "descriptive" or "discovery" science.

## Problem-Solving Discoveries

Finding cures for diseases has always been important. In the nineteenth century, solving medical problems was urgent because much of Europe's expanding population was packed into filthy industrial cities where infectious pathogens thrived. In these crowded and polluted cities, people became even more vulnerable to epidemics of typhoid, cholera, diphtheria, influenza, and other diseases. A second threat to human health during this period was the increase in international commerce that aided the transmission of pathogens from one continent to another. Cholera, for example, traveled by trading ships from Asia to Europe several times during the nineteenth century.

One approach to solving such medical problems is problem-solving science, which uses scientific experimentation and systematic observation. Two important persons stand out as practitioners of problem-solving science during the nineteenth century. Louis Pasteur (1822–1895) and Robert Koch (1843–1910) were contemporaries and bitter rivals. Both made major medical discoveries in the realm of problem-solving science that became turning points in medical history. Pasteur and Koch are the two scientists most responsible for developing the germ theory of disease, which states that specific microorganisms cause specific diseases. Identifying the pathogen responsible for a disease meant that one could then research ways to eradicate the pathogen. Both Pasteur and Koch identified several disease-causing microorganisms.

Pasteur's and Koch's work with microorganisms was based upon earlier studies made by an amateur Dutch scientist, Antoni van Leeuwenhoek (1632–1723). Although the existence of microorganisms had been known since the fifteenth century, Leeuwenhoek added considerably to the body of knowledge about these microscopic creatures. He built his own microscopes and made systematic observations and descriptions of the microorganisms that he found in rainwater. Leeuwenhoek was the first to describe the classes of bacteria that Pasteur and Koch would later link to specific diseases.

Until Pasteur's and Koch's work became known during the second half of the nineteenth century, the view that disease was caused by miasmas (vapors) and chemical poisons prevailed among scientists. Even though Lazzaro Spallanzani (1729–1799) in 1765 and Theodor Schwann (1810–1882) in 1839 demonstrated in laboratory experiments that microorganisms could not arise spontaneously from nothing, scientists adhered to the idea of spontaneous generation.

## Louis Pasteur's Contributions

French chemist Pasteur was the first to show that microorganisms do not arise spontaneously from nothing, as so many scientists believed. In 1861 Pasteur designed an ingenious and simple experiment involving cleverly designed glass tubes to prove that microorganisms cannot arise spontaneously. It followed from his experiments that the organisms already exist in the air and on surfaces.

Although there was increasing evidence for the accuracy of the germ theory of disease, many physicians of the time were not yet convinced. Despite their skepticism, Pasteur continued to use his problem-solving approach to finding the pathogens responsible for several diseases. Among his discoveries was the microorganism that caused puerperal fever, also called childbed fever. However, he never published his findings on this microorganism. Pasteur also developed vaccines for anthrax and rabies.

In addition to applying his understanding of microorganisms to the medical field, Pasteur was able to contribute his knowledge to several commercial industries. First, he demonstrated the means by which airborne microorganisms contaminated beer and wine during production. He instructed producers how to avoid this contamination and, in so doing, rescued the ailing French beer and wine industry from economic ruin. Similarly, Pasteur rescued the French silk industry by demonstrating how to quickly identify an illness in silkworms, isolate the infected silkworms, and properly feed the silkworms to prevent reintroduction of the pathogen. In this way, further infection of silkworms was prevented. Although Pasteur never actually identified the pathogen, he was able to teach silk producers how to avoid its lethal effects on silkworms.

Finally, Pasteur used his knowledge of microorganisms to develop a technique of heating food products, especially milk, to kill contaminating pathogens. This technique is now called "pasteurization."

## Robert Koch's Contributions

Like Frenchman Louis Pasteur, German scientist Robert Koch searched for the microorganisms responsible for specific diseases. In 1876 Koch isolated the anthrax germ from sick farm animals, grew the anthrax pathogen in his laboratory, and noted the production of "spores" that he discovered could lie dormant for years. He then reintroduced spores into healthy animals. This induced anthrax disease in the healthy animals, thus proving that the anthrax spores caused anthrax.

Koch identified the pathogen responsible for tuberculosis in 1882 and for cholera in 1883. Although English physician John Snow had demonstrated in 1854 that dirty drinking water could cause cholera, the responsible pathogen was unknown until Robert Koch identified the *Vibrio cholerae* bacteria in his laboratory. His discovery of this pathogen led to improved public sanitation standards and the protection of drinking water. In the twentieth century, environmental regulations would be added to sanitation as a public health measure.

One of Koch's significant contributions was a set of principles he developed in 1879 that could be used to definitively identify the pathogen responsible for a disease. The principles came to be known as Koch's postulates. They are:

- The specific organism must be proven to be present in every instance of the infectious disease;
- The organism must be capable of being cultivated in pure culture [grown in the laboratory];
- Inoculating an experimental animal with the culture will reproduce the disease;
- The organisms can be recovered from the inoculated animal and grown again in a pure culture.[1]

Koch's students used his methods to identify the microbes responsible for numerous diseases, including typhoid, diphtheria, pneumonia, gonorrhea, meningitis, and plague. It is a testament to the soundness of Koch's postulates that they continue to be used today. For example, when a mysterious respiratory illness called SARS (severe acute respiratory syndrome) broke out in southern China in the spring of 2003, scientists used Koch's postulates to identify the disease. Scientists first determined that the suspected pathogen, a coronavirus, was present in sick people but not in healthy ones. Next, they isolated the virus from the tissues of sick patients and grew the virus in a laboratory culture. Then the laboratory-grown virus was introduced into healthy animals. After demonstrating that the healthy animal had become ill with SARS, the doctors isolated the virus again, this time from the sick animals' tissues, and grew the virus in lab cultures. "The Koch's postulates have been fulfilled, so we can now say for certain that the new coronavirus is the cause of SARS,"[2] said Klaus Stohr, a World Health Organization virologist.

Pasteur's and Koch's problem-solving research and contributions to the germ theory of disease also led the way to two additional medical innovations: chemotherapy and antiseptic practices. Early in the twentieth century, Paul Ehrlich (1854–1915) and other scientists experimented with various chemical compounds to treat specific diseases by attacking the causative microorganisms—a practice known as chemotherapy. Chemotherapy is used to treat people suffering from cancer. Ehrlich referred to these drug compounds as "magic bullets" because the drugs could kill the pathogenic microorganisms without harming healthy tissue. Today there are thousands of pharmaceutical drugs available to provide chemotherapy.

The use of antiseptic methods was another medical advance based on the germ theory of disease. Surgeon Joseph Lister (1827–1912) suspected that infections in wounds were caused by microorganisms carried to the wound on the unwashed hands of surgeons. He urged surgeons to wash their hands and to decontaminate wounds and surgical equipment with antiseptic chemicals. Contemporary medicine still makes use of the infection control techniques that Lister advocated, but his methods have been greatly expanded. The Centers for Disease Control provides health care professionals with detailed instructions on how to prevent the transmission of specific pathogens. These instructions include proper use and decontamination of medical equipment, methods of protecting medical personnel, and even the use of negative air pressure in rooms holding isolated ill patients—preventing airborne pathogens from escaping the room.

## Accidental Medical Discoveries

Pasteur and Koch's discoveries resulted from systematic efforts to cure or prevent disease. However, significant medical discoveries are sometimes made totally by accident rather than as an attempt at problem solving.

An example of an accidental medical discovery is the case of Georgia physician Crawford Long (1815–1878). Long was asked by some young men near his home to prepare some nitrous oxide for use in a "frolic," a party at which participants intentionally intoxicated themselves with the gas.

Long suggested using ether instead, saying that it was just as good as nitrous oxide for inducing intoxication. He prepared the ether, attended the frolic, and participated in the intoxication. At this point, Long made an important discovery. He had bruised himself while intoxicated by the ether and observed that he felt no pain at the time. Shortly after, Long began using ether as anesthesia in his surgical practice. Long's discovery and use of surgical anesthesia led to a new medical specialization: anesthesiology.

Another man who made an accidental medical discovery was Wilhelm Röntgen (1845–1943). He stumbled upon a new kind of radiation while working on an unrelated problem in his lab. The German physicist was experimenting on the behavior of electricity when he noticed a mysterious glowing light in his darkened lab. Physicist Graham Farmelo describes the discovery:

> He discovered that this emanation went unhindered through a piece of black paper. He then demonstrated that it passed through a playing card. . . . When he examined the extent to which the rays penetrated metals, he had perhaps the biggest surprise of all. As he put a small piece of lead in the path of the rays, he saw not only the object's dark shadow, but a fainter shadow in the shape of his thumb and finger as well. That shadow in turn enclosed another set outlining the bones of his hand.[3]

Röntgen called the penetrating light an X ray, the X suggesting how little was known about the mysterious rays.

The discovery of X rays was greeted with some skepticism by physicians, at least until they saw the photographs of broken bones made with X-ray technology. The public was not so skeptical, and getting X-ray photos, or "bone portraits," became highly popular.

One of the most important and lasting results of Röntgen's accidental discovery was giving physicians the ability to make a noninvasive diagnosis of certain injuries or illnesses. A second far-reaching result was that the field of medicine eventually developed a new specialization: radiology, in which various types of radiation are used to diagnosis and treat disease. X rays are just one technology used in radiology today. During the twentieth century new means of making diagnostic medical images emerged that were inspired by or directly related to Röntgen's discovery. Computerized tomography (CT) developed from X-ray technology and is considered the next generation of medical imaging after X-ray photographs. Developed and introduced in 1972 by electrical engineer Godfrey Hounsfield, CT combines X rays with the ability of computers to manage and analyze huge amounts of data. The result is a cross-sectional, highly detailed image of the interior of the human body.

CT can image bones, calcium deposits, and cartilage, but soft tissue is not easily "seen" by CT scans. For that, physicians turn to magnetic resonance imaging (MRI). MRI scans use radio waves and magnets to create images of the internal organs. Like CT, MRI depends heavily on computers to organize and store the raw data coming from the scan. With an MRI image, the bones disappear and the soft tissues become clear to the viewer, often in very sharp detail.

Another medical-imaging technology is positron-emission technology (PET) scans. PET scans measure the amount of photons emitted by the decay of a radioactive tracer ingested by the patient. PET scans are particularly useful at monitoring biochemical and metabolic processes such as oxygen uptake, blood flow, and glucose metabolism in human tissues. Brain tumors, strokes, and seizure disorders can be diagnosed by PET scans.

Two additional medical imaging devices are ultrasound and mammography. The first is frequently used to examine a fetus, and the second is used to diagnosis breast cancer.

## Discovery Science

Whereas X-ray technology was discovered by accident, other important medical advances have been achieved through pure descriptive scientific research, sometimes called discovery science. Discovery science is research done for no other reason than to describe something or to find out how it works. No particular health problem is under consideration. Discovery science often involves careful ob-

servation and description of the object of study. As biologists
Neil Campbell, Jane B. Reece, and Eric J. Simon write:

> Discovery science enables us to describe life at its many lev-
> els, from ecosystems down to cells and molecules. [Charles]
> Darwin's careful description of the diverse plants and animals
> he collected in South America is an example of discovery sci-
> ence, sometimes called descriptive science. A more recent
> example is the sequencing of the human genome; it's not
> really a set of experiments, but a detailed dissection and de-
> scription of the genetic material.[4]

Antoni van Leeuwenhoek's careful observation and description of bacteria is a prime example of discovery science.
Leeuwenhoek made his living selling cloth and men's clothing, but his true calling was to observe and document what
he called "little animals" by using microscopes that he made
himself. He made careful notes and drawings of the bacteria
he found in rainwater and from the surface of his teeth.
These early observations of bacteria laid the foundation for
the germ theory of disease that linked together specific microorganisms with specific diseases.

Another example of discovery science is the work of Austrian monk Gregor Mendel (1822–1884). Mendel was curious about certain characteristics of garden peas, such as the
color of the flower and the texture of the seed. He concocted
an elaborate experimental breeding program, resulting in his
discovery of the fundamental patterns of inheritance. Because Mendel was interested in mathematics, he analyzed
these inheritance patterns, and this led to the discovery of
mathematical laws governing heredity. He published the results of his work in 1865, but little attention was paid to the
diffident monk's research. Nearly thirty years later, other
scientists rediscovered what came to be known as the
Mendelian laws of inheritance. Today Mendel is considered
to be the founder of genetics.

## The Discovery of the Structure of DNA

A third example of great discovery science, also in the field
of genetics, is the discovery of the structure of DNA (de-

oxyribonucleic acid), as modeled by James Watson (1928– ) and Francis Crick (1916– ). Watson and Crick were not attempting to solve any particular medical problem when they began their DNA modeling project. They simply wanted to know how DNA was structured because they, like most scientists during the mid–twentieth century, intuited that knowing the structure of DNA would open up a whole new world to medical science. By the mid–twentieth century, scientists already knew that DNA carried genetic information. How it accomplished this task was a mystery. The structure turned out to be the key to the mystery.

A number of scientists were researching the problem during the 1950s. British scientist Rosalind Franklin (1920–1958) was taking X-ray diffraction photos of DNA molecules at her lab in England. Other scientists were attempting to model the structure. American scientist Linus Pauling, for example, came up with an early model that proved to be faulty. Maurice Wilkins, a fellow researcher in the same laboratory as Rosalind Franklin, gave James Watson one of Franklin's photos without her knowledge. When Watson saw the photo, he recognized that the molecule was in the form of a double helix. Watson and Crick used this crucial piece of information to create a model of the DNA molecule that proved to be correct, and they introduced the double helix to the world immediately.

Watson and Crick's discovery was unusual. As medical historians Meyer Friedman and Gerald W. Friedland point out:

Never before had such a discovery been made by the simple combination of blackboard scrawling, absorption of the experimental work of others, perusal of other scientists' publications, and manipulation of plastic balls, wires, and metal plates. Not once in their several years of working together did either Watson or Crick touch or look directly at a fiber of DNA.[5]

Wilkins, Crick, and Watson won a Nobel Prize for their discovery of the structure of DNA in 1962. Many scientists believe that Rosalind Franklin also deserved the Nobel for her key contribution. However, the Nobel is never awarded posthumously, and Franklin had died of cancer in 1958.

## DNA Structure: The Impact of the Discovery

The discovery of DNA's double-helix structure was an important turning point for medical science. Many new technologies and treatments developed directly from the knowledge that Watson and Crick presented to the world. One such advance is DNA sequencing, a technique used to determine the sequence of nitrogenous bases along the linear length of a DNA molecule. DNA sequencing has become a key tool used in medicine. Many medical applications are based on the determination of an organism's DNA sequence because every living organism has its own unique sequence. Diagnosis of disease-causing organisms is an obvious use of DNA sequencing. Genetic diseases such as cystic fibrosis can be diagnosed in a fetus in the very early stages of pregnancy.

Infectious diseases can also be identified by amplifying small amounts of the DNA of pathogens found in the tissues or blood of sick people. The DNA of the SARS virus, for example, was sequenced, and the virus was identified and named in only six days—a stunning achievement. Identifying an infectious disease is especially important if strict infection control measures need to be implemented immediately, as was the case with SARS.

Another outcome of knowing the structure of DNA is that pharmaceutical drugs can be developed to address human health problems. Knowing the DNA structure of human insulin, for example, led to the mass production of this human hormone through genetic engineering. Insulin has now been made readily available and at a lower cost to diabetics, whose bodies lack the ability to produce or properly make use of insulin. Vaccines can be developed to respond to specific pathogens once the structure of the pathogen is known. For example, the first genetically engineered vaccine was developed to provide immunity to the disease hepatitis B.

"Designer drugs" are developed regularly by pharmaceutical companies to address specific health problems. An example is a tissue plasminogen activator that reduces blood clotting and lowers the risk of heart attack. Some designer drugs also inhibit or disrupt the metabolic processes of bacteria or viruses, thus rendering them harmless. An example is the class of drugs called protease inhibitors, which inhibit the entrance of the human immunodeficiency virus (HIV, the cause of AIDS) into human cells. Development of this class of drugs was based on knowledge of the DNA structure and function of the pathogen HIV.

Yet another possibility is manipulation of genes themselves. Genes are distinct nucleotide sequences in DNA. By knowing the DNA structure of specific genes, changes could theoretically be made in the faulty genes that cause disorders such as cystic fibrosis or sickle-cell disease. At this time, though, there are no lasting and effective gene therapy treatments, although much promising research is being done.

## Problems Associated with Genetic Medical Discoveries

There are ethical problems associated with new genetic treatments and procedures. For example, what should be done about a fetus that has been diagnosed with an incurable genetic disease? Gene therapy promises to correct genetic disorders such as cystic fibrosis, but changing the human genetic code opens the door to eugenics and manipulation of the human genome to produce a "better" human being. Determining what is "better" poses many moral issues. Should we decide that it is "better" to have a certain skin or eye color or to grow to a certain height?

Another problem is the possibility of discrimination against individuals with particular genetic histories. A woman who carries the familial gene for breast cancer is more prone to developing breast cancer, yet she may never develop the disease. Some genes only cause a disease in the presence of certain environmental factors. If the person never encounters those environmental factors, then he or she will never develop the disease. Should medical insurance companies be allowed to refuse to insure such a person? Should these persons be denied employment because they *might* someday prove to be a health risk for the employer? These are just a few of the potential problems that genetic discoveries pose for humankind.

## The Continuing Search for Health

Despite these ethical problems, the search for human health continues. Medical discoveries are made every day. Some discoveries will prove to be turning points capable of changing the course of medical history. Genetic research, in particular, is moving rapidly toward solutions to many human health problems. One of the most encouraging contemporary trends is the sharing of information among scientists around the world. For example, Erick Lander, director of the Whitehead Institute for Genome Research, has said that the DNA sequences established daily in his laboratory are posted to the Internet each day for other scientists to see. Humanity continues to apply innate creativity and persistence toward achieving that long-standing goal sought since the beginning of civilization—good health.

## Notes

1. Quoted in Roy Porter, ed., *The Cambridge Illustrated History of Medicine*. Cambridge, UK: Cambridge University Press, 1996, p. 185.

2. Quoted in *Arizona Daily Star*, "Tests Confirm SARS Virus Identity," April 17, 2003, p. A13.

3. Graham Farmelo, "The Discovery of X-Rays," *Scientific American*, November 1995, p. 86.

4. Neil Campbell, Jane B. Reece, and Eric J. Simon, *Essential Biology*, 2nd ed. San Francisco: Benjamin Cummings, 2003, pp. 13–14.

5. Meyer Friedman and Gerald W. Friedland, *Medicine's 10 Greatest Discoveries*. New Haven, CT: Yale University Press, 1998, p. 224.

# Chapter 1

# Human Body Structure and Function

# Vesalius and the Study of Human Anatomy

John Galbraith Simmons

Although the respected Greek physician Galen died in A.D. 200, his teachings on human anatomy prevailed for well over one thousand years. Andreas Vesalius (1514–1564), a Belgian physician and scientist trained at the University of Padua in Italy, was the first to challenge Galen's version of human anatomy. Vesalius conducted his own anatomical dissections on human cadavers and found that Galen's teachings, based on animal dissections, did not always apply to humans. Vesalius used the empirical method to discover for himself the truth about the structure of the human body. Galen's version of anatomy was established dogma, and initial responses to Vesalius's findings were outrage and skepticism. He convinced his critics by refuting Galen's teachings with observable facts demonstrated in his dissections. Vesalius published his profusely illustrated textbook on human anatomy entitled *De Humani Corporis Fabrica (The Fabric of the Human Body)* in Latin in 1543. The book was not only a scientific milestone but also a noteworthy addition to the history of printing and book arts. In fact, a hand-colored copy of the *Fabrica* that was presented to Holy Roman Emperor Charles V sold for $1,652,500 in 1998. Science writer John Galbraith Simmons reviews the contribution of Vesalius to human anatomical knowledge in this excerpt from his book *Doctors and Discoveries*. He is also the author of *The Scientific 100: A Rating of the Most Influential Scientists, Past and Present.*

John Galbraith Simmons, *Doctors and Discoveries: Lives That Created Today's Medicine.* New York: Houghton Mifflin Company, 2002. Copyright © 2002 by John Galbraith Simmons. All rights reserved. Reproduced by permission of the publisher.

In 1543, from Basel, [there] issued a work of art and science that would influence the annals of Western medicine forever after. *De humani corporis fabrica* was one of the first anatomy texts to systematically provide descriptions derived from actual dissection of the human body. Its brilliantly detailed drawings represented a break with the scholastic model of the body based on the work of Galen [130–200], then over a thousand years old and, not surprisingly, rife with errors. Above all, the *Fabrica* embodied the Renaissance and its new vision of humankind, less encumbered by religion, unbound by dogma. Its author, Andreas Vesalius, is as a consequence traditionally classed with such historic figures in medicine as William Harvey [1578–1657] and Ambroise Paré [1510–1590].

Andreas Vesalius was born to Isabella Crabbe and her husband, Andreas, on December 31, 1514, in Brussels. The paternal side of his family was steeped in medicine, from his father, apothecary to the Hapsburg emperor Charles V, to his great-great-grandfather, a renowned physician. The Vesaliuses were prosperous and possessed a library, and young Andreas became absorbed by books. Other details of his early education are lacking—it is said that he dissected animals—but he entered the University of Louvain in 1528. He received an extensive education there before going on to study medicine at the University of Paris in 1533. At that conservative institution he did not learn a great deal, he said, but he became committed to anatomical studies. Dissection of human corpses had been common in medical schools since the fourteenth century. One of Vesalius's teachers was Johann Guinther of Andernach [1505–1574], a translator of Galen's anatomical work, but not much of an anatomist himself. Another professor was Jacobus Sylvius [1478–1555], remembered for helping to develop a rational terminology for anatomy.

## First Dissections

Vesalius did not graduate before being compelled to leave Paris after Charles V invaded France in 1536. Returning to the Low Countries, Vesalius soon became known for his anatomical knowledge, and it is during this period, as he later recounted, that he went to great trouble to obtain his first skeleton, from an executed prisoner. Bodies were customarily left at the gallows after hangings, and the flesh would soon rot and be eaten off the bone by animals. "After I had brought the legs and arms home in secret . . . I allowed myself to be shut out of the city in the evening in order to obtain the thorax which was firmly held by a chain. I was burning with so great a desire. . .that I was not afraid to snatch in the middle of the night what I so longed for. . . ." Vesalius subsequently conducted dissections before fellow students. But he soon moved on to Padua, a hub of culture and learning during the Renaissance. The faculty at the University of Padua awarded Vesalius his medical degree with high distinction in 1537.

Young Vesalius's anatomy demonstrations were popular among students. They were distinctive in two ways. First, Vesalius dissected the cadavers himself. This contravened the usual procedure, in which the professor read from a Galenic text while the body was opened by a menial, or prosector. In addition, and as a consequence, Vesalius began to employ drawings to clarify the various structures of the body. Success with this method led him to publish his charts. The *Tabulae anatomicae sex (Six Anatomical Charts)*, with drawings by Jan Stefan van Calar, appeared in 1538. They depict the reproductive organs in both the male and female, the liver, and the vascular system. The influence of Galen remained strong in this early work, with the liver drawn as a five-lobed organ, and the heart is as that of an ape. Nevertheless, the charts were an immediate success and were widely plagiarized.

## Publication of the *Fabrica*

Over the next six years Vesalius worked, as he had hinted he would, on a larger and more comprehensive work. He had the advantage of a good supply of cadavers, which emboldened him to put realism before Galenic dogma. In 1543—within weeks of the publication of Copernicus's *De revolutionibus*—appeared Vesalius's masterpiece, *De humani corporis fabrica libri septem (Seven Books on the Structure of the Human Body)*. Beautifully printed by Johannes Oporinus [1507–1568] of Basel, the books represent a marriage of objective description to the new realism in art characteristic of the Late Renaissance. There has been much discussion over the identity of the artist or artists responsible for the plates. It is thought today that several were at work, among them Vesalius himself, but also the artists of the celebrated school of Titian, considered the greatest of the Venetian painters.

Although a revolutionary work, the *Fabrica* could not escape the influence of Galen, which still permeated thinking about the body. Thus, elements of Galenic anatomy strongly persist, while the book as a whole moves medical thought in another direction entirely. The *Fabrica* aimed to elucidate the real human body for the benefit of students. It is at once a descriptive catalog of the human body and a didactic guide to dissection. Bones and muscles are detailed in Books I and II, and Book III attempts to describe the vascular system. Book IV, on the nervous system, shows how Vesalius could be led astray by the Galenic classification of nerves. Book V describes the abdominal and reproductive organs—the liver is now the real, human liver. In Book VI, Vesalius expresses clear suspicion concerning the septum of the heart. Galen had assumed it must be permeable in order to allow the flow of venous blood, which he believed was produced in the liver, to enter the arterial system. Book VII describes the brain.

Publication of a volume that was, in effect, an assault on established authority was bound to raise some hackles. *De fabrica* quickly won attention, some of it negative. It was denounced by Vesalius's former teacher Sylvius of Paris, among others. Sylvius went to extraordinarily vituperative lengths to denounce Vesalius—calling him a madman—though with no great results. The *Fabrica* became an authoritative work within a short time.

It seems odd that the publication of the *Fabrica* concluded Vesalius's career as an anatomist, but essentially that is what happened. Vesalius would continue to follow developments in anatomy, and he saw to press a second, lavish edition of the *Fabrica* in 1555. But, perhaps with the help of his father, in 1544 he sought and obtained appointment as imperial physician to Emperor Charles V. It used to be thought that

Vesalius had hoped that by entering royal service he would evade the enmity aroused by the *Fabrica*. More likely, though, the move represented fulfillment of ambition. . . .

Vesalius's personality has been the subject of debate over four centuries. He has been described in first-hand accounts as "choleric" and also characterized as disputatious and querulous, wrathful, schizoid, depressed, a butcher at heart, and avaricious. But he has also been endlessly admired. As evidenced by his writings, Vesalius was aggressive, well aware of his own historic significance, and possessed of a broad grasp of the whole range of medicine in his time. "I could have done nothing more worthwhile," he wrote, "than to give a new description of the whole human body, of which nobody understood the anatomy."

# William Harvey's Discovery of Blood Circulation

Farokh Erach Udwadia

Like Andreas Vesalius (1514–1564), who challenged the ancient Greek Galen's concept of anatomy, English physician William Harvey (1578–1657) challenged Galen's concept of blood circulation. Galen taught that there were two types of blood with separate pathways through the human body. Through careful observation and experimentation, Harvey came to understand that the blood was expelled from the heart's left ventricle into arteries that carried it to all parts of the body. Then blood was returned to the heart by way of the veins. In the following selection Farokh Erach Udwadia describes how Harvey was able to prove that blood moved through the body in a circle rather than through two separate systems as taught by Galen. It would be nearly fifty years later, in 1661, that another scientist, Marcello Malpighi (1628–1694), would discover blood capillaries that provided the link between the arterial and venous circulation discovered by Harvey. Udwadia is professor emeritus of medicine at Grant Medical College and the J.J. Group of Hospitals in Mumbai, India.

The discovery of circulation by William Harvey (1578–1657) will rank as one of the greatest discoveries in science and medicine. Harvey was the most brilliant star in the Baroque century. His epoch-making work outshone every discovery of the past and formed the foundation on which many subsequent discoveries in medicine were made.

Harvey was the son of an alderman in the English fishing port of Folkestone. He studied humanities at Cambridge and went on to study medicine at Padua—a centre of learning to which flocked the rich and poor from all corners of Europe. In Padua he was the student of Fabrizio D'Acquapendente [1533–1619]. He and his fellow students seated within the tiered lecture hall of this university must have heard and seen with breathless admiration Professor D'Acquapendente lecture on anatomy and demonstrate anatomical facts through dissection. Fabrizio D'Acquapendente was the first to describe valves within the venous system and this was of great interest to his pupil William Harvey.

The scientific temper of Harvey must surely have developed in this university, which was famous for its free thinkers, its great teachers and the renowned scholars engaged in unravelling the secrets of nature. The great Galileo [1564–1642] was also working and teaching at Padua in this era. Harvey was acquainted with his work—perhaps he peered at the heavenly bodies through the telescope devised by Galileo and acquired an interest in their motion and in the principles underlying motion and movement. Significantly, the study of movement and motion (e.g., of falling bodies, of planets, of the pendulum) was all-consuming in this era. Even though Harvey was a physician, the impact of the above studies in natural sciences may well have had a conscious or subconscious effect on his resolve to study the motion or movement of blood in the human circulation.

On his return to London in 1602, he married the daughter of Lancelot Browne, physician to Queen Elizabeth I and James I and joined the staff of St Bartholomew's hospital as reader in anatomy and surgery. He spent almost all his time in research and investigations on the vascular system and announced his discovery of circulation in 1616. His classic work *Exercitatio anatomica de motu cordis et sanguinis in animalibus* was published 12 years later in Frankfurt in which he described circulation, as we know it today.

## Harvey's Revolutionary Concept

The stupendous magnitude and significance of this discovery can only be understood if one contrasts Harvey's concept of the circulation with that prevailing in the early seven-

# The Discovery of Capillaries Using the Microscope

*Historians believe that the first microscopes were made by Dutch brothers Johannes and Zachiarias Janssen. Italian Marcello Malpighi was the first to develop techniques for using the new instrument, and he made many observations relevant to the medical sciences. In this selection Malpighi describes seeing the circulation of blood in the capillaries.*

The man who worked out basic microscopical technique and discovered many new facts about man, animals and plants was Marcello Malpighi (1628–94). After studying medicine at Bologna, he taught at Bologna and Pisa, where he gave Borelli [Giovanni, 1608–1679] anatomy lessons in return for lessons on mathematics and physics. In 1661 he added the final piece of evidence to Harvey's work on the circulation by direct observation of blood in the capillaries:

'I saw the blood, flowing in minute streams through the arteries, in the manner of a flood, and I might have believed that the blood itself escaped into an empty space and was collected up again by a gaping vessel, but an objection to the view was afforded by the movement of the blood being tortuous and scattered in different directions and by its being united again in a definite path. My doubt was changed to certainty by the dried lung of a frog which to a marked degree had preserved the redness of the blood in very tiny tracts, which were afterwards found to be vessels, where by the help of a glass I saw not scattered points but vessels joined together in a ring-like fashion. And such is the wandering of these vessels as they proceed from the vein on this side and the artery on the other that they do not keep a straight path but appear to form a network joining the two vessels. Thus it was clear that the blood flowed along sinuous vessels and did not empty into spaces, but was always contained within vessels, the paths of which produced its dispersion.'

Roberto Margotta, *The History of Medicine*. New York: Smithmark, 1996, pp. 108–10.

teenth century. The old Galenic [Galen, 130–200] concept taught that venous and arterial blood were two distinct types of blood with different pathways and different functions relating to three major organ centres within the body—the liver which was responsible for growth and nourishment, the heart controlling vitality, the brain responsible for reason and sensations. The venous blood originated in the liver, and was distributed to all parts of the body through venous channels; it was used up and mediated growth and nourishment. The arterial blood contained blood plus *pneuma* (air) due to an intrinsic 'pulsatile faculty' within the arterial system. Galen explained the composition of arterial blood (venous blood + air) in the left ventricle by postulating invisible pores in the interventricular septum through which venous blood reached the left ventricle. He explained the presence of air in this blood by postulating that air was conveyed to the left ventricle from the lungs via the pulmonary vein. The latter also served as a channel through which sooty vapours formed by the mixing of blood with air in the left ventricle travelled back to the lungs and were exhaled. Galen had no concept of the pulmonary circulation and his doctrine was therefore theoretical, lacking both in observation and experimentation. However bizzare his concept may appear to us, it afforded a plausible explanation in that day and age.

Harvey's concept of the circulation was revolutionary when compared to the then prevailing concept. He postulated and proved through experiment and observation that the blood was expelled out by the left ventricle through the aorta and was distributed by the arterial system to all parts of the body; it then became venous and was carried by the veins to the right atrium and from there to the right ventricle. It was now propelled by the right ventricle, through the pulmonary artery and its branches, into the lungs where it was transformed into arterial blood. After passing through the pulmonary veins, it entered the left atrium and then returned to the left ventricle. The blood was therefore in constant motion, in continuous circulation.

Like all great discoverers Harvey had his precursors. The Galenic doctrine that the left ventricle contained air or blood mixed with air, which reached it from the right ventricle through the invisible pores in the septum had been refuted by both Leonardo [da Vinci (1452–1519)] and Vesalius. Michael Servetus, a Spanish theologian and physician had postulated the existence of the pulmonary circulation and denied the porosity of the septum. Realdo Cremona (1516–1559) of Cremona who succeeded Vesalius to the chair of anatomy also denied the permeability of the septal wall. Andrea Cesalpino of Arezzo (1524–1603) botanist and physician discovered sex in plants and gave a correct concept of the circulation in the human body. His concepts were embodied in his work *Des Plantes* published in 1583. His house in Arezzo bears a plaque—'here lived Andrea Cesalpino, discoverer of the circulation of the blood and the first author of the classification of plants'.

## Harvey's Experiments

Harvey crystallized earlier ideas into a definite hypothesis proven by numerous observations and experiments which were lacking in the postulates of earlier workers. The principles of research in natural sciences followed by Galileo, Newton [Isaac, 1642–1727], Keppler [Johann, 1571–1630] were, for the first time, applied with astounding results to medicine. Harvey experimented on over 80 animals to measure the rate of blood flow. He calculated the blood flow to be 8640 oz/hour—a quantum that could not be replenished by food or by tissues hour by hour. He thus deduced that blood flowed continuously in a circle through the heart to the arteries, to the veins and back to the heart. Keppler, Galileo and Newton studied with mathematical precision the movements of falling bodies on earth and of heavenly bodies in space. Harvey studied the movement of blood in the human body, showed that it moved in a circle and used mathematical calculations to deduce this result. Harvey did not rest his theory of circulation solely on the mensurations stated above. He performed scores of animal experiments using cannulation, ligation and perfusion. He announced his discovery in the Lumelian lecture of 1616 delivered from notes in English and Latin, stating that the heart was a force pump that drove the blood in constant circulation through the vessels. It contracted when it emptied and forced blood into the vessels, and dilated when it filled on receiving blood from the veins. His epoch-making book on circulation *Exercitatio anatomica de motu cordis et sanguinis in animalibus* was published rather shoddily in Frankfurt, years later. It immediately divided the medical world into two hostile camps.

## Opposition to Harvey's Ideas

The most violent opposition to Harvey's view on the circulation was from the medical faculty in Paris. Jean Riolan of Paris declared that if dissection had proved Galen wrong, it was because nature had over the centuries changed. Guy Paten, Dean of the Paris faculty of Medicine dubbed Harvey's theory as 'paradoxical, useless, false, impossible, absurd, harmful'. Harvey was stoutly defended by numerous physicians from England, Germany, France and Holland, many of whom proved his experiments correct. One of his great defenders was Descartes [1596–1650] who in his treatise in physiology in AD 1662, stated that blood in the body was in a state of perpetual circulation. In fact, he felt that Harvey's concept of circulation of blood supported his mechanistic philosophy. Descartes, however, differed from Harvey in his explanation of the significance of the action of the heart. He believed (and he was of course in error) that the chief activity of the heart was in diastole, when its innate heat rarefied and expanded drops of blood within its chambers forcing these into the arteries. These very small drops of blood became animal spirits, which, on reaching the brain, nerves and muscles induced perception and motion. The heart was thus akin to an engine imparting motion to the body.

Harvey's other great original work was in embryology. His book *Exercitationes de generatione animalium* was published 8 years after his death. Harvey postulated very correctly the theory of epigenesis stating that all living beings develop from an egg: *omne vivum ex ovo*. Thus the organism does not exist as a preformed entity within the ovum but develops gradually with the building up of various tissues and organ systems. Harvey postulated this concept without the use of a microscope and was proved correct by Von Baer [Karl Ernst, 1792–1876] who had the advantage of its use.

Harvey rose to be the royal physician to the Stuart kings James I and Charles I. He kept aloof from all political and religious controversies, but sided with the Royalists during the civil wars. His house during the civil war was sacked by a violent mob, with the loss of valuable scientific notes. After the execution of Charles I, Harvey returned to his brother's country house where he died in 1675 [sic]. His books and possessions were donated to the Royal College of Physicians to fund a library and to establish an annual Harverian oration in his honour.

The only lacuna in Harvey's postulate of the circulation was the link between the arterial and venous systems. Though he could not prove the presence of this link directly through observation, he concluded from simple ligation experiments on the forearm that such a link must exist. He also proved, by similar experiments, that the function of the venous valves was to direct blood always towards the heart. The direct proof of a link between the arterial and venous circulation was provided by the discovery of capillaries by Marcello Malphigi [1628–1694] in 1661. The circle postulated by Harvey in the movement or motion of blood was now complete.

# Santiago Ramón y Cajal Establishes the Science of Neuroanatomy

Geoffrey Montgomery

Santiago Ramón y Cajal (1852–1934) may be unique among great scientists. Not only did he establish the science of neuroanatomy (study of the structure and function of neurons and the nervous system), but he also was the leader of a gang of delinquents when he was a youth. Growing up in the Aragon region of Spain, Ramón y Cajal led a group of boys who were famous locally for their vandalism and petty thievery, so much so that they were listed in the village "Index of Bad Companions." Ramón y Cajal's father attempted to keep his son on the straight path by demanding that he follow a rigorous course of study. The boy was interested in art, but his father found that no more acceptable than vandalism. For a while, the boy hid his drawings, but everything changed one day when Ramón y Cajal saw an image on the ceiling formed by a beam of light coming through shuttered windows. He was seeing an optical phenomenon known as a "camera obscura." From that experience, Ramón y Cajal developed a passion for photography that led to a lifelong fascination with the anatomy of the human eye—in particular, the retina, where images are formed. He became a physician and conducted research into the anatomy of human neurons, especially those in the eye. In this article from *Grand Street*, science writer Geoffrey Montgomery reviews Ramón y Cajal's contribution to the development of the new science of neuroanatomy.

Santiago Ramón y Cajal would come to be generally considered the father of modern neuroscience. Nowhere was his revolutionary approach to the nervous system better displayed than in his study of the retina, that transparent sheet of neural tissue where light becomes transformed into the electrochemical language of the brain. It was in his analysis of the retina's exquisite cellular structure, wrote Cajal, that "I felt more profoundly than in any other subject of study the shuddering sensation of the unfathomable mystery of life." Yet Cajal's entry into the nervous system was in fact crucially conditioned by his occupation of the photographic dark room, and his revelations of the structure and function of retinal nerve cells were both guided and ultimately limited by his equation of eye and camera.

## Cajal's Interest in Photography

It was only in the summer of 1868, when Cajal was sixteen, that Don Justo [Cajal's father] realized that his son's passion for image-making might have some application in his training for medicine. That summer, Don Justo introduced his son to his beloved subject of human anatomy by climbing with him one moonlit night over a cemetery wall. There the two picked through a pile of exhumed bones for the most "perfect and least weathered crania, ribs, pelves, and femurs," which they took back for scrutiny in the family barn. Don Justo taught Cajal to overlook no detail in his observation of bone structure, and for Cajal's artistic leanings "osteology constituted one more subject for pictures." Within two months, to the amazement of his father, Cajal had formulated a detailed mental map of all the bones, muscles, arteries, and nerves of the human body.

That same year, in the city of Huesca, where Don Justo had sent his truant son for a solid dose of schooling and discipline, Cajal gained his first admittance to the photographic darkroom. A group of photographers known by a friend of his had set up a laboratory in the underground chambers of a ruined church. Here Cajal watched in wonder as the light-sensitive salts of silver were mixed into a colloidal film, which was then laid thinly over a plate of glass, and as albumen-covered paper for positive prints was sensitized. "All of these operations astonished me, but one of them, the development of the latent image by means of pyrogallic acid, positively stupefied me'."....

It had been known since 1727 that certain compounds of silver blacken upon exposure to light. The first attempt to use a sheet of paper coated with silver nitrate to record a portable camera obscura image [images projected using a darkened box device with an aperture] was made by Thomas Wedgwood, scion of the Wedgwood pottery family, around 1800. Wedgwood failed because his coatings of silver salts were insufficiently sensitive to the relatively weak camera image. Furthermore, he lacked a fixer: that is, he could lay a leaf directly on his coated paper under the sun and make a negative image, but any further exposure to sunlight spread a shadow of liberated silver across the white figure of the leaf. The whole paper turned black. Wedgwood had no way of stopping the light-recording process—of "fixing" his images.

The first fixed photograph was made by William Henry Fox Talbot in August 1835; it showed the view through a latticed window in his home at Lacock Abbey. "When first made," Talbot noted by the side of this paper negative, "the squares of glass about 200 in number could be counted, with help of a lens." In 1839 Daguerre [Jacques, 1789–1851] announced his own method of fixing camera images on polished silver plates: a method dominant for the next two decades because of its greater rendering of detail, but ultimately without offspring, as Daguerre's negative images could not serve as a template for positive copies. Talbot was impelled to improve his process. The image of the latticed window had required a camera exposure of many minutes; it was only when the sun had visibly blackened the two hundred squares of light on the coated paper that Talbot ended the exposure. Such exposure times made portraiture impractical. But in 1840 Talbot discovered that a latent image could be formed on his photographic paper in a far shorter period of time and then developed into a visible image through the action of pyrogallic acid. . . .

## The Human Retina

The word "retina" derives from the Latin translation of a Greek term for the one-third-millimeter-thick sheet of transparent tissue lining the back of the eye: "netlike tunic." Two other Greek names for the retina compared it to a spider web and to glass; long before its light-sensing function was known, the retina itself was seen as a kind of latticed window. Its transparence fitted Greek theories that tied the retina to the conveyance of the "visual spirit" flowing from the brain to the eye's crystalline lens—the place where mind and image supposedly met.

Yet by the nineteenth century, scientists realized that if the retina contained the eye's true light-receptors, elements within the tissue must be colored so as to absorb light. In 1876 Franz Boll discovered that the purple rod cells lying within a frog's retina bleached yellow upon exposure to light. Descartes [Rene, 1596–1650] had described how the imaging function of the retina could be proved by placing the eyeball of an ox or dead person in the aperture of a dark room; remove the white sclera from the back half of the eye, and one could see projected there the inverted scene outside. In 1878 Willy Kuhne of the University of Heidelberg set out to prove that a living retina could record such a scene using visual purple as its photographic pigment. Kuhne secured the head of an albino rabbit in place before a barred window for a three-minute exposure.

The rabbit was then decapitated and its retina removed. In a yellow image against the purple of this gossamer tissue were the window's six skylit panes. Kuhne fixed this "optogram" in alum and then drew a copy for all the world to see—a curious complement to the latticed window of Talbot's first photograph. The three-century-old analogy between eye and camera seemed deeper than ever.

That year, Santiago Ramon y Cajal coughed up blood. The young physician had already been stricken with malaria during military service in Cuba, and now he had contracted tuberculosis. Cajal had by then begun his investigations with a microscope and was studying anatomy in hopes of gaining an academic appointment, for Don Justo felt that his malaria-weakened son would be unable to maintain a medical practice. Now consumption had seized him. Cajal saw his death foretold in the artificially encouraging manner of his father's questions and his own emaciated frame.

But a long interval in the country, with his sister as nurse, served to restore Cajal's strength. In his autobiography, Cajal also credits photography with reviving his spirits and will to live, as it "obliged me to take continual exercise and, by offering me the daily solution of artistic problems, it flavored the monotony of my retreat. . . ." After his marriage, when Cajal was beginning his academic career, his passion for photography led him to begin manufacturing ultrarapid gelatin silver-bromide plates; these fast emulsions were then unavailable in Spain. Indeed, Cajal's photographs of bullfights, "and especially one of the president's box crowded with beautiful young ladies . . . created a furor." Cajal was compelled to manufacture these fast emulsions—whose standard formula he had improved—for general distribution, and might have begun a new Spanish industry if not for his preoccupation as director of Zaragoza's Anatomical Museum.

Cajal had become entranced with the invisible universe revealed by the microscope; he once peered through his lens for twenty consecutive hours in order to observe a white blood cell crawling out of a capillary. In 1880 he began publishing his findings; by 1884 he had the chair of Anatomy at Valencia. He specialized in histology, the study of the microstructure of tissues, publishing a book on the subject in 1885 filled with 203 woodcuts—the first Spanish histology text to contain original illustrations. Just as he had found the formula for ultrarapid gelatin silver-bromide emulsions in a foreign journal and subsequently improved it, Cajal was always searching for new techniques to visualize the cellular composition of the tissues he studied. At the time, the standard stains for nerve cells colored only the cell bodies and the thick beginnings of their fibers. The fiber's tangled terminations and interlinkings were impossible to see. Commencing his analysis of the nervous system, "that masterpiece of life," Cajal borrowed the superior microdissection technique that Max Schultze had pioneered in the retina.

The nerve tissue was softened in solution, and then, with a needle, the cells' spidery fibers were teased apart. In Cajal's hands, the method enabled the isolation of the larger nerve cells in the body. But for the fine transparent cells of tissue such as the retina, Cajal thought, the method required the patience of a Benedictine monk. One did not merely have to count the angels dancing on the head of a pin; one also had to dissect them.

## Tissue Staining

[In 1887] Cajal was in Madrid to serve as a judge in the examinations for anatomy professorships. While in the capital he paid visits to the laboratories of fellow microscopists. Luis Simarros [Madrid psychologist] had just returned from Paris with samples of several novel methods for preparing neural tissue, among them the "black stain" (*reazione nera*) discovered in 1880 by the Italian histologist Camillo Golgi [1843–1926]. Cajal had read a brief, dismissive note about Golgi's stain but had never before witnessed its workings. The procedure for black staining was relatively simple: bathe tiny slices of brain tissue in potassium bichromate, and then treat this tissue with a solution of silver nitrate crystals. Many samples failed to stain. But in those that did, a latent image of spectacular appearance developed: individual nerve cells were blackened from their cell bodies to their finest branching twigs. Under the microscope, the dark-stained cells were framed against the surrounding tissue like wintry trees, stripped of leaves, standing black against the sky before dawn.

Finally Cajal had a method of penetrating the tangled thicket of the nervous system, of tracing ramifying fibers to their terminations. Within a year, Cajal had mastered and improved Golgi's black stain. Like Talbot increasing the sensitivity of his silver salt negatives, Cajal developed a method of double impregnation to maximize the chance of staining his cells. Just as importantly, still daunted by the crowded complexity of adult nervous tissue—"a forest so dense that . . . there are no spaces in it, so that the trunks, branches, and leaves touch everywhere"—Cajal reverted to the embryonic brains of birds and mammals. "Since the full-grown forest turns out to be impenetrable and indefinable, why not revert to the study of the young wood, in the nursery stage . . . ?" (Moreover, the insulating sheath of myelin that covers axonal fibers on adult nerves, which is not stained by the Golgi method, is largely absent in embryos and neonates.)

The pre-Cajal period in neuroanatomy had settled one important issue: all fibers ramified back to the bodies of nerve cells. But still unresolved was the nature of the relationships between these fibers. The dogma adhered to by Golgi and nearly all other researchers was that the fibers of the brain formed a unified whole, merging together in one vast and continuous plexus. For Cajal, this reticular theory was a "species of protoplasmic pantheism," precluding the specific nerve linkages required for reflex action and the doctrine of the association of ideas. According to the reticular hypothesis, nerve impulses could travel along no specific pathways, but instead fed into a "sort of unfathomable physiological sea, into which, on the one hand, were supposed to pour the streams arriving from the sense organs, and from which, on the other hand, the motor . . . conductors were supposed to spring like rivers originating in mountain lakes."

## Cajal's Theory of the Neuron

In a fever of graphically illustrated publications, Cajal showed instead that each nerve cell retained its individuality. Its branches did not merge with those of other trees of the neural forest, but instead communicated with them through intimate contact, across a narrow cleft that came to be called the synapse. Cajal's neuron theory underlies all modern attempts at a biological understanding of brain function. Synapses connect neurons along specific pathways, and the implications of this specificity of neural wiring were nowhere clearer than in the retina—for Cajal, "the oldest and most persistent of my laboratory loves."

Max Schultze had shown that we have in effect two retinas in each eye—one for day, and one for night. Night vision is mediated through the rod cells and utilizes the visual purple studied by Kuhne; day and color vision works through the retina's cones, which use three other related photopigments. Rod vision is color-blind and coarse, says Cajal, producing "an image with little detail, comparable roughly to an ordinary photograph out of focus." The cones, on the other hand, give "colored pictures, detailed and brilliant, like a photograph in colors on an autochrome plate."

Rods and cones occupy the retina's innermost layer. In order for their light-recording signals to be sent to the brain, they must pass their signal to bipolar cells, which in turn signal retinal ganglion cells, whose axonal fibers form the optic nerve connecting the eye and brain. Schultze had carried the cellular anatomy of the retina to its highest level before Cajal, but without the black stain he had been unable to trace the connections between rods, cones, and bipolar cells. He assumed, however, that they merged in a common plexus.

## Cajal's Study of the Retina

Cajal's first foray into the retina proved this view false. The cells of this outpost of the brain—for the retina is an outgrowth of the same embryonic tissue as the central nervous system—are independent and communicate through synaptic contacts. "This important point established," wrote Cajal, "I proposed a very simple question to myself. Since the impression received by the rod is different from that taken up by the cone, it is necessary from every point of view that each of these specific impressions should be conveyed through the retina by a specific channel." That is, the rod and cone signals must pass through separate classes of bipolar cells.

"Knowing what I was looking for, I began to explore eagerly and repeatedly the retina of fishes and mammals. . . . and finally, as the reward of my faith, there deigned to appear most clearly and brilliantly those two types of bipolar cells demanded by theory and guessed by reason." Cajal also found that in the fovea, the small cone-rich center of the retina that is the place of highest visual acuity (we read by flicking letters on a page across our foveas), bipolar cells synapse with single cones. This allows the foveal cones' fine-grained sensitivity to be transmitted individually to the brain.

Cajal spent the last years of his long life running the

Madrid institute that had been constructed in his honor, extending his study of vision to the compound eye of insects. In 1906 he shared the Nobel Prize with his great adversary, Camillo Golgi, who, on the Stockholm stage, reportedly refused to speak to the Spaniard who had stolen his black stain. Golgi, though his grand vision of neural structure was utterly mistaken, felt the Nobel should have been his alone.

# A Monk Uncovers the Laws of Heredity

Venita Jay

Gregor Johann Mendel (1822–1884) came from a family of poor Austrian peasants who sacrificed so that he might be educated. Although suffering from health problems and a rather delicate mental state, he finished his studies and was ordained as a priest in 1847. Mendel became ill when confronted with human suffering, and this made him unsuitable for work as a village pastor. He entered a monastery, became a teacher, and with the encouragement of others, began a series of carefully controlled studies of inheritance patterns in the lowly garden pea. Mendel studied the inheritance of color and texture in peas, the colors of pea flowers, and several other characteristics. He theorized that the characteristics were passed from parents to the next generation by something he called "elements." These elements were genes, though Mendel did not know this at the time. He worked out mathematical formulas that predicted the inheritance patterns. In this selection author Venita Jay reviews Mendel's life and explains why his becoming a monk provided him with the right environment and resources to conduct his research. Jay details how Mendel's research with generations of garden peas led to the discovery of the laws of heredity. The science of genetics developed out of Mendel's groundbreaking work. Jay is an ophthalmic pathologist in the department of pathology at the Hospital for Sick Children in Toronto, Canada.

On August 6, 1847, Gregor Johann Mendel was ordained as a priest in Brunn Moravia. Luckily for medicine, Mendel's

Venita Jay, "Gregor Johann Mendel," *Archives of Pathology and Laboratory Medicine*, vol. 125, March 2001, p. 320. Copyright © 2001 by the College of American Pathologists. Reproduced by permission of the author.

personality and psychosomatic disposition rendered him unsuitable for practical pastoral duties. It was 18 years later that the results of his famous experiments with the garden pea were presented to the Brunn Natural History Society. In the following year [1866], the landmark work, "Experiments on Plant Hybrids," was published. Even the enigmatic Mendel, who elucidated the fundamental principles of genetics, was perhaps unaware of the monumental nature of his work. Upon his death in 1884, no one had yet recognized him as the founder of a new and powerful science; the belated discovery of this cloistered monk would come years later.

## Early Life

Born Johann Mendel in July 1822, in Heizendorf, Silesia (then in Austria), Mendel hailed from a humble family of peasants devoted to farming and gardening. Johann Schreiber, a priest from a Moravian parish, recognized the immense talent in the young Mendel and encouraged the family, which was under dire financial circumstances, to send Mendel for higher education. Schreiber was an expert fruit grower with a special interest in natural history and would have a lasting influence on Mendel. It was with all of Mendel's strength and endurance and the support of his family that he was able to complete his 2-year course of philosophical studies.

When Mendel's father died, the financial hardship facing his family became more severe. Mendel tried private tutoring, but with his perpetual struggle to make ends meet, he could see no satisfactory worldly existence compatible with his intellectual ideals. He thus turned to theology as a vocational choice, and joined the Augustinian Monastery in Brno (Brunn) in 1843.

At the time, Brunn was a thriving cultural center in Moravia. The abbot of this monastery, Franz Cyrill Napp, was an enigmatic figure. An ardent linguist proficient in ancient Oriental languages, Napp had many other passions, including horticulture, viniculture, and fruit growing. Many exotic plants were grown in Napp's monastery. It was in this monastery that the young Mendel stepped in, taking the name Gregor.

There was intense interest in animal and plant breeding in Moravia, and Napp was intrigued by the principles of breeding and heredity. Napp was intimately involved with the Moravian-Silesian Agricultural Society. The astonishing results of some area sheep breeders on combining and improving valuable traits were discussed in detail at the meetings of the society. The question of plant improvement was particularly significant for fruit growers. No doubt, Mendel's interest in heredity was aroused by these discussions.

For 4 years, Mendel pursued his theological studies, and he was ordained as a priest in August 1847. But it soon became apparent that Mendel was unfit for pastoral duties, as the very sight of suffering made him ill. The intuitive Napp realized this and excused Mendel from pastoral duties and assigned him to teaching. In the abbey, Mendel's life was enriched not only by Napp, but also by several other intellectuals, scientists, and botanists.

Mendel twice failed to pass the official examination required for natural science teachers. He thus lacked the state qualifications to teach and settled into a career of teaching in a local school. Napp, who saw tremendous potential in Mendel, arranged for Mendel's university studies in Vienna, with the expenses covered by the monastery. Napp himself had originated from a poor family and supported young men from similar social circumstances.

## Discovering the Patterns of Inheritance

From 1856 to 1863, Mendel conducted his famous plant breeding experiments with the garden pea (Pisum sativum). These experiments took place in a narrow garden in the abbey, which measured 35 m long and 7 m wide. Mendel essentially found the same pattern for all 7 traits he studied, and he derived the mathematical formula that defined the laws of heredity. Mendel's work remains a classic, outlining the results of experimental work with painstaking observations on 7 pairs of contrasting characters. These characters included those affecting the seed (wrinkled or round, yellow or green, and gray or white seedcoat) and those affecting the plant (distribution of flowers, shape and color of pods, and length of stem). Mendel's laws of segregation and the law of independent assortment of characters are now recognized as the fundamental principles of heredity. He noted that each trait was inherited as a separate unit; these units of heredity would later be named genes. Mendel introduced the terms dominant and recessive.

Mendel elucidated the basic patterns of inheritance by performing carefully planned experiments on the common garden pea, an extremely wise choice of experimental model. Pea plants proved to be excellent subjects for simple genetic experiments, as they had some easily recognizable, clear-cut differences in external characteristics.

When Mendel read his paper entitled "Experiments on Plant Hybrids" in 1865 before the Brunn Natural History Society, little discussion followed. This work was published in the proceedings of the society in the following year (1866), but would remain in obscurity for more than 30 years.

For years, Mendel maintained a scientific correspondence with Carl Naegeli, a leading German scientist. Naegeli steered Mendel in the direction of the hawkweed, which proved to be a complicated and unfortunate experimental model. Two years after publication of his paper on the garden pea, Mendel was elected abbot of the monastery. His life thereafter became involved in administrative problems. In particular, Mendel was saddened by a dispute concerning the taxation of the monastery property.

The founder of genetics, Mendel died January 6, 1884, after a long bout with chronic nephritis. In his final years, the conflict with government officials on religious taxes took a toll on his health. Yet, Mendel was an enigmatic figure whose life was marked not only by remarkable successes, but also by many adversities and disappointments. A combination of factors, including dire financial situations, inadequate nutrition, and illness, forced him into a vocational choice borne out of the necessity to survive. Failure to pass the board examinations for teaching certification was a blow to him, but had Mendel been successful, he would have had little opportunity to devote long hours to his experiments with the garden pea.

Mendel was indeed before his time—the monumental significance of his work was not recognized by his peers. At the dawn of the 20th century, 3 researchers, Hugo DeVries, Karl Correns, and Erich von Seysenegy Tschermak, independently discovered the mendelian principles. Unappreciated in life, one posthumous honor after another has been bestowed on this extraordinary monk.

# The Race to Discover the DNA Double Helix

Michael D. Lemonick

Although the Austrian natural scientist Gregor Johann Mendel (1822–1884) had determined the laws that govern genetic inheritance in the 1800s, his contribution went unnoticed for years. In the first decade of the twentieth century scientists rediscovered his findings, and the search began to discover the means by which genetic information is passed from one generation to the next. Deoxyribonucleic acid (DNA) was the key to the problem. DNA provides the instructions that control protein synthesis, and hereditary information is transmitted through protein synthesis. The next step was for scientists to understand how DNA is structured and how it replicates itself.

In this selection from *Time*, senior science writer Michael D. Lemonick describes the race to determine the structure of DNA and the competition that developed among the scientists working on the problem. Two young scientists, Francis Crick (1916– ) and James Watson (1928– ), became the first to accurately describe the double helix of paired bases at the heart of the DNA molecule. Watson and Crick did not do laboratory research but instead preferred to make models in hopes of logically deducing the structure of DNA. A key piece of information necessary to their model building was an X-ray diffraction photo of the DNA double helix made by researcher Rosalind Franklin (1920–1958), given to Watson and Crick by Maurice Wilkins (1916– ) who worked in the same laboratory as Franklin. Many historians believe that Franklin was herself on the verge of discerning the structure of DNA. Watson and Crick saw Franklin's photos, and quickly developed a model of the DNA molecule that they introduced to the world in an article in *Nature* in 1953. For their efforts, Watson, Crick, and Wilkins won a Nobel Prize in 1962. Franklin did not receive the Nobel because it is only given to living scientists. She died of breast cancer in 1958. Lemonick is the author of *Other Worlds* and *The Light at the Edge of the Universe*.

On Feb. 28, 1953, Francis Crick walked into the Eagle pub in Cambridge, England, and announced that he and James Watson had "found the secret of life." At least that's what Watson remembers; Crick's memory is different. The exact words don't matter that much because the fact is, they had done it. Earlier that day, the two scientists had pieced together the correct solution to a problem that researchers around the world were racing to solve. They had built a model of de-oxyribonucleic acid (DNA) that showed by its very structure how DNA could be everything they fiercely believed it to be: the carrier of the genetic code and thus the key molecule of heredity, developmental biology and evolution. Watson and Crick weren't necessarily the smartest scientists in the contest (though they were plenty smart). They weren't the most experienced; their track records in this area of science, in fact, were essentially nonexistent. They didn't have the best equipment. They didn't even know much biochemistry.

But despite these dismal odds, they made a discovery that in the half-century since has transformed science, medicine and much of modern life—though the full impact has yet to be felt. The tale of how this unlikely pair solved the most basic mystery of molecular biology is a reminder that brilliant minds and top-notch training aren't necessarily enough to penetrate the secrets of nature. You also need resilience, dogged persistence, plus a fair amount of luck—and as Watson inadvertently proved with the 1968 best seller *The Double Helix*, his controversial inside account of the discovery, a bit of arrogance doesn't hurt.

By the time Watson arrived in Cambridge in the fall of 1951, the brash and brilliant 23-year-old was obsessed with DNA. He had originally set out to become a naturalist (since childhood, he had had an interest in birds), but during his third year at the University of Chicago, Watson read a book titled *What Is Life?*, by Erwin Schrodinger, a founder of quantum physics. Stepping boldly outside his field of expertise, Schrodinger argued that one of life's essential features is the storage and transmission of information—that is, a genetic code that passes from parent to child. And because it had to be both complex and compact enough to fit inside a single cell, this code had to be written at the molecular level.

Impressed by these arguments, Watson switched from birds to genetics and went to Indiana University in 1947 to study viruses, the simplest form of life on the planet and thus the one in which the code might be especially easy to find. By then, scientists had strong evidence that Schrodinger's genetic code was carried by DNA, thanks to a series of brilliant experiments on pneumococcal bacteria, first by Fred Griffith of the British Health Ministry and later by Oswald Avery at the Rockefeller Institute (now Rockefeller University) in New York City.

But while biologists freely used the word gene to mean the "smallest unit of genetic information," they didn't have a clue what a gene actually is. And with far more self-assurance than a newly minted 22-year-old Ph.D. had any right to possess, Watson decided he would figure it out. His first stop was Copenhagen for a postdoctoral fellowship with the biochemist Herman Kalckar, who was studying DNA's chemical properties. The fellowship ended in a hurry. "Herman," writes Watson in *The Double Helix*, "did not stimulate me in the slightest." Even worse, he decided Kalckar's research would not immediately lead to an understanding of the gene.

During a conference in Naples, Italy, in the spring of 1951, Watson happened to sit in on a lecture by Maurice Wilkins of King's College, London, who was using X-ray diffraction to try to understand the physical structure of the DNA molecule. When you shine X rays on any sort of crystal—and some biological molecules, including DNA, form crystals—the invisible rays bounce off atoms in the sample to create complex patterns on a piece of photographic film. In principle, you can look at the patterns and get important clues about the structure of the molecules that make up the crystal. In practice, the patterns in DNA are hellishly hard to disentangle.

But Watson was elated. Wilkins' image suggested that DNA had a regular crystalline structure. By figuring out what that structure is, moreover, one might be in a better position to understand how genes work. Here was someone who appreciated what Watson already believed but which many scientists didn't yet accept: that the genetic code was somehow tied up in the physical structure of DNA. He realized he needed to understand X-ray diffraction and wanted to join Wilkins in London but never got an opportunity to ask him. So Watson wangled the next best position—a fellowship at the Cavendish Laboratory in Cambridge, where the director, Sir William Lawrence Bragg, had (with his father Sir William) developed X-ray crystallography in 1912–14.

It was there, in the fall of 1951, that Watson initially met Crick. (He actually met Crick's wife Odile first. Her only comment afterward: "He had no hair!"—a reference to Watson's crew cut.) Like Wilkins, Crick was a physicist who switched into biology; like Wilkins and Watson, Crick had been impressed with Schrodinger's *What Is Life?* He wasn't actually studying DNA, though; at age 35, thanks in part to a hiatus for military work in World War II, he was still pursuing his Ph.D. on the X-ray diffraction of hemoglobin, the iron-carrying protein in blood. Watson, meanwhile, had gone to Cambridge to use X-ray diffraction to understand the structure of another protein, myoglobin.

But whatever their formal duties, both men were determined to figure out what genes were, and both were convinced that understanding the structure of DNA would help them do that. "Now, with me around the lab always wanting to talk about genes," writes Watson in *The Double Helix*, "Francis no longer kept his thoughts about DNA in a back recess of his brain. . . . No one should mind if, by spending only a few hours a week thinking about DNA, he helped me solve a smashingly important problem."

The two men turned out to be utterly compatible. "Jim

and I hit it off immediately," writes Crick in his book, *What Mad Pursuit*, "partly because our interests were astonishingly similar and partly, I suspect, because a certain youthful arrogance, a ruthlessness and an impatience with sloppy thinking came naturally to both of us." (Crick had got in trouble more than once at the Cavendish for pointing out the sloppy thinking of his bosses.)

Both men also loved to think out loud, for hours at a stretch, during walks along the river Cam, at meals at the Cricks' flat, at the Eagle and, of course, in the lab, where their incessant chatter drove their colleagues crazy. (Watson and Crick were quickly relegated to a separate office, where they would disturb only each other.) Most important, both were as tenacious as pit bulls. Once they clamped their minds onto the problem of DNA structure, they couldn't let go until they solved it—or someone else got there first.

The likeliest someone, both men believed, was Linus Pauling. To a later generation, Pauling would be best known as an antiwar activist and the slightly batty advocate of vitamin C as the antidote to colds and cancer. But at mid-century he was the world's premier physical chemist, the man who had literally written the book on chemical bonds. A few months before Watson arrived, in fact, Pauling embarrassed the Cavendish by winning the race to figure out the structure of keratin, the protein that makes up hair and fingernails. (It was a long, complex corkscrew of atoms known as the alpha-helix.) While he did rely on X-ray crystallographs for hints to what was going on at the molecular level, Pauling depended more heavily on scaled-up models he built by hand, using his deep knowledge of the ways atoms can bond together. Cavendish scientists, relying mostly on X rays, hadn't bothered to consult their colleagues in the chemistry department about what was or wasn't possible for atoms to do, and became hopelessly sidetracked.

The defeat was humiliating—"the biggest mistake," Bragg would one day say, "of my scientific career"—and Crick and Watson knew it could easily happen again. Pauling surely understood that the structure of DNA was the next big challenge, and once he turned his powerful brain to the problem, he would certainly crack it. "Within a few days of my arrival," writes Watson, "we knew what to do: imitate Linus Pauling and beat him at his own game." To do so, they would need X rays of DNA, but they would have to look outside Cambridge. The Cavendish's crystallographers were interested in proteins; DNA was the province of King's College, London; and while actively competing with Americans was fine, it just wouldn't do to poach—openly, at least—on fellow Brits.

Fortunately, Crick was on good terms with Wilkins, the man whose DNA images had originally sparked Watson's interest. Unfortunately, Wilkins was on very bad terms with his King's College colleague, the accomplished but prickly Rosalind Franklin. At 31, she was already one of the world's most talented crystallographers and had recently returned to her home country to take a position at King's after a stint at a prestigious Paris lab.

Franklin believed deeply in the primacy of experimental data: Pauling might have been lucky with his flashy model building, but the best way to understand DNA, she insisted, was to make high-quality X-ray images first and speculate afterward about what they meant. "Only a genius of [Pauling's] stature," writes Watson, summarizing Franklin's attitude, "could play like a ten-year-old boy and still get the right answer." Wilkins made the mistake of declaring publicly that Franklin's images suggested that DNA had a helical shape. Franklin was incensed. He had no right, she believed, to even be working on X-raying DNA, something she was led to believe was her exclusive domain at King's College.

They remained collaborators in name but essentially stopped talking. To find out what she was doing, Wilkins had to go to a seminar Franklin gave in November 1951. He invited Watson to come along. (Crick, whose interest in DNA was well known, thought it might cause too much of a flap if he showed up.) Wilkins had warned Watson that Franklin was difficult; for his part, Watson had a generally piggish attitude toward women at the time. He liked "popsies"—young, pretty things without brains—but strong, independent women rather baffled him. In *The Double Helix*, he puts Franklin down in a passage that he later had the decency to renounce:

"By choice she did not emphasize her feminine qualities. Though her features were strong, she was not unattractive and might have been quite stunning had she taken even a mild interest in clothes. This she did not. There was never lipstick to contrast with her straight black hair, while at the age of 31 her dresses showed all the imagination of English bluestocking adolescents."

Then came the professional assessment: "Clearly Rosy [a nickname she abhorred, and which her adolescent-minded antagonists therefore insisted on using] had to go or be put in her place. The former was obviously preferable because, given her belligerent moods, it would be very difficult for [Wilkins] to maintain a dominant position that would allow him to think unhindered about DNA."

## The Human Genome Project

*A gene is a "discrete unit of hereditary information consisting of a specific nucleotide sequence in DNA," according to biologists Neil Campbell, Jane B. Reece, and Lawrence G. Mitchell. Once the mystery of DNA and genes began to unravel, scientists became interested in mapping the genome (a complete set of an organism's genes) of the human species. This project is called the Human Genome Project.*

The information obtained from studying individual genes is interesting and valuable, but in recent years geneticists have also undertaken a much broader approach, with the goal of systematically mapping entire genomes. They aim to determine the precise locations of all of an organism's genes—and noncoding DNA segments, as well—along the DNA molecules of its genome. The most ambitious research project made possible by DNA technology is the Human Genome Project, officially begun in 1990. This is an international effort to map the entire human genome, ultimately by determining the complete nucleotide sequence of the DNA of each human chromosome (the 22 autosomes and the $X$ and $Y$ sex chromosomes). The project

For the moment, though, the men were stuck with "Rosy's" data, and Watson briefed Crick as soon as possible on what he had seen and heard. But Watson, overconfident to the point of arrogance, hadn't bothered to take notes. "If a subject interested me," he would write, "I could usually recollect what I needed. This time, however, we were in trouble, because I did not know enough of the crystallographic jargon." A key point was the amount of water present in Franklin's DNA samples. Watson remembered the number incorrectly, by a lot. . . .

The King's College group, meanwhile, pushed ahead with its DNA research. Franklin kept working to perfect her X-ray images. In May 1952 she took one that would prove crucially important—though until the day she died, she would never realize it. By increasing the humidity in her lab apparatus, she and graduate student Raymond Gosling discov-

---

is proceeding through three stages that focus on the DNA more and more closely. These stages are genetic (or linkage) mapping, physical mapping, and, finally, DNA sequencing. [Scientists announced in April, 2003 that the project was 99.9% complete.]

In addition to mapping human DNA, the Human Genome Project includes mapping of the genomes of other species important in biological research, including *E. coli* and other prokaryotes, *Saccharomyces cerevisiae* (yeast), *Caenorhabditis elegans* (nematode), *Drosophila melanogaster* (fruit fly), and *Mus musculus* (mouse). These genomes are of great interest in their own right, and the sequences completed so far have already brought us important biological insights. In addition, work on these genomes is useful for developing the strategies, methods, and new technologies necessary for deciphering the human genome, which is much larger. The technological power for this daunting task will come in large part from advances in automation and from utilization of electronic technology, including computer software.

Neil Campbell, Jane B. Reece, and Lawrence G. Mitchell, *Biology*. 5th ed. Menlo Park, CA: Benjamin Cummings, 1999, p. 376.

ered that DNA could assume two forms. When sufficiently moist, the molecule would stretch and get thinner, and the pictures that resulted were much sharper than anything anyone had ever seen. They called the wetter version the B form of DNA.

Wilkins was intrigued; the pictures convinced him more firmly than ever that the DNA molecule was helical, and he proposed to collaborate with Franklin in exploring the B form in detail. But Franklin, who still thought there was no evidence of a helix in her pictures, went into a rage, according to Wilkins. "She exploded," writes Brenda Maddox in her sympathetic 2002 biography *Rosalind Franklin: The Dark Lady of DNA.* "Rosalind had good reason. . . . Undervalued at King's, she had just achieved extraordinary results by working in virtual isolation. Now what she saw as a less able colleague of higher rank was proposing to elbow in and spoil the clarity of her investigation." Alarmed by what had become a very public quarrel, lab director Randall [J.T.] declared that from now on Wilkins would work with the B form of DNA and Franklin would have exclusive rights to the A form. Unwittingly and indirectly, he had just handed Watson and Crick a crucial piece of information.

Through the summer and fall of 1952, Watson and Crick kept talking, trying to fit together the still unconnected pieces of the DNA puzzle. One piece was a discovery that had been made years earlier by the Austrian refugee Erwin Chargaff. Analyzing the DNA of many different organisms, he found that while the overall proportions of the four DNA bases varied among species, the number of adenine molecules always equaled the number of thymine, and guanine and cytosine were similarly matched. (Chargaff visited Cambridge during this period and was appalled at how little basic chemistry Watson and Crick knew—and offended by how little this seemed to bother them.)

But progress on the greater problem was slow. "On a few walks our enthusiasm would build up to the point that we fiddled with the models when we got back to our office," writes Watson. "But almost immediately Francis saw that the reasoning which had momentarily given us hope led nowhere. . . . Several times I carried on alone for a half hour or so, but without Francis' reassuring chatter my inability to think in three dimensions became all too apparent."

In December 1952, they got some bad news. In a letter to his son Peter, then a graduate student at Cambridge, Pauling revealed that he would soon publish a paper on the structure of DNA. It looked as if Watson and Crick had lost the race. Peter received his father's paper on Jan. 28 and walked into Watson and Crick's office to tell them about it. "Giving Francis no chance to ask for the manuscript," writes Watson, "I pulled it out of Peter's outside coat pocket and began reading." The senior Pauling had come up with a three-stranded molecule with the sugar-phosphate backbone at the center. Almost immediately, Watson realized it didn't make sense. "I could not pinpoint the mistake, however, until I looked at the illustrations for several minutes. Then I realized that the phosphate groups in Linus' model were not ionized. . . . Pauling's nucleic acid in a sense was not an acid at all."

But of course DNA was an acid. Pauling, the world's greatest chemist, had made a mistake in basic chemistry—an unimaginable blooper. Watson and Crick retired to the Eagle to drink a toast to Pauling's failure. They were more nervous than ever, though. The paper was scheduled to be published in March; once it was out, someone would notice the error, and Pauling would work that much harder to vindicate himself. They had at most six weeks to figure out DNA.

Watson also knew he had to warn Wilkins and Franklin about Pauling's near miss. On Friday, Jan. 30, he went to London. Wilkins wasn't in his lab, so Watson dropped in on Franklin. What happened next—from Watson's point of view, at least—was recorded in great detail in *The Double Helix*. The passage shows how formidable Franklin could be but also demonstrates Watson's adolescent delight in needling her. He tried to engage Franklin in debate about the idea that DNA was helical, which she still insisted was unsupported by evidence. "Rosy by then was hardly able to control her temper," he writes, "and her voice rose as she told me that the stupidity of my remarks would be obvious if I would stop blubbering and look at her X-ray evidence.

"I decided to risk a full explosion," he continues. "Without further hesitation I implied that she was incompetent in interpreting X-ray pictures. If only she would learn some theory, she would understand how her supposed antihelical features arose from the minor distortions needed to pack regular helices into a crystalline lattice." The explosion occurred. "Suddenly, Rosy came from behind the lab bench that separated us and began moving toward me. Fearing that in her hot anger she might strike me, I grabbed up the Pauling manuscript and hastily retreated toward the open door. My escape was blocked by Maurice [Wilkins], who, searching for me, had just then stuck his head through." Franklin shut the door on both men. "Walking down the passage," Watson continues, "I told Maurice how his unexpected appearance might have prevented Rosy from assaulting me. Slowly he assured me that this very well might have happened. Some months earlier she had made a similar lunge toward him."

United in their belief that Rosy was impossible—there's no evidence that either man felt he had contributed to her reaction—Watson and Wilkins began chatting. "Now that I need no longer merely imagine the emotional hell he had faced during the past two years," writes Watson, "he could treat me almost as a fellow collaborator rather than as a distant acquaintance." In the course of that conversation, Wilkins trotted out one of Franklin's images of the B form of DNA. Labeled Photograph 51, it was her best—and, writes Watson, "the instant I saw the picture my mouth fell open and my pulse began to race. The pattern was unbelievably simpler than those obtained previously. Moreover, the black cross of reflections which dominated the picture could arise only from a helical structure."

DNA must be a helix after all, and on a cold train ride back to Cambridge, Watson decided that two helical sugar-phosphate backbones made more sense than three. "Thus by the time I had cycled back to college and climbed over the back gate, I had decided to build two-chain models. Francis would have to agree. Even though he was a physicist, he knew that important biological objects came in pairs."

It wasn't just the clarity of Franklin's picture that excited Watson. It was also the fact that the pattern repeated itself every 34 angstroms (an angstrom is one ten-billionth of a meter). That gave Crick and Watson crucial information about the angles between bonded molecules. Even better, the image suggested that the bases attached to the backbone were neatly stacked one on top of the other.

But were the two backbones on the inside of DNA or on the outside? Inside was a lot more straightforward; with the attached bases pointing outward, whatever code they might carry would be easily accessible. There seemed no chemically viable way to parse it, however, although Watson spent several days trying. Finally, he writes, "as I took apart a particularly repulsive backbone-centered molecule, I decided that no harm could come from spending a few days building backbone-out models." This would raise the tricky question of how to pack strings of bases against one another. But Watson put aside that worry for the moment.

On Feb. 8, 1953, the Cricks had Wilkins and Watson to lunch, and the Cavendish scientists learned several things. First, it was O.K. with Wilkins if they proceeded with their model building (a good thing, since they had already started and had no intention of stopping now). More important, they evidently also learned that the King's group had prepared a report on its DNA studies for the Medical Research Council, which funded the work. It wasn't a confidential document, so Watson and Crick got hold of a copy. In it were some more crucial clues, including the fact that DNA had a particular type of structural symmetry that implied that the molecule was made of two chains running in opposite directions.

But there remained the problem of how to fit the bases together. Watson kept trying to do it by pairing like with like—an A attached to one backbone linked to an A on the other. Chemically, it would work. The bases were different enough in size and shape, though, that this scheme led to either a gap between bases or misshapen backbones. Worse yet, when Watson happened to show his idea to Jerry Donohue, an American crystallographer doing a stint at the Cavendish, Donohue informed him that the bases came in more than one chemical form. Watson was using the form prescribed in standard textbooks. But the textbooks, Donohue insisted, were wrong.

It took about a week for Watson and Crick to see that Donohue was right. The Cavendish machine shop would have to build new pieces for their models. Watson couldn't wait. He spent the afternoon of Feb. 27 cutting his own pieces out of cardboard. Then he went out to the theater.

On Feb. 28, armed with his new cardboard bases, Watson began trying to match like with like again—and then he had an insight. "Suddenly," he writes, "I became aware that an adenine-thymine pair held together by two hydrogen bonds was identical in shape to a guanine-cytosine pair held together by at least two hydrogen bonds." If the bases were joined up this way, the backbones wouldn't be bumpy. Moreover, such an arrangement neatly explained what Chargaff had discovered in 1950. If A and T were always paired, there naturally had to be equal amounts of these two bases; same thing for G and C.

"Even more exciting," writes Watson, "this type of double helix suggested a replication scheme . . . always pairing adenine with thymine and guanine with cytosine meant that the base sequences of the two intertwined chains were complementary to each other. Given the base sequence of one chain, that of its partner was automatically determined. Conceptually, it was thus very easy to visualize how a single chain could be the template for the synthesis of a chain with the complementary sequence."

He consulted Donohue. It made sense. Crick showed up about 40 minutes later; it made sense to him too. There were still details to work out, and Watson feared a repeat of their botch job in late 1951. "Thus," he writes, "I felt slightly queasy when at lunch Francis winged into the Eagle to tell everyone within hearing distance that we had found the secret of life."

But of course they had. Wilkins and Franklin would be informed within a few days—although they never told Franklin of the crucial role her photograph had played. The rest of the world would learn about the double helix in a one-page letter to *Nature*, which appeared on April 25, 1953. It began with the now famous understatement: "We wish to suggest a structure for the salt of deoxyribose nucleic acid (D.N.A.). This structure has novel features which are of considerable biological interest."

In retrospect, what they found is utterly straightforward and so elegant that Pauling or Wilkins or Franklin or someone would have come up with it, possibly within weeks. The reason we remember Watson and Crick instead is summed up nicely by Crick himself. "The major credit I think Jim and I deserve," he writes, "is for selecting the right problem and sticking to it. It's true that by blundering about we stumbled on gold, but the fact remains that we were looking for gold."

# Chapter 2

# Disease and Disease Prevention

Turning Points

IN WORLD HISTORY

# Leeuwenhoek and the Discovery of Bacteria

William Bulloch

Antoni van Leeuwenhoek (1632–1723) was a Dutch retailer of cloth and men's clothing with a fascination for careful observation using microscopes. Although van Leeuwenhoek did not invent the microscope, he built as many as four hundred, grinding the lenses himself. At the time of his death he owned nearly two hundred fifty microscopes. He spent much of his free time peering through the microscope at the little creatures he found swimming in rainwater. He came to call the creatures "little animalcules" and he categorized them according to shape and locomotion. Although later scientists would make the connection between bacteria and disease, it was van Leeuwenhoek who was the first to systematically observe and describe these microscopic organisms. William Bulloch, professor emeritus of bacteriology at the University of London until his death in 1941, reviews van Leeuwenhoek's scientific contribution in this selection from his book on the history of bacteriology.

[Antoni van] Leeuwenhoek was born in Delft in Holland 24 October 1632, and died in Delft 26 August 1723, nearly 91 years of age. His father was a basket-maker, and Antony was sent to school near Leyden. In 1648, being then 16, he went to Amsterdam and was placed in a draper's shop to learn the business. In this shop he rose to be book-keeper or cashier, and after some years returned to his native Delft and remained there from 1654 to 1723, a period of 70 years. In Delft he bought a house and shop and set up as a draper and haberdasher. He also held the office of Chamberlain of the Council Chamber of the worshipful Sheriffs of Delft. . . .

From 1660 nothing was heard of Leeuwenhoek outside Delft, but in 1673 he suddenly became known as an amateur scientist offering a paper to the Royal Society for publication in the *Philosophical Transactions*, whose first editor was Henry Oldenburg (?1615–77), Secretary of the Royal Society. Oldenburg carried on a large correspondence with students of science all over Europe. Indeed his correspondence was so extensive as to arouse suspicion and he was committed to the Tower [tower of London prison] for a couple of months and was visited there by John Evelyn the diarist, who was one of the original fellows of the Royal Society. Oldenburg, to his credit, was one of the few who stayed in London during the Great Plague in 1665, and he was also there during the Great Fire of 1666. One of Oldenburg's correspondents was the famous Reinier de Graaf (1643–73), the discoverer of the Graafian follicle. He was a friend of Leeuwenhoek and practised in Delft. In 1673 he introduced Leeuwenhoek to Oldenburg's notice in a letter in which he says: 'I am writing to tell you that a certain most ingenious person here (i.e. Delft) named Leewenhoeck has devised microscopes which far surpass those which we have hitherto seen manufactured by Eustachio Divini and others.'

Apparently in the period from 1660 to 1673 Leeuwenhoek, the draper of Delft, had in his spare time acquired the art of making lenses and mounting them to form microscopes, and he had begun to turn his lenses on to all manner of objects. De Graaf had himself examined many of Leeuwenhoek's preparations.

## Letters to the Royal Society

The first letter of Leeuwenhoek to the Royal Society dealt with mould, the mouth parts and eye of the bee, and on the louse. From this time for the next fifty years he sent letters to the Royal Society covering an enormous field of observations. He was not much of a scholar of languages and knew only Dutch, but many of his letters were translated into Latin and English and no doubt suffered thereby. All his observations were communicated in letters only, all written by himself in a beautiful hand. In the Library of the Royal Society are still preserved about 200 of these letters. Leeuwenhoek was elected F.R.S. (member of the Royal Society) on 29 January 1679–80 (o.s.) and his election was unanimous. He was greatly gratified by this recognition among fellow scientists, and on the receipt of his fellowship diploma wrote to say that he held himself 'most straitly pledged . . . to strive with all my might and main, all my life long, to make myself more worthy of this honour and privilege'. Leeuwenhoek never came to London to sign the register nor did he ever attend a meeting of the Royal Society, although on one occasion before his election he paid a visit to England (1668).

In Delft in his later years Leeuwenhoek became an object of curiosity to visitors, many of whom called to see his microscopes. Among well-known visitors were people of title, including the [Russian] Tsar Peter the Great, who at that time (1698) was staying in Holland to learn shipbuilding. . . .

All the microscopes made by Leeuwenhoek were of the single or simple type. They were in fact magnifying glasses but he himself left no description of them or how he made them, and he had some secret method for the examination of the smallest creatures which he studied. He left behind him 247 finished microscopes and 172 lenses merely mounted between small plates, an amazing total of 419 lenses which he had made with his own hands. . . .

## Leeuwenhoek's Discoveries

I may now tell the reader something of what Leeuwenhoek found with his microscopes which entitles him to be called 'the father of protozoology and bacteriology'. In his famous 18th letter, dated 9 October 1676, he tells us—I quote (Clifford) Dobell's translation of the original Dutch letter in the Royal Society—that in September 1675 he 'discovered living creatures in rain which had stood but a few days in a new tub that was painted blue within'. He described four sorts of animals of which one was undoubtedly Vorticella. The fourth sort 'which I saw a-moving were so small that for my part I can't assign any figure to 'em. These little animals were more than a thousand times less than the eye of a full-grown louse.' Several writers have thought that the animalcules so described were bacteria, but Dobell thinks that they were probably a species of Monas. In the same 18th letter Leeuwenhoek also described animalcules which he found in water from the river Maas, from a well in the courtyard of his house in Delft, and in sea-water which he obtained at Scheveningen when he visited that village in July 1676. Leeuwenhoek also gave a long and detailed account of 'incredibly many very little animalcules of divers sorts' which he discerned in infusions of peppercorns in water. It is not possible to identify all the forms he found in pepper water although the majority were probably protozoa. Some, however, may have been bacteria, especially those which were 'incredibly small, nay so small in my sight that even if 100 of these very wee animals lay stretched out one against another they could not reach to the length of a grain of coarse sand'.

If there is any doubt about the bacterial nature of the smallest creatures described by Leeuwenhoek in 1676 there can be none about those he described in 1683. In his 39th letter, dated 17 September 1683, he gave an unequivocal description of bacteria which he had found on his own teeth. Not only did he discover bacteria but he described and figured all the morphological types known to-day, viz. cocci, bacteria, and spiral forms. . . .

Leeuwenhoek found the same animals on the teeth of two women and a child about 8 years old. The substance on the teeth of an old man 'who leads a sober life and never drinks brandy or tobacco' showed 'an unbelievably great company of living animalcules a-swimming more nimbly than any I had ever seen up to this time. The biggest sort . . . bent their body into curves in going forwards . . .' Leeuwenhoek washed out his own mouth with strong wine vinegar but still found animalcules on his teeth. He estimated that 'there are more animals living in the scum on the teeth in a man's mouth than there are men in a whole kingdom'. These 'animals' described and figured by Leeuwenhoek are clearly bacteria. . . .

Leeuwenhoek returned to the subject of the animalcules on the human teeth in his 75th letter, dated 16 September 1692. In it he tells us that since 1683 he had not been able to find living creatures on his teeth, and he attributed this to the fact that he drank very hot coffee in the morning. But having carefully cleansed his mouth and taken material from his back teeth with the help of a magnifying mirror, 'I saw with as great wonderment as ever before an unconceivably great number of little animalcules. These animalcules, or most all of them, moved so nimbly among one another that the whole stuff seemed alive and a-moving.' He tried to measure the size of them by comparing them with a grain of coarse sand such as is used for scouring pewter and he found that the grain of sand was 1,000 times longer than the diameter of one of the animalcules, 'consequently then such a grain of sand was far more than a thousand millionfold bigger than one of the little creatures aforesaid'. In addition to the smallest animalcules of rounded form he saw others whose bodies were 'quite 5 or 6 times longer than they were thick and therewithal their body was of equal thickness all along so that I couldn't make out which was their head or which their tail end'. Their motion was slow. . . .

Leeuwenhoek frequently expresses the feelings of pleasure he had when studying the minute creatures with his lenses. He sometimes refers to them as beasties (*beesjes*) or little creatures (*cleijne Schepsels*), and he must have spent many hours watching them. His observations are classical, and Dobell (1923) has made a just estimate of his position in the bacteriological world when he wrote that Leeuwenhoek 'was the first bacteriologist and the first protozoologist and he created bacteriology and protozoology out of nothing'.

# Semmelweis Reduces the Spread of Childbed Fever

Robert P. Hudson

English physician Edward Jenner noticed connections between cowpox and immunity to smallpox, and his observation led to the development of a vaccination against smallpox. Austrian physician Ignaz Phillipp Semmelweis (1818–1865) observed that the death rate from puerperal (childbed) fever was much worse among women who gave birth in the hospital than those who gave birth before they arrived at the hospital. His observation eventually led to improved sanitation methods in hospitals, but his initial investigations turned up no immediate answers. The key to the mystery came when Semmelweis learned of the death from childbed fever of a male professor. Semmelweis found that the man had been cut by a scalpel while doing an autopsy on a woman who had died of puerperal fever. In the nineteenth century doctors did not use antiseptic practices, and as a result, they spread infection among patients. Although Semmelweis did not fully understand what was causing the puerperal infections, he instituted cleanliness practices such as washing his hands and using a chlorine solution—mainly to reduce odors. In this selection from his book *Disease and Its Control*, physician Robert P. Hudson describes how the mortality rate from childbed fever dropped dramatically after Semmelweis convinced others to adopt his more hygienic practices. Hudson is a professor of the history of medicine at Kansas University Medical Center.

Obstetrics is ordinarily the happiest of medical specialties. In the vast majority of cases the obstetrician is not even dealing with disease. Excepting disappointment over the sex of the new citizen, the "patient" is almost invariably satisfied with her obstetrical encounter. The mortality of childbirth has now been reduced to near zero, and the prospective mother can choose how little pain she wishes to bear. But the giving of birth was not always such a benign affair. In the nineteenth century the happiness accompanying an announcement of pregnancy was usually beclouded by a realistic fear. The morbidity and mortality associated with childbirth were a source of genuine concern to patients and physicians alike. The chief reason for this widespread anxiety was the often fatal complication, childbed fever.

When the placenta separates from the uterine wall after delivery of a child, a large wound remains, which has been likened to an amputation stump. Ordinarily this presents no danger because the uterus harbors no bacteria. But with the cervix widely dilated following the birth process, bacteria present in the vagina have access to the placental wound, and from there through the open veins and lymphatics to the bloodstream and the body at large. Normally the probability is small that pathogenic bacteria will be present in the vagina to ascend into the uterus after delivery. Any number of factors can enlarge this probability, but for our purposes the most important is the intrusion of a contaminated hand or instrument. . . .

[In Vienna Austria] in the late eighteenth century the empress Maria Theresa, free for a while from the demands of war, turned her attention to the general well-being of her subjects. One manifestation of this monarchical altruism, one that was not finally accomplished until four years after her death, was the General Hospital of Vienna and its famous division, the Vienna Lying-in. At its dedication the Lying-in was the largest such institution in the world, a distinction that would have been a source of a good deal less pride if all concerned had known then what was seen in retrospect, that the total burden of postoperative and obstetrical infection was greater in hospitals than in homes and that the heaviest mortality was occurring in the larger hospitals.

The Vienna Lying-in was a teaching hospital, providing

instruction to medical students and young physicians in its
First Division, and after about 1840 or so, separate supervi-
sion of aspiring midwives in its Second Division. In order to
keep track of the progress of labor, expectant mothers underwent periodic pelvic examinations. The presence of students increased the incidence of such intrusions, at times
several-fold. In the absence of an established germ theory,
physicians, nurses, and students engaged in handwashing
largely for esthetic purposes, not with the idea of preventing
disease. Interspersed with their attendance on women in
labor, students and physicians were frequently involved in
autopsies, many on women dead of puerperal fever. It was in
this setting on July 1, 1846, that a young Hungarian physician arrived to assume his duties as assistant at the First Obstetrical Clinic.

## Mysterious Mortality Rates

Ignaz Phillip Semmelweis (1818–1865) was born in a region
that is now located in Budapest. He began the study of law
at the University of Vienna but switched to medicine, receiving his degree in April, 1844. In his position as assistant
in obstetrics, Semmelweis was soon confronted with a set of
statistics that had long disturbed medical attendants. Over
the preceding years, figures revealed that the mortality from
childbed fever in the First Division was some three times
greater than in the Second. In truth the figures were even
worse than Semmelweis first realized, because seriously ill
patients from the First Division were frequently transferred
to the General Hospital, where their deaths were not
recorded as puerperal fever. Such transfers rarely occurred
from the Second Division. . . .

For a year Semmelweis accumulated data and struggled to
make sense of the facts confronting him. Why were women
who were admitted after giving birth on the way to the hospital (*Gassengeburt*, or streetbirths, they were called) rarely affected by puerperal fever? Why had the death rate jumped
suddenly from 0.84 percent in 1821 to 7.8 percent in 1822,
the year following Doctor Klein's [physician and teacher who
did not use antiseptic practices] appointment to the chair of

obstetrics? And why the appalling difference between the medical student and midwife wards in the first place? "Everywhere questions arose," he wrote; "everything remained without explanation: all was doubt and difficulty. Only the great number of the dead was an undoubted reality."

Depressed by such questions and by political considerations that forced him to repeat his two-year period as ordinary assistant, Semmelweis left for Venice to freshen his spirits. Soon after his return he learned of the death of Professor Kolletschka who, in the course of a post-mortem had suffered a scalpel wound at the hands of one of his students. From the autopsy protocol Semmelweis learned that Kolletschka had been "affected with lymphangitis, phlebitis in the same upper extremity, and he died from pleurisy, pericarditis, peritonitis, and meningitis, and a few days before his death metastasis occurred in one of the eyes." Reading this, Semmelweis's thinking took a crucial leap. . . .

With this, the puzzling pieces fell into place. Kolletschka, though a man, had in effect died of childbed fever. In his case the disease was transmitted from the dead body to his bloodstream by a scalpel wound. In the case of childbed fever the disease was carried unwittingly on the hands of medical attendants from women sick or dead of puerperal fever to normal lying-in women. The women who gave birth on the way to the hospital were spared childbed fever because they avoided the pelvic examinations that spread the disease.

Also comprehensible was the sudden jump in the incidence of puerperal fever in 1822, when Klein took over the obstetrical unit. Klein's predecessor had refused to accede to demands from his superiors that the various aspects of labor be taught directly from cadavers. Instead he had insisted on using manikins of the pelvis and child, or phantoms as they were called. Under administrative pressure, when Klein took over he agreed to use fresh cadavers for instructing midwives as well as medical students. Many of the cadavers, of course, had reached their tragic end as a result of puerperal fever, and were thus a rich source of infective material easily transmissible from the classroom sessions involving dead bodies to women in labor on the wards. Similarly clear were the statistics that had first attracted Semmelweis's attention. Medical personnel in the First Division were customarily involved in autopsies, an infrequent situation in the Second Division for either teachers or pupils.

Perhaps no disease in history has matched puerperal fever in demonstrating the role that medical ignorance, understandable though it may be, can play in binding the physician directly to his patient's death. Practices such as bloodletting at times undoubtedly abetted the disease instead of recovery, but precision is elusive here because the medical intervention cannot be separated from the natural course of the disease. In the case of puerperal fever the relationship between the medical attendants and the deaths of their patients was now starkly visible. The confessions of physicians, before and after Semmelweis, who were gradually moved to conclude that they had been agents in the spread of childbed fever, makes for some of the most poignant reading in the annals of disease.

Convinced of the mechanism by which puerperal fever was being spread, Semmelweis now faced the problem of remedying the situation. He had concluded that the agents responsible for childbed fever were cadaveric particles, that is, morbific or dead materials, passed from the sick and dead to healthy women on the hands of medical attendants. Finding that he could not remove the odor of this morbific matter with soap and water, he reasoned that some of the particles must survive even a thorough washing. In order to destroy the odor, which he equated with the morbific material, he decided first on a chlorine solution, switching later to the cheaper chlorinated lime. Before moving from the autopsy room to a woman in labor or from one patient to another, all medical attendants were required to undergo a chlorine rinse.

The efficacy of Semmelweis's method was soon apparent. In 1846, before chlorine was adopted, the mortality rate was 2.7 percent in the Second Division and 11.4 percent in the First Division. In 1848, after a full year of the chlorine wash, for the first time in the history of the Vienna Lying-in, the mortality rate in the First Division was lower than in the Second, 1.27 percent versus 1.33 percent.

# Pasteur, Koch, and the Science of Bacteriology

John R. Green

In this selection from his book on the history of medicine, physician and author John R. Green points out that several scientists contributed to knowledge of how infections are spread by bacteria. German pathologist Jacob Henle (1809–1884) was the first to point out the relationship between infectious agents and disease. But it was not until the work of Frenchman Louis Pasteur (1822–1895) that interest in the connection between bacteria and disease really began to be applied to public health. First, Pasteur was able to demonstrate in the laboratory that bacteria did not arise spontaneously from nothing, as most scientists believed. Then he introduced the "germ theory of disease" in 1865, positing that many diseases were caused by specific microorganisms. When the French silk industry was threatened with ruin by a silkworm disease, Pasteur investigated and was able to find and isolate the responsible pathogen. He did the same for anthrax affecting livestock. He was also responsible for the technique of "pasteurization," by which contaminant bacteria in milk and other foods are killed at high temperatures. Pasteur's work directly led to the growth of bacteriology as a science. Green, a professor at Arizona State University, also reviews the work of German Robert Koch (1843–1910), who developed six postulates to determine which organism causes a specific disease. These postulates are still in use. Pasteur's and Koch's work would inspire Joseph Lister (1827–1912), who developed antiseptic practices in hospitals to prevent the spread of disease.

John R. Green, *Medical History for Students*. Springfield, IL: Charles C. Thomas, 1968. Copyright © 1968 by Charles C. Thomas. Reproduced by permission.

Bacteriology actually dominated the medicine of the last quarter of the nineteenth century. During the first century before Christ, Marcus Varro (116–27 B.C.) mentioned the idea that small animaliculae may cause disease. Hugo of Lucca, Theodoric and Henri de Mondeville introduced their revolutionary treatment of wounds with concern about contamination by the air in the thirteenth century but had no idea of bacteriology. Fracastoro [Girolamo, 1478–1553] advanced the theory that invisible living semina scattered disease. His work on infection was published in 1546 and contained the first scientific statement of the true nature of contagion, infection, disease germs and the modes of transmission of various diseases. Kircher [Athanasius, 1602–1680] said that he saw "innumerable small animals" in putrefying meat and "worms" in the blood of plague patients. It is not actually known what he did see and it would have required a most excellent microscope to visualize what he described. His publication, however, in 1658, was a clear statement of the germ theory of contagious disease, based upon microscopic studies. On the contrary, Leeuwenhoek [A., 1632–1723], who has been described as the "Father of Protozoology and Bacteriology," sketched "little animals" but made no attempt to associate these organisms with disease. No one doubted that Leeuwenhoek saw the structures that he illustrated. His work was described in some 200 letters to the Royal Society during the latter part of the seventeenth century.

Some historians consider Agostino Bassi (1771–1856) the founder of the parasitic theory of infection. He carried out experiments at the University of Pavia and described methods of preventing muscardine of silk worms by segregation and by treatment of infected places with calcium chloride, potassium nitrate and other chemicals. He published *On Contagions* in 1844 and stated that "smallpox, spotted fever, bubonic plague and syphilis are caused by living parasites, animal or vegetable."

Jacob Henle (1809–1884) had called attention to the probability that living parasitic agents caused infectious diseases in 1840. Anthrax bacilli were seen in the blood of dead sheep in 1849 and 1850. "Monads" which were round or oval shapes were seen in the stools of patients with cholera in 1854. The term *vibrions* had also been introduced in the early years of the century for long or short moving rod-like organisms as seen under the microscope.

## Louis Pasteur

However, it was Louis Pasteur (1822–1895) who excited a new interest in Leeuwenhoek's "little animals." Pasteur was a chemist and his eminence in science was a result of imagination, intuition, patience, persistence and industry. Pasteur made at least six outstanding contributions to his fields of chemistry, bacteriology and industrial chemistry. His first accomplishment occurred in 1848, when he was twenty-six years of age, and had to do with the study of tartaric acid crystals under the microscope in relation to polarized light, with the demonstration of its rotatory activity to the left or right. The study of alcoholic fermentation and lactic acid fermentation in sour milk six years later led him to maintain that organisms were introduced by air and were not spontaneously generated. He demonstrated this by boiling an infusion in an open flask with the observation that putrefaction occurred. However, if the boiling was done after the flask had been hermetically sealed, the solution remained pure. This was the crucial experiment that suggested antisepsis to [Joseph] Lister eleven years later. Pasteur saved the French wine industry by finding that souring of wine was due to parasitic growths and that these could be destroyed by heating the wine for a few minutes at a temperature of 50 to 60 degrees Centigrade. This process was developed in 1864 and has since been extended to other fields, including the purification of milk and is known as "pasteurization." He was able to rescue the French silk industry in 1865 by the finding of silk worms feeding on damp mulberry leaves which contained innumerable "vibrions." He demonstrated that the disease could be prevented by the proper feeding of the silk worms. Unfortunately, Pasteur suffered a "stroke." He was paralyzed on his left side but recovered over a period of three months. He then resumed work and entered into the fifth phase of his major contributions, namely, that of the isolation of the microbes of anthrax in

sheep and in chicken cholera and the introduction of vaccination for these diseases in homage to Jenner. His final major
contribution was that of the discovery of the cause and treatment of rabies in 1885 when he was sixty-three years of age.

Pasteur's work created a wave of worldwide enthusiasm
and led to the creation by his government of the Pasteur Institute in 1888. Pasteur taught that the areas of religion and
science "are distinct, and woe to him who tries to let them
trespass on each other in the so imperfect state of human
knowledge." As a scientist he claimed absolute liberty of research. His seventieth birthday was celebrated by an international gathering at the Sorbonne. The eulogy was given
by Lord Lister, following which Pasteur was presented to

## Joseph Lister and Antiseptic Surgery

*French chemist Louis Pasteur demonstrated the connection between
disease and specific microorganisms. He also showed that bacteria did
not suddenly arise spontaneously. Instead, microorganisms existed
everywhere, including in the air. Joseph Lister heard about this work
and realized that unseen microorganisms could easily infect surgical
wounds and injuries. He instituted antiseptic practices in surgery and
radically reduced infection rates.*

If a patient did not die from the pain of an operation in the
early nineteenth century, there was a good chance that infection
would finish them off. In many cases gangrene set in before the
wound healed and there was little that could be done about it.
There are stories of patients having repeated amputations on a
leg in an effort to stop the infection reaching the body, to no
avail. The first method of preventing infection during an operation was developed by Joseph Lister (1827–1912).

Lister was Professor of Surgery at Glasgow University. He
was concerned about the number of patients who died from infection and blood poisoning after operations. He set about trying to reduce this by improving the cleanliness of operations.

The French chemist Louis Pasteur (1822–1895) was a major
influence on Lister. Lister read about Pasteur's discovery of
germs and decided that to prevent infection, he needed to en-

the Assembly by the President of France.

Meanwhile, a man twenty-one years younger than Pasteur gave bacteriology an impetus that it had never known previously. He was Koch.

## Robert Koch

Robert Koch (1843–1910) graduated in medicine from the University of Göttingen where he had been deeply influenced by Jacob Henle. Henle's theory of contagion and his importance in creating microscopic anatomy provided Koch "with both inspiration and tools to continue in an expert fashion." During the years that Pasteur was working on the disease of the silk worm and the problems of the wine industry, Koch was

sure that the germs present in the air did not get into wounds. Lister conducted an experiment on an 11-year-old boy, who had been run over by a cart and had fractured his leg, leaving the bone exposed. Once Lister had cleaned the wound, he placed a dressing covered with carbolic acid over it. Lister knew that carbolic acid had been used to disinfect drains and cesspools and therefore thought that it may have the power to kill germs. The boy survived and did not suffer from the gangrene that was common with these types of injuries.

Following on from his success, Lister decided to develop his theory further by inventing a carbolic spray which could be used to spray the operating area. In addition, Lister insisted that the operating theatre was kept clean, that the surgeon wore clean clothes, and that instruments were regularly disinfected.

At first Lister was regarded as an eccentric and nurses resented the extra work that his obsession with cleanliness caused. But deaths from blood poisoning and gangrene were reduced and before he died, Lister's services to medicine were recognised and he was awarded a knighthood. Today the terms, 'Before Lister' and 'After Lister' are used to describe surgery.

British Broadcasting Company, "BBC: Medicine Through Time," 2003. www.bbc.co.uk.

practicing medicine in the country. His wife bought him a microscope with her housekeeping money and Koch was able to trace the elusive anthrax bacillus through its stages by means of his methods of culturing the organism. He demonstrated his work to Cohn [Ferdinand Julius, 1829–1890], Weigert [Carl, 1845–1904] and Cohnheim [Julius Friedrich, 1839–1884], as well as to other well-known scientists and they were all favorably impressed. During the following year (1877) he introduced his techniques of drying bacterial forms on cover slips, staining them with aniline dyes and photographing them for study and comparison. Because he had now advanced to the first rank in medical science he was brought to Berlin in 1878 to work in bacteriology and was given Löffler and Gaffky to work with him as his assistants. In 1881 he was successful in developing a new method of obtaining pure cultures of bacteria by using a meat infusion mixed with warm gelatin which hardened after being poured upon glass plates. Some scientists consider this to be Koch's greatest contribution to medical science because it enabled bacteriologists to obtain pure cultures of microorganisms. Using this method, he discovered the tubercle bacillus in 1882 and thus completed the long history of the search for the cause of this old disease. Koch's postulates regarding the specificity of an organism in relation to the cause of a disease were contained in his publication on tuberculosis and are as follows: (1) the microorganism must be demonstrated in every case of the disease; (2) the microorganism must be cultivated in pure culture; (3) the microorganism must be inoculated from culture to a susceptible animal and must produce the same disease, and (4) the microorganism must be recovered from the animals that have been infected by it.

Koch was able to discover the cholera vibrio in 1883 and developed tuberculin in 1890. He also found that bubonic plague was almost always transmitted by rat fleas. Emil von Behring (1854–1917) was one of Koch's students at the Berlin Institute for Infectious Disease and he became an outstanding bacteriologist. One of his major contributions was the discovery of bacterial toxins against which the body was able to form antitoxins. From this concept he was able to develop immunization for diphtheria and tetanus.

# The Mosquito as Culprit in Malaria and Yellow Fever Infection

Ralph H. Major

The tropics had long been ravaged by the diseases malaria and yellow fever. When Europeans began traveling to the tropics in the nineteenth century, they also became infected with these diseases. In this article Ralph H. Major, a professor of medicine at the University of Kansas, describes a series of scientific discoveries that led to the conquest of malaria and yellow fever. French army physician Charles-Louis-Alphonse Laveran (1845–1922) discovered the infective agent when he found that the blood of all malarial patients showed evidence of a specific parasite. Mosquitoes came under suspicion as the carriers of these parasites. When British surgeon Ronald Ross found the same parasite in the stomach of mosquitoes and in the blood of malaria patients, the mosquito was determined to be the carrier of the malaria parasites. Humans became infected when bit by the mosquitoes, and today, an insect that carries a disease to humans is called an "insect vector." Cuban physician Carlos Finlay (1833–1915) promoted the idea that the mosquito also was the cause of yellow fever. Eventually the argument that mosquitoes were spreading disease became widely accepted. Eradication programs directed at mosquitoes dramatically lowered the incidence of both malaria and yellow fever. However, since the 1970s, as mosquitoes have become more resistant to pesticides, tropical diseases, especially malaria, have returned with a vengeance.

Ralph H. Major, *The History of Medicine*. Springfield, IL: Charles C. Thomas, 1954.

In the latter years of the nineteenth century, several note-worthy discoveries were made which took their place beside the astounding advances already recorded.

## Malaria

In 1880, Alphonse Laveran [1845–1922] a French Army physician stationed at Constantine, was engaged in the study of malaria. He noted at autopsy the constant presence of pigment granules, especially in the liver and in the cerebral blood vessels, and began an intensive study of the pigment in the blood vessels and in the blood. He wrote:

> In 1880, at the military hospital of Constantine, I discovered on the edges of the round pigmented bodies in the blood of a patient with malaria filiform elements resembling flagella which moved about with great vivacity, displacing the neighboring red cells: from that time I had no doubts on the parasitic nature of these bodies which I had discovered in malarial blood.

Laveran sent a memoir describing his discovery to the Paris *Académie des Sciences*. This was read and published the same year but was received with great skepticism. However, he continued his investigations and found that these bodies were invariably present when the blood was examined during the chill before the administration of quinine. In 1882, he went to Rome, where he again found the same parasites in the blood of malarial patients and demonstrated them to Baccelli [Guido, 1832–1916], Bastianelli [Giuseppe], Celli [Angelo], Grassi [Giovanni-Battista, 1854–1925], Marchiafava [Ettore], and other Italian scientists. Golgi [Camillo, 1843–1926] in 1886, showed that the attack of fever commences at the moment the merozoites are liberated and pointed out the difference in the appearance of the tertian and quartan parasites. In 1889, Celli and Marchiafava differentiated the malaria parasites into the three types recognized today—tertian, quartan, and aestivo autumnal. Celli later formed a society for combatting malaria and suceeded in stamping out the disease in the Roman Compagna, a hot bed of malaria since the days of the ancient Roman republic. All of this work was accomplished by the study of fresh preparations. Dimitri Romanowsky [1861–1921] of St. Petersburg devised in 1891 a stain which stained the parasites and has since been of great value in the study of malaria. The skepticism regarding Laveran's discovery continued, however, for several years. Gradually, as techniques improved, the truth of his claims was established. Osler [William, 1849–1919] observed in the first edition of his *Principles and Practice of Medicine*, 1892: "So far as I know, not a single observer, who has had the necessary training and the material at his command, has failed to demonstrate the existence of these parasites." In a later passage, Osler adds: "We do not know how the parasite enters, or how or in what form it leaves the body; how or where it is propagated, under what outside conditions it develops, whether free or in some aquatic plant or animal."

## Mosquito Transmission

Five years were to elapse after Osler wrote these words before the answer was found. In 1883, Albert F.A. King [1841–1914] had already published a paper in which he gave 19 reasons for believing that malaria is transmitted by the mosquito, although he was apparently unfamiliar with Laveran's great discovery. Laveran, himself, became convinced in 1884 that the disease was transmitted by mosquitoes and stressed the fact that mosquitoes were extremely numerous in areas where malaria was prevalent. Meanwhile, Sir Patrick Manson [1844–1922], who had demonstrated while in China in 1879 that filariasis is transmitted by the bite of a mosquito and that the life cycle of the *filaria Bancrofti* takes place in the mosquito, returned to England and became interested in the subject of malarial transmission by mosquitoes.

In 1894, Ronald Ross [1857–1932], a surgeon in the Indian Medical Service, returned for a leave and saw Manson in London. Ross had been studying malaria in India 13 years but had made little headway and had never even seen the malarial parasite. Manson demonstrated to him at the Charing Cross Hospital the parasites in the blood of a patient who was suffering from malaria and also expounded the mosquito theory to him. On his return to India, Ross continued his work with new enthusiasm, aided by better technique and a better microscope of his own invention. In 1895, he demonstrated the parasites in the stomach of an anopheles mosquito which had fed on a malarial patient. This was the same year that W.G. MacCallum [1874–1944] of Johns Hopkins showed that the so-called flagella were really sexual forms of the parasite. In 1898, Ross demonstrated the parasites in the salivary glands of the anopheles mosquito. . . .

The importance of these discoveries is difficult to exaggerate. Malaria has been one of the greatest killers of history. While never appearing with the dramatic suddenness of an outbreak of bubonic plaque or of yellow fever, striking a community, destroying thousands in a few days or weeks, and then moving to fresh victims, malaria comes in quietly and unobstrusively but settles down as a permanent inhabitant, exacting its daily toll year by year and, as time rolls on, century by century. From the days of Aristophanes until the period of the conquistadores of Peru in the seventeenth century, the disease exacted a huge toll of life on four continents with no remedy available. Laveran had now made it possible to differentiate malaria from a group of fevers with which it had long been confused; Ross had proved that it was transmitted by the mosquito, the destruction of which must be accomplished if the disease were ever to be controlled or eradicated. Malaria still exacts a heavy toll, but the mortality from this disease has definitely declined since the work of Laveran and Ross.

## Yellow Fever

The mode of transmission of yellow fever was demonstrated less than five years later. Yellow fever had been present on the American continent since the time of Columbus. As early as 1493, an epidemic appeared in Santo Domingo. From that time, the disease appeared in epidemic form in various American cities, one of the most destructive outbreaks being the epidemic of 1793 in Philadelphia, where, in four months, 4,041 deaths were recorded, Philadelphia then having a population of 40,000. In 1870, a Napoleonic army, which had landed in the West Indies, was almost completely destroyed by yellow fever.

In 1881, Carlos Finlay [1833–1915], a Cuban physician, at the International Sanitary Conference held in Washington, expressed his belief that yellow fever was transmitted by the bite of a mosquito. He published an article in the *American Journal of the Medical Sciences*, 1886, describing his experiments on five men who were subjected to the bites of mosquitoes which had bitten patients suffering from yellow fever. In all of the subjects, yellow fever developed. Finlay's experiments, however, either were ignored or failed to impress most investigators.

In 1900, following the Spanish-American War, an outbreak of yellow fever appeared in Havana. The army sent the well-known Yellow Fever Commission, consisting of Walter Reed [1851–1907], James Carroll [1854–1907], Jesse Lazear [1866–1900], and Arístides Agramonte [1868–1931], to study the disease. In Havana, they worked in close collaboration with Major W.C. Gorgas [1854–1920], who was the sanitary chief of Havana, and with Carlos Finlay, whose insistence on the mosquito theory they listened to with much skepticism but agreed to test.

The commission soon proved that yellow fever was transmitted by the bite of a mosquito, known then as the *Culex fasciatus*, later as the *Stegomyia fasciata*, and now called the *Aëdes aegypti*. They showed further that the disease was not transmitted by contact or other means. In the course of their experiments, Carroll submitted to the bite of an infected mosquito, developed yellow fever, but recovered. Lazear was bitten accidentally by an infected mosquito and died of yellow fever. Gorgas now initiated a thorough campaign of mosquito extermination. In three months, yellow fever was eradicated, and Havana, for the first time in 150 years, was free of the disease. Four years later, Gorgas was placed in charge of sanitation during the construction of the Panama Canal. Here he was largely responsible for the successful completion of this project, at which De Lesseps [Ferdinand Marie, 1805–1894] had previously failed. De Lesseps and the French had not lacked engineering skill, but the high mortality of their workers from yellow fever and malaria had doomed their efforts to failure.

# Dr. David Ho, the AIDS Detective

Christine Gorman and Alice Park

In 1996 *Time* magazine honored David Ho (1952– ) with the title of "Man of the Year" for his work on HIV (human immunodeficiency virus) and the disease caused by HIV, AIDS (acquired immunodeficiency disease). In this profile of Ho accompanying his designation as Man of the Year, authors Christine Gorman and Alice Park trace the doctor's career and his two great contributions to AIDS research. First, Ho discovered that the HIV virus is most active immediately after infection, which means that the infected person needs to be treated immediately rather than after symptoms have appeared. Second, he developed a combination drug therapy of AZT and protease inhibitors to arrest the progression of the disease. Although the drug "cocktail" did not work for everyone and was not a cure for AIDS, the drug combination did provide a new lease on life for millions. The number of deaths from AIDS dropped by two-thirds in the two years after the introduction of protease inhibitors (1997–1999). Ho, who has called AIDS "the plague of our millennium," is now working on a vaccine against HIV.

Dr. David Ho [1952– ] doesn't look like a gambler. With his boyish face and slender build, he could more easily pass for a teenager than for a 44-year-old father of three—or, for that matter, for a world-renowned scientist. In fact, when he was an undergraduate at the California Institute of Technology back in the 1970s, Ho hung around the blackjack tables in Las Vegas, tilting the odds in his favor by memorizing each card as it was played. He got so good at counting cards that he was thrown out of several casinos.

Today Ho is still something of a gambler, though in a very different field and for much bigger stakes. The director of the Aaron Diamond AIDS Research Center in New York City, he has come up with a daring strategy for flushing out the virus that causes AIDS. As he explained at the 11th International Conference on AIDS in Vancouver, Canada, [in 1996], Ho (like more and more doctors) is using powerful new drugs called protease inhibitors [drugs that stop viral reproduction] in combination with standard antiviral medications. But unlike most doctors, he gives the so-called combination therapy to patients in the first few weeks of infection. . . .

Like so many promising HIV treatments, Ho's strategy could fail. It could even backfire if it is mistakenly touted as a kind of "morning after" treatment that allows people to relax their guard and engage in risky sexual behavior. By desensitizing the virus to medications, it could jeopardize a patient's ability to respond to future treatments. Worse yet, it could inadvertently create a mutant strain of virus resistant to all currently available drugs—a kind of super HIV—that could lead to a second, even more devastating AIDS epidemic.

There are other problems. Even if the treatment works, it isn't practical. HIV-positive patients would have to start taking the drugs immediately after infection, before they realize they're sick. And even if the drug cocktails can be made to work in the later stages of infection, they are far too expensive to do much good for the 20 million people in the developing world who are infected with HIV. In the long run, scientists believe, only an AIDS vaccine will stop the global epidemic. . . .

## A Team Effort

David Ho would be the first to say that he cannot take all the credit. It was an immunologist from Los Angeles named Michael Gottlieb who in 1981 reported the first cases of what was then called gay pneumonia. It was the U.S. Centers for Disease Control that alerted doctors to the gathering epidemic and established that the infection was transmitted through blood transfusions, tainted needles and un-protected sex. It was Dr. Luc Montagnier's laboratory at the Pasteur Institute in Paris that first isolated the killer virus in 1983. It was Dr. Robert Gallo and his colleagues at the National Cancer Institute in Bethesda, Maryland, who made it grow in the lab, which allowed for the development of an antibody test. It was the National Institutes of Health that funded the basic research on HIV and AIDS. It was the big drug companies like Burroughs Wellcome and Merck that brought a growing list of anti-HIV drugs to market.

But Ho, working alone or in concert with others, fundamentally changed the way scientists looked at the AIDS virus. His breakthrough work in virology, beginning in the mid-1980s, revealed how HIV mounts its attack. His tenacious pursuit of the virus in the first weeks of infection helped show what the body does right in controlling HIV. His pioneering experiments with protease inhibitors helped clarify how the virus ultimately overwhelms the immune system. His work and his insights set the stage for an enormously productive shift in the treatment of AIDS away from the later stages of illness to the critical early days of infection.

Once, not so long ago, researchers believed that nothing much happened after HIV gained entry into the body. The virus simply hunkered down inside a few of the immune system's T cells—the linchpins of the body's defensive forces—for anywhere from three to 10 years. Then something, no one knew what, spurred the microbial invader to awaken. In this picture, the AIDS virus spent most of its life hibernating before starting its final, deadly assault.

[In 1995 and 1996], Ho and his colleagues . . . demonstrated that this picture of the virus is wrong. There is no initial dormant phase of infection. Ho showed that the body and the virus are, in fact, locked in a pitched battle from the very beginning. . . .

Suddenly the entire picture of AIDS had changed. As long as doctors thought that the virus was not very active through the early and middle years of infection, it made sense to conserve forces and delay treatment so they would be ready for the virus when it emerged from hibernation. Now it was becoming clear that the immune system needed all the help it could get right from the start.

But where would that help come from? Boston's Martin Hirsch and other virologists had already started looking to cancer research for inspiration. Oncologists have learned that it is often better to combine the firepower of several different chemotherapeutic drugs than to rely on any single medication to destroy cancer cells. Too often, they have found, the one-drug approach allows a few malignant cells to survive and blossom into an even more lethal tumor. The AIDS researchers faced a similar problem with HIV. Whenever they prescribed a single drug, such as AZT, for their patients, a few viral particles would survive and give rise to drug-resistant HIV.

Now that the protease inhibitors had become available, doctors were eager to combine them with the old standby AZT and a third drug called 3TC. A couple of mathematical models—created by one of Ho's collaborators, Alan Perelson of the Los Alamos National Laboratory—suggested that HIV would have a hard time simultaneously undergoing the minimum three mutations necessary to resist combination therapy. He placed the odds at 10 million to 1. It was at least worth a try.

## Hope at Last

For once in the history of HIV, a strategy that ought to work seemed in fact to succeed. Within weeks of starting combination therapy, 7 out of 10 men and women with AIDS begin to get better. Blood tests show that in many of them, the viral load has dropped below detectable levels. Relieved of the burden of fighting HIV, their long-suffering immune systems can finally tackle the deadly fungal and bacterial infections that have taken hold in their lungs, intestines and brains. Fevers break; lesions disappear; energy returns.

With the virus under control in at least some AIDS patients, doctors are considering how to rebuild their battered immune systems. After a decade of fighting HIV, many of the body's defensive reserves have been thoroughly depleted and cannot be regenerated from within. Researchers plan to grow replacement cells in the laboratory for transplant into recovering patients. Before the advent of combination therapy, no one would have considered such a rescue effort because the unchecked virus would have rapidly destroyed the new implants. . . .

Even if the virus stages a comeback, that doesn't necessarily mean that combination therapy has totally failed. It may be that additional ingredients could eliminate the virus completely. Ho has already started using a combination of four drugs in another early-intervention trial. And he has access to new, experimental medications that can better penetrate the brain and perhaps the testes. These drugs may help patients in later stages of the disease whose infections have become resistant to current treatments.

There is still a long way to go, both in the quest for an effective treatment and in the search for a way to prevent infection in the first place. In the flush of the new optimism, some scientists are more hopeful about the prospects for gene therapy, which could possibly make the immune system impervious to HIV attack. Another promising line of research centers on a group of molecules called chemokines, which may one day be used to shield cells from HIV. Other scientists, including Ho, are intensifying their search for a vaccine. [In 1996], the [National Institutes of Health] increased its budget for AIDS-vaccine research 18%—to $129 million—and named Nobel-prizewinning molecular biologist David Baltimore to head the effort.

It has taken the collaborative work of thousands of scientists and physicians to get this far. It will take even greater cooperation and well-funded coordination to overcome the remaining hurdles. But the worst fear—the one that seeded a decade with despair, the foreboding sense that the AIDS virus might be invincible—has finally been subdued.

# Chapter 3

# Medical Procedures

Turning | Points
IN WORLD HISTORY

# Trepanation: Primitive Surgery

Charlotte Roberts and Keith Manchester

Archaeologists have discovered human skulls with clear evidence of having undergone cranial surgery called trepanation. These skulls have been found all over the world and date back to the Neolithic period (late Stone Age). Trepanation, which is still done in some less-advanced cultures, usually involves drilling holes in the skull. Scholars think that the purpose of trepanation in ancient times was to relieve severe headaches or to allow the escape of spirits or demons that were thought to have possessed the patient. It is unlikely that scientists will ever know exactly how trepanation was discovered as effective. Probably it was an accident. Yet the procedure is important because trepanation was a very early attempt by humans to provide medical care to a suffering person. A surprising number of ancient people survived this medical procedure, and in some cases, such as swelling of the brain or head wounds, the trepanation may have actually helped. Anthropologists Charlotte Roberts and Keith Manchester, both of the University of Branford in England, describe the archaeological evidence of ancient cranial surgery.

Trepanation is a practice known since very early times and is seen today in developing countries. The operation involves, for whatever reason, incision of the scalp and the cutting through and removal of an area of skull. The result is the exposure of the membranes (dura) covering the brain. Survival of the patient, for patient he or she must be regarded in this surgical operation, probably depended upon the skilful avoidance of perforation of these membranes and the avoidance, either by luck or good judgement, of the major blood vessels within the skull. It should be noted that the proportion of survivors of this operation in antiquity was high. The evidence for survival is, of course, the healing and remodelling of the bone around the operation site. Several examples exist of individuals having undergone more than one trepanning operation, having survived a preceding one. A notable specimen, the Cuzco skull from Peru, shows no less than seven trepanned holes, all showing signs of healing. Perhaps equally surprising are the size of trepanned areas, particularly where survival has occurred. For example, a Neolithic skull from Latvia possessed three trepanning defects in the skull. The largest single hole measured 68 × 55 mm, and all three merged to produce an opening 120 × 60 mm in size. Surprisingly, this individual survived his horrific surgical trauma and died over 1 year later, possibly from some other disease unrelated to the trepanation.

Ancient examples of trepanation number well into the thousands and their distribution is world-wide. Perhaps because of the excellence and extent of archaeological excavation and post-excavation skeletal analysis, Europe affords many of these examples, and Piggot [Stuart] (ibid.) suggests that central and northern Europe may be the original home of trepanation. The Americas, Australia, Asia, Africa and Melanesia have also produced examples. A late palaeolithic origin has been claimed and certainly in the Neolithic period it was an active practice. Although flourishing in the Neolithic period in Europe, perhaps more than at any other time, the operation has been performed during all periods since.

## Methods Used

The technical object of operation was clear, but the actual surgical procedure adopted was variable. Dependent upon the era and the technologies available, the operation may have been carried out with a flint scraper or blade, or a metal implement which may or may not have been adapted specifically for the purpose. Recent work has provided evidence for the type of instrument used. . . .

Initial incision of the scalp is a very bloody procedure, but the haemorrhage can be minimized by turning back the scalp flaps created; no doubt this was realized and carried out by early surgeons.

After cutting the soft tissues, the outer skull surface was exposed. At this point the pattern varied. Five types of trepanation have been identified from skeletal material worldwide. The scraped type involved the bone surface being removed and bevelled edges to the wound were created towards the central hole in the skull. The gouge method removed a larger piece of skull by delineating a circular area on the skull and gouging the area with an implement. The bore and saw method usually involved the use of a drill-type implement in which a series of holes were made in a circle between which saw marks were subsequently made. The saw method consisted of the creation of four saw marks in a square to enable a piece of bone to be removed from the skull. The final method involved the creation of a small hole

## A Roman Child's Trepanned Skull

*Here, Italian archaeologists describe the trepanned skull of a child who lived in ancient Rome. The child was hydrocephalic, a condition in which serous fluid builds up inside the skull and causes great enlargement of the cranium. No doubt the trepanation was meant to relieve this condition. The child survived the operation, but only for a few weeks. The authors are from Italy's National Archaeological Museum, the University of Gabriele D'Annunzio, and the University La Sapienza.*

In 1995, the skeleton of a hydrocephalic child was excavated from a cemetery that was probably part of a villa in suburban Rome, on the site of the ancient town of Fidenae. The child was 5–6 years old, on the basis of the teeth, and was dated to about the end of the first or the start of the second century AD on archaeological context. The remarkably well-preserved cranium of this child is a fine example of trepanation, which may have been intended to alleviate the clinical signs of an endocranial space-occupying lesion. . . .

with a drill (which can strictly be called a trephination).

These types of trepanation appear in differing frequencies in different parts of the world and eras. For example, the scraping method appears more frequently in Europe and the sawing method in South America. Studies of the site of trepanation indicate that many were performed on the left side of the frontal and parietal bones; rarely were these operations performed over the skull sutures. Hippocrates, writing in the fifth century BC (and many other authors), recommended not to trepan over the sutures for fear of lacerating a major vein. One can imagine the agony suffered by the patient in antiquity. Such agony may not have been physical, since after cutting the soft tissues the operation is relatively painless, particularly if pain relief is assisted by alcohol or by herbal preparations; drugs such as opium, henbane and mandrake have all been quoted as herbs used for inducing anaesthesia and analgesia in particular population groups.

During all of these processes the bone dust created may

---

The lesion would have progressed slowly, allowing a compensatory expansion of the neurocranium. The possible causes include traumatic, infectious, and neoplastic disease. Whatever the cause of the disease, the Fidenae child provides the most ancient direct evidence of a specific surgical treatment aimed at the alleviation of the symptoms of an intracranial expanding lesion. . . .

The trepanned child was buried in a cemetery that contained graves of commoners, probably from a rural community. This finding suggests that a complex and costly surgical procedure was executed as a last therapeutic resort on a suffering child of modest origins. Because of the special care and expertise required for cranial trepanations in children, reflected in Galen's (Greek physician 130–200 A.D.) writings, it is plausible that the child was operated on by an experienced surgeon in the city of Rome.

Renato Mariani-Costantini et al., "New Light on Cranial Surgery in Ancient Rome," *Lancet*, January 2000, p. 305.

have been collected. In more recent periods human skull dust has been used among developing societies as a magical remedy; it is known that trepanation was also undertaken to produce amulets. Whatever method was employed by whichever society, the end result was the removal of a piece of skull and the exposure of the membranes covering the brain. The post-operative care of this bloody and potentially infected area of operation is equally impressive, particularly in view of the survival of many victims. . . .

In Britain it is apparent that the scraping method was accompanied by better survival than the other methods. Perhaps the gradual scraping of the skull allowed more precise and controlled penetration of the inner table of bone and hence less likelihood of brain injury. Osteitis and bone scarring surrounding the hole in the skull has been attributed to chemical irritants applied post-operatively. These features are, however, more likely to be due to sepsis of the wound. Doubtless some closure of the skin wound must have been made, either by drawing together the skin flaps or by the application of a pad, possibly of vegetation. It was noted, for instance, in historic times in Melanesia that the operation site was covered with materials such as wood bark, banana leaf and coconut shell.

## Motives for Operating

The technique of operation is plain to see. The motive for the operation is not known for certain in most cases, and most likely lies in the culture of the societies who practised this operation. The popular and somewhat romantic notion that trepanation was carried out solely for magico-ritual reasons is hardly credible. Such a reason there may have been for carrying out the operation on a corpse, and this undoubtedly did occur. In these cases no healing would be expected and post-mortem damage may be implicated for the lesion. The absence of documentation from the long periods of prehistory permits only speculation. It is difficult to imagine living people submitting themselves willingly to such a horrific operation with a high mortality merely for ritual reasons, although they may have had no choice. So many trepanned skulls have been found in the chambered tombs of the Seine-Oise-Marne area of France that it is probable that the operation had some ritual significance; roundels of human skull bone have been found in early prehistoric graves, suggesting that such objects were treated as fetishes by prehistoric people.

To the contemporary mind, however, the bizarre behaviour of the schizophrenic, the strange uncontrollable fits of the epileptic, and the incapacitating head pain of migraine may have seemed sufficient justification to 'let the evil spirit out of the brain'. These illnesses are without skeletal manifestation and must, therefore, remain speculative. There is clear documentary evidence, at least from Hippocratic times, that the operation was also carried out for justifiable clinical reasons, even by modern standards. Hippocrates (Greek physician c 460–360 B.C.) recommended trepanation for wounds of the head and haematoma. Calsus (medical historian 25–45 A.D.) also proposed the operation for cranial injuries. It has been noted in many examples that trepanation may be related to the site of cranial fracture, and recent evidence suggests infection of the sinuses may have initiated trepanation, where a skull with two healed and one unhealed trepanations also had evidence of frontal sinusitis and intracranial infection.

Whatever the ailment being treated in the past, it is certainly clear that the association of increased intracranial pressure and head wounds was recognized. There are several other lesions of the skull that may be considered in a differential diagnosis for trepanation; thinning of the parietal bones resulting in a hole (usually in old age), tumours producing holes in the tables of the skull, enlarged parietal foramina and post-mortem damage. However, with the advent of the use of sophisticated methods of analysis such as the scanning electron microscope, these differential diagnoses, should be easily eliminated.

# Surgical Anesthesia

Meyer Friedman and Gerald W. Friedland

Surgery without anesthesia was an excruciating experience for patients, and physicians long sought some way of relieving their suffering. In this selection from their book *Medicine's 10 Greatest Discoveries*, physicians Meyer Friedman and Gerald W. Friedland tell the story of the discovery of ether, a chemical substance that brings on sleep and that can serve as surgical anesthesia, and a similar compound, nitrous oxide—also known as "laughing gas." According to the authors, "ether frolics" were held in nineteenth-century America, where participants would intentionally intoxicate themselves with ether or nitrous oxide. A young Georgia physician, Crawford Long, was the first to use ether as a surgical anesthetic after observing the effects of ether at one of the "frolics." Crawford made no attempt to capitalize on his discovery, but others did. An intense rivalry developed among physicians and dentists to be the first credited with the use of anesthesia, and the first to profit from it.

Physician Meyer Friedman, who died in 2001, was director of the Harold Brunn Institute at San Francisco's Mount Zion Hospital and Medical Center. He was the author of numerous books on medical topics and is credited with discovering the connection between "type A" behavior and cardiovascular disease. Physician Gerald W. Friedland is professor emeritus at Stanford University School of Medicine and has written several books and articles on radiology.

The first important advance in the development of anesthesia was the discovery in 1275, by the famous Spanish alchemist Raymundus Lullius [1232–1316] that if vitriol (sulfuric acid) was mixed with alcohol and distilled, a sweet, white fluid would result. At first Lullius and his contemporaries called the fluid sweet vitriol; it was later called ether. Quite a future was in store for this simple chemical compound, even though six centuries would pass before its ultimate fate would be discovered.

In 1605 the famous alchemist Paracelsus [1493–1541], a Swiss physician, employed ether to relieve pain. He was a medical, not a surgical, doctor, so he was not able to invent surgical anesthesia. After testing it on experimental animals, though, he administered ether to his medical patients who were in extreme pain. Amazingly, it would be the middle of the nineteenth century before anyone would again think to use ether for pain relief.

## Priestley and Laughing Gas

Another great advance was made by the English chemist Joseph Priestley [1735–1804], who discovered nitrous oxide, later called laughing gas, in 1772. Priestley did not recognize nitrous oxide as an anesthetic agent, but he did make a number of other enormously important discoveries, including the existence of oxygen and carbon monoxide. . . .

After Priestley, the "pneumatic medicine" (medication by inhalation of various gases) he had helped to found became a kind of fad in England. One of its leading exponents was Thomas Beddoes [1760–1808], the physician and chemist from Berkeley, England, who was a neighbor of Jenner [Edward, 1749–1823]—whose vaccination process Beddoes had initially opposed and later strongly supported. Beddoes, a liberal like Priestley, was forced to leave his position as reader [lecturer] in chemistry at Oxford. In 1794 he traveled to Bristol, where he opened a Pneumatic Medicine Institution. Four years later he appointed Humphrey Davy [1778–1829], a brilliant twenty-two-year-old surgeon-chemist as superintendent.

Davy's youth was similar to Jenner's, in that he did very poorly at school, which he left at age thirteen. Without the qualifications to train as a physician, Davy apprenticed himself to a surgeon-apothecary. During his apprenticeship Davy developed an enormous interest in chemistry, which he essentially taught himself. It was he who introduced the term *laughing gas* for nitrous oxide, having inhaled it at the age of seventeen and feeling so exhilarated that he burst out laughing. Later he developed an inhaler for use with the gas.

In 1800 Davy published an astonishing book, the record of his research of the previous two years, in which he discussed in enormous detail the chemical, physical, and physiological properties of nitrous oxide. The book was hailed as the work of a genius, particularly as its author was twenty-one at the time of publication and had been working on it for only two years.

In the book Davy recounted the eruption of a wisdom tooth. His entire gum became inflamed and painful, to the extent that he had to take nitrous oxide three times in one day, after which the pain in his jaw was temporarily relieved. He went so far as to suggest that nitrous oxide could be used

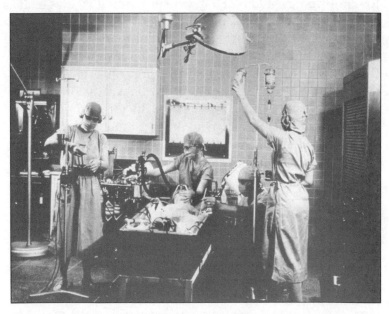

*Many important advances in medicine would have been impossible without the discovery of anesthesia. Here, doctors perform open heart surgery in the 1950s.*

for surgical operations, but Davy did not pursue this idea because he thought he had more meaningful work to do. That work included poetry; he was a poet of note, known and admired by the leading poets of his time. . . .

## Anesthesia in America

After Davy, the focus on nitrous oxide research moved to the United States, where William Barton [1786–1856] wrote a medical thesis at the University of Pennsylvania in 1808, confirming Davy's observations about nitrous oxide. Barton mentioned in his report that he had received a violent and very painful blow to the head, which nitrous oxide enabled him not to feel at all. Like Davy, he suggested using laughing gas as anesthesia during surgery. Again like Davy, he chose not to develop his idea further. Another thirty or so years would pass before the thought would be put to practical use.

When the concept of anesthesia was finally introduced, the people most interested were dentists and surgeons. Dentists needed only a very light anesthesia; surgeons needed, and still need, a deep anesthesia. Thus, there arose a division between dental and surgical anesthesia, and in discussions of the history of anesthesia it has, by common consent, become customary to focus on the history of surgical anesthesia.

Various American chemists realized after making anesthetics that inhaling them made people feel happy and gay. As a result, the chemists who made them organized "ether frolics" and "laughing-gas parties." As it happened, the first to use ether as a dental anesthetic was a chemistry student, William E. Clark, who had watched and participated in ether frolics himself. His dentist was Dr. Elija Pope. Clark suggested one day that Pope use it for dental extractions, no doubt figuring that a little frolic could only help with the pain. In January 1842 Pope's patient, a Miss Hovey, became the first person to have a tooth extracted painlessly, while under the influence of ether.

## Crawford Long, Georgia Physician

The initial use of anesthesia for surgical purposes was by Dr. Crawford Long [1815–1878]. Born in Danville, Georgia, in

1815, Long was a graduate of Franklin College of Athens (Georgia) at the age of fourteen. He was a member of what must be the most distinguished graduating class in collegiate history, since every member would become famous. One became a governor, one a secretary of the treasury, two were senators, two Confederate generals, and (including Long himself) three became eminent scientists.

Long earned his medical degree at Transylvania University in Lexington, Kentucky, and at the University of Pennsylvania in Philadelphia, at the time the finest medical school in the country. He trained in surgery in New York City for eighteen months, then returned to Georgia in 1841 to establish a medical practice in Jefferson. The town was inhabited by only a few hundred souls, although Long's practice soon became larger than that, as he was an excellent doctor, kind and very devoted. His reputation spread. . . .

## First Surgery Using Anesthesia

Shortly after his wedding, several of the young men of Jefferson asked him to make some nitrous oxide for them, so that they could have laughing-gas parties. Long's response was that ether was just as good, and he promptly made some, which they all tried. The jollity was infectious, and ether frolics soon became fashionable in Jefferson and its environs.

At the jollifications he had helped to introduce, Long made an observation of profound importance. After a typical episode, he would be bruised from thrashing about under the influence of the ether, but could never remember feeling any pain when the actual bruises occurred. Long remembered these painless bumps when one of his patients, James N. Venable, had surgery scheduled several times for two cysts on his neck, but canceled each time because of the pain he feared he would have to undergo. Long invited him to some ether frolics to see that ether would not hurt him and was able in this way to convince Venable that ether was harmless. On March 30, 1842, Long poured some ether into a towel, let Venable inhale from it, and saw him become unconscious. Long removed one of the two cysts, without Venable's feeling any pain whatsoever. When Venable regained consciousness, he could not believe what had happened. Long had to show him the cyst to prove to Venable that it was gone. The experience was so successful that nine weeks later Long removed the second cyst, with the same happy result.

Long continued to give ether to his patients. In July 1842 he amputated a boy's toe painlessly, and by October 1846 he had administered surgical anesthesia successfully to eight patients. On each occasion there were numerous witnesses who confirmed what had happened, a fact that would be meaningful in what was to come. In addition, Long was the first to use anesthesia for an obstetrical procedure, in December 1845. So by the time he was twenty-six, he had become the first person in the long history of medicine to use surgical anesthesia and, by the time he was twenty-nine, the first person to use obstetrical anesthesia.

Long moved to Atlanta in 1850 and a year later to Athens, Georgia. During the Civil War news reached Athens that a division of federal cavalry was approaching, with orders to burn the city. Long reached home just as his daughter Frances and her younger brother were fleeing. He gave Frances a glass jar containing a roll of papers on which he had recorded evidence of his discovery of surgical anesthesia. Frances buried the jar in a wooded area, from which it was recovered after the war.

Long practiced surgery and anesthesia until June 16, 1878, when he died suddenly from a massive cerebral hemorrhage while delivering a baby to the local congressman's wife. His dying words were, "Care for the mother and child first."

Dr. Long certainly was the first person to employ ether to abolish both consciousness and pain in patients undergoing surgery. But he did not publish this stunning achievement until 1849, seven years after his discovery. Moreover, were it not for the competing claims of two dentists and one physician in 1846, it is doubtful that Long would ever have published his article.

## Jackson Tries Ether

It is now time to describe the three other claims. Before doing so, however, we should mention that the physician,

Charles Jackson [1805–1880], and probably one of the dentists, William Thomas Green Morton [1819–1868], had visited the tiny village of Jefferson in the spring of 1842, at the precise time that Dr. Long had given ether to his first patient. It is almost inconceivable that this earthshaking event did not serve as a focus of admiring discussion among the four hundred citizens of Jefferson. It is also almost inconceivable that Dr. Jackson and the dentist were not immediately apprised by the villagers of the ether discovery.

We emphasize this visit because Jackson, on returning to Harvard University after his visit to Jefferson, claimed he had suffered a sore throat of such intensity that he had given himself some ether, which rendered him unconscious as he sat in his chair. He claimed that this strange medical episode had taken place in February 1842, conveniently a month earlier than Long's first anesthetic procedure. His chair is still part of the anesthesia exhibit at Massachusetts General Hospital in Boston. Many who were aware of Jackson's personality and previous claims, however, doubted the validity of his new discovery.

Jackson was born in Plymouth, Massachusetts, in 1805 and received his M.D. with honors from Harvard in 1829. He was on the medical faculty there and at Massachusetts General Hospital, and had an encyclopedic knowledge. He worked hard, publishing more than four hundred papers, and all the evidence is that Harvard was proud of him.

Although he was undoubtedly brilliant, he also had sociopathic tendencies. His colleagues remembered him as being overcompetitive, deceitful, sly, manipulative, and highly suspicious. At different times in his career he falsely claimed a number of discoveries that had been made by other persons— which, curiously, did not seem to have bothered Harvard. In any event, he was never disciplined for these indiscretions. . . .

## Wells and Dental Anesthesia

It is appropriate now that we describe the role of Horace Wells [1815–1848] in the discovery of anesthesia. Wells was born in Hartford, Vermont, in 1815 and graduated from Harvard Dental School in 1834. He taught there for many years, was very learned, and wrote articles in the dental journals of the day.

Wells, however gifted, was an unstable man. He intermittently gave up his practice, once going to France to buy art, which he sold for a profit in the United States, and on another occasion leaving to manufacture portable baths and stoves. He was highly religious and once considered entering the ministry. Overexuberant at times, he still was easily depressed, and the opinions of others unduly swayed him.

On December 10, 1844, Wells attended a nitrous oxide party given by Dr. Gardner Q. Colton. He sat next to someone inhaling the laughing gas, who severely bruised his leg but who felt no pain. Wells immediately recognized that laughing gas might work as a dental anesthetic. He himself had a badly decayed tooth, so the next day he asked Colton to give him laughing gas while a colleague removed the tooth. As he did so, Wells felt no pain. When he had recovered from the anesthesia, he called out excitedly that this was the greatest discovery in the history of the world.

Before we continue Wells's story, it is opportune at this time to introduce the second dentist, William Thomas Green Morton, in our account of the discovery of surgical anesthesia.

Morton probably was the mysterious dentist who visited Jefferson in 1842. He had been taught dentistry at Harvard by Wells, who later took him as a partner in his private dental practice. In 1844, however, Morton decided to study medicine at Harvard and had Jackson as his preceptor. This strange union of distinctly sociopathic personalities resulted in so many conflicts and such confusion that even the U.S. Congress was baffled.

Morton, hearing of Wells's discovery of the anesthetic power of nitrous oxide, became tremendously enthusiastic about it. A medical student at Harvard, he arranged for Wells to demonstrate his discovery before a surgical, not a dental, class of students. Dr. John C. Warren [1778–1856], the world-famous physician then at Harvard, speedily approved the demonstration.

This historic demonstration was scheduled for the surgical amphitheater at the Massachusetts General Hospital in Boston in January 1845. Wells's fragile ego, though, was about to receive an unexpected blow. The apparatus he used to administer the laughing gas involved a wooden mouthpiece and a stopcock attached to a 2-liter bag of oiled silk. This was not large enough to anesthetize the patient; he needed at least 30 liters—but that, of course, he did not know. Another problem was that his patient was a terrified boy with a bad tooth. Wells was only able to administer a partial anesthesia, the boy screamed, and—instead of the applause he expected—he heard hisses and boos and was bodily thrown out of the amphitheater. Wells was devastated, although the boy said when he recovered that he could not remember any pain. The medical students who had seen the demonstration remained unimpressed, and Wells went into a deep depression.

He recovered, however, and within a short period used laughing gas to anesthetize forty patients during his dental procedures. All of these patients furnished him with written affidavits declaring that they felt no pain, and witnesses were present at each procedure. Still, no one at the hospital believed his story.

## Morton Claims Discovery

Morton, shortly prior to Wells's debacle before the Harvard surgeons and medical students, began to associate with Jackson as well as with Wells. Jackson, unaware of the probable fact that Morton, like himself, had visited Jefferson and had become quite familiar with the anesthetic power of ether, confided to Morton that ether was an outstanding anesthetic. Morton's immediate response was "Ether? What is it?"

Morton later claimed under oath that when Jackson told him about ether, he already had been experimenting with it but had hidden this activity from Jackson. He later insisted that he had anesthetized a fish, some insects, and a puppy, as well as himself; but one of his fellow medical students later told the U.S. Congress that Morton had never done any experiments at all.

Apparently Morton did try to anesthetize two dental students with ether; but both became agitated, not anesthetized. At this point Morton realized that he would have to join up with Jackson, who he knew possessed genuine knowledge. Jackson pointed out that Morton had used impure commercially made ether, and that for anesthetic purposes they would have to make the ether themselves. This they did and decided that they could make a lot of money through the strategic employment of secrecy. Jackson had the idea of mixing ether with aromatic oils, to disguise its true nature; he and Morton patented it as Letheon and tried to keep its contents secret.

Morton used this new product on Eben Frost on September 30, 1846. Jackson told Morton exactly how to administer the anesthesia and was convinced that it would work—and it did. Morton extracted the patient's tooth painlessly; witnesses were present; and the *Boston Journal* heralded the new discovery in an article published the very next day.

## Morton's Successful Demonstration

Morton now approached John Warren about a test. His request was similar to the one he had made on Wells's behalf two years before. Again Warren said yes, and his house surgeon, Dr. C.F. Heywood, wrote Morton proposing that at 10 A.M. on Friday morning, October 16, 1846, surgical anesthesia be given to a patient having a tumor of the jaw removed. A young surgeon, Dr. Henry Jacob Bigelow [1818–1890], arranged the details of the demonstration, inviting all of Boston's leading surgeons (but, oddly, no medical students).

Morton did not appear. An alarmed Bigelow went to Morton's office, where he found an equally alarmed Morton packing his bags to leave town. Bigelow managed to persuade him to go ahead. Letheon, after all, he encouraged Morton, could be effective. Bigelow and Morton arrived at the surgical amphitheater at Massachusetts General Hospital just as Warren was about to make his incision. Morton made up an excuse on the spot (something about waiting for his instrument maker to complete a new inhaler). He then administered the Letheon.

Unlike Long, who had poured his ether onto a towel, Morton used an inhaler. What he feared would happen did not happen—or only partially happened—because, like Wells, he had problems with his inhaler. In Morton's case, the inhaler had a wooden spigot but no valve. During the incision the patient felt no pain, but later began to speak incoherently and became agitated. Afterward the patient said that he had felt as though his neck were being scratched, and he was apparently aware that an operation was proceeding.

This time there were no boos or hisses. The visiting surgeons and Warren himself were stunned by the favorable outcome. At the next operation Morton anesthetized a patient for Dr. Heywood, again using Letheon. The patient was having a large tumor removed from his left arm and, thanks to Morton's improved inhaler with brass inspiratory and expiratory valves (still on exhibit at the Massachusetts General Hospital), the anesthesia worked very well. The patient was unconscious throughout, could remember no pain, and groaned only occasionally toward the end of the procedure.

## Controversy Erupts

After this second, highly successful anesthesia, Warren, Heywood, and Bigelow learned that Morton and Jackson had patented Letheon. They said publicly that this was unethical. When Jackson heard their statement, he withdrew his name from the patent but entered into a written agreement with Morton according to which Morton would pay him $500 and 10 percent of all future profits from the use of Letheon.

When Dr. Warren learned of these machinations, he prohibited the use of Letheon and banned Morton and his new anesthesia from the Commonwealth of Massachusetts. Morton was therefore forced to reveal that Letheon was just ether, since without some degree of medical cooperation he would never be able to work as an anesthetist again. Warren asked Morton why he had tried to conceal the ether with aromatic oils. Morton lied, replying that the oils made a more powerful anesthetic. These claims notwithstanding, he and Jackson later canceled their patent application.

On November 9, 1846, Bigelow delivered a lecture before the Boston Society of Medical Improvement on the new anesthesia, and on November 18 published reports of Morton's two successful cases in the *Boston Medical and Surgical Journal*.

Within days of the publication of Bigelow's article, worldwide attention was being paid to the new anesthesia. In the glow of all this publicity, Jackson, Morton, and Wells each claimed to have discovered it. The other claimants to the throne—William E. Clark, who had given the first dental anesthesia, and Crawford Long—at this point were silent. Clark wanted no part of all the publicity, and Long could not be bothered either—and would not have been, except for the efforts of his home state senator.

Shortly thereafter Jackson and Morton signed an agreement, with the help of advisers and lawyers, claiming to be codiscoverers of surgical anesthesia. Wells learned of the agreement and felt it was a slap in the face. It may have been a contributing factor in his taking his own life in 1848 by opening a vein in his arm and inhaling ether as he did so.

The strange story of the discovery of surgical anesthesia continued to become stranger. Within days of signing the agreement with Morton, Jackson, ever the deceitful schemer, wrote to the French Academy of Sciences and stated that he was the sole discoverer of surgical anesthesia. When Morton heard of the claim, he went back to his lawyers and advisers, broke off the agreement, and thereafter claimed that he had been the sole discoverer.

## U.S. Congress and Ether Controversy

This bickering between Jackson, Morton, and for a short while Wells about who first discovered surgical anesthesia became so bitter that the U.S. Congress in 1847 stepped in to decide who indeed was the first discoverer. This matter, eventually called the Ether Controversy, preoccupied Congress for sixteen years, despite the onset of the Civil War.

Morton's claims were supported by two powerful friends. The first was Daniel Webster [1782–1852], the best-known orator and lawyer of his time, founder of the Whig Party, and a vastly influential United States senator. The second was Oliver Wendell Holmes [1809–1894], professor of anatomy at Harvard, already famous as an essayist, novelist, and poet. Despite all this firepower on Morton's behalf, Congress decided that Morton definitely did not discover surgical anesthesia. Many witnesses substantiated the fact that he had learned everything he knew about ether from Jackson, and they also testified that they had heard Morton assert frequently that Jackson had, in fact, invented the anesthesia.

William Morton came to be called the Great Pretender in congressional reports, because of his initial "pretending" to Jackson that he knew nothing about ether. He went on to limit his practice to anesthesia, but shortly after the notable developments of 1846, he underwent severe financial and emotional problems. In 1868, at age forty-nine, he died a relatively young man for reasons that remain obscure.

Congress also decided that Wells had definitely not invented surgical anesthesia, because he attempted only dental anesthesia. In any case he had by then committed suicide and was no longer available to claim the prize.

The contest, therefore, was between Jackson and Long, at least as Congress had come to see it. Given the powerful advocates on both sides of the question, Congress was unable to decide on the identity of the discoverer of surgical anesthesia. Incredibly, it asked the coclaimants to resolve the question themselves! They ordered Jackson to visit Long in Georgia, which he did. As was his wont, Long was courtly, pleasant, and deferential to the older man, but the two were unable to settle the dispute. Shortly after leaving Georgia, Jackson became demented and remained so for the rest of his life.

Thus, Long was the only claimant to lead a normal life after 1846; the others died either harassed or insane. Long remained calm in response to the tumult and continued to treat the whole affair as if it were of little consequence. . . .

The American College of Surgeons, meeting in Atlanta in 1921, named Long the discoverer and created the Crawford Long Association, which in 1926 erected a statue of Long in Statutory Hall in Washington, D.C. Later a hospital in Atlanta was named the Long Memorial Hospital in his honor, and since that time most surgeons throughout the world have accepted Crawford Long as the discoverer of surgical anesthesia. We too have decided to award the honor to this backwoods surgeon.

# Organ Transplants and Organ Rejection

Joseph Palca

Physicians knew that something mysterious occurred in the human body that caused it to reject transplanted organs, although not enough was known about the immune system to explain the rejections. After a successful kidney transplant from one identical twin to another in 1954, Joseph E. Murray (1919– ) began looking for a way to prevent organ rejections from persons who were not genetically identical, as the twins were. He and other scientists targeted the major histocompatibility complex (MHC), for its key role in rejection. MHC is a gene complex unique to each person's immune system. E. Donnall Thomas (1920– ) used this crucial information about the MHC to help him successfully transplant bone marrow. In this article from *Science*, Joseph Palca reports on the careers and research of the two physicians who won Nobel Prizes for their clinical research on organ transplantation. Palca is a science correspondent for National Public Radio, and he also writes for print publications. Palca won the American Chemical Society's 1998 Grady Stack Award for his reporting on chemistry-related topics. He was the only radio reporter to ever win this award.

To the delight of clinical researchers, the Nobel Prize in Physiology or Medicine [in 1990] [went] to two medical doctors who led the way in using transplanted organs and tissue to treat human patients. Joseph E. Murray [1919– ] emeritus professor of surgery at Harvard Medical School, performed the first successful kidney transplant in a pair of

Joseph Palca, "Overcoming Rejection to Win a Nobel Prize," *Science*, vol. 250, October 9, 1990, p. 378. Copyright © 1990 by American Association for the Advancement of Science. Reproduced by permission.

identical twins. E. Donnall Thomas [1920– ] of the Fred Hutchinson Cancer Research Center in Seattle, first demonstrated that bone marrow cells could be safely transplanted from one individual to another. "They were really pioneers," says Emil Frei, III, director of the Dana-Farber Cancer Institute. "They opened the field that everybody plays in today."

What makes Frei and others particularly pleased is that Thomas and Murray are representatives of what some fear is a diminishing breed: physicians who have spent their careers in clinical research. In recent years, most medicine Nobels have been awarded for more basic research. "I was totally surprised by this," says Thomas. "I really felt the prize would never go to patient-oriented research."

## First Kidney Transplant

Thomas and Murray helped turn what had been a medical pipe dream into a reality. From the beginning of this century researchers had known that there was some "biological force" preventing the transplantation of organs between individuals. But chance threw Murray an opportunity to overcome that force. While a resident at the Peter Bent Brigham Hospital (now Brigham and Women's Hospital) in the late 1940s, Murray joined a team of clinicians who were studying end-stage renal disease. The Harvard researchers, led by David Hume and John Merrill, had been experimenting with transplanting a third kidney taken from a cadaver into the thigh of patients with renal failure. Although the organ wasn't instantly rejected by the recipients' immune system, it was obviously an awkward approach. Murray began developing surgical techniques in dogs that would make a true replacement possible.

Then, in late 1954, Richard Herrick turned up at Peter Bent Brigham Hospital with endstage renal failure. His identical twin brother Ronald Herrick was prepared to donate a kidney and Murray reasoned that, since Ronald's healthy kidney would be genetically identical to Richard's diseased kidney, there should be no problem with rejection. The operation, performed on 23 December 1954, was a "spectacular success," says Murray. Murray spent the next decade looking for ways to overcome the rejection problem. The key insight, says Murray, came from work by two Boston hematologists, William Dameshek and Robert Schwartz, who demonstrated that the compound 6-mercaptopurine would prevent a host animal from rejecting a foreign protein. Working with George Hitchings and Gertrude Elion of Burroughs Wellcome (themselves winners of the Nobel Prize in 1988), Murray developed a drug regimen based on 6-mercaptopurine that suppressed the immune system and allowed the transplanted kidney to establish itself in its new host. Murray performed the first successful transplant from an unrelated donor in 1962.

The excitement generated by the successful organ transplants "led to the enormous increase in research" in the rejection phenomenon, says immunologist David H. Sachs of the National Cancer Institute. Specifically, immunologists began to unravel the nature of the major histocompatibility complex (MHC) that is not only important in rejecting foreign tissue but, as later research has shown, plays a central role in other immune reactions.

## Bone Marrow Transplants

Understanding the MHC turned out to be crucial for the success of the bone marrow transplants pioneered by Thomas. Bone marrow cells are the precursors of all cellular components of blood, including cells responsible for cellular immunity. When these marrow cells stop functioning, as in aplastic anemia, or become cancerous, as in certain forms of leukemia, the body's immune defenses are decimated and severe illness and death usually follow.

Thomas, who began his medical career with Murray at Harvard, reckoned that if he could first eradicate the diseased marrow and then replace it with healthy marrow cells, he could restore patients with these diseases to health. But he faced two major hurdles. First, he had to overcome the host's own immune defenses against the foreign tissue. Then, if the new bone marrow started producing immune cells, these new cells might attack their new host, causing a kind of autoimmune reaction called graft-versus-host disease, a potentially fatal complication.

In 1963, Thomas moved to the University of Washington and began assembling a team of researchers, including Rainer Storb and Dean Buckner, to work on overcoming these problems. Their technique involved a combination of whole-body irradiation to wipe out a patient's own marrow cells and a drug called methotrexate to suppress an immune response. They also began typing tissues based on MHC, vastly improving the odds of finding suitable donors. Since those early experiments, the Seattle team has made steady improvements in their techniques. The results have been remarkable: "What was once a high risk, last ditch operation with a 12 or 13% survival is now a curative approach which works in 40 to 50% of patients with leukemia," says Richard J. O'Reilly, chief of marrow transplantation at Memorial Sloan Kettering Cancer Center.

# Chapter 4

# Pharmaceuticals

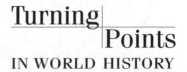

Turning Points
IN WORLD HISTORY

# Aspirin and the Development of the Pharmaceutical Industry

Anne Adina Judith Andermann

The active ingredient in the aspirin tablets taken for headaches and fever is salicylate. This chemical compound occurs naturally in willow bark, wintergreen, and other plants. Native Americans, ancient Chinese, and other cultures have long used these plants to reduce pain and fever. Aspirin, on the other hand, is a nineteenth-century product developed by a pharmaceutical industry in its formative state. In this article from the *McGill Journal of Medicine*, historian and medical student Anne Adina Judith Andermann tells the story of Felix Hoffmann, a chemist at Friedrich Bayer & Company, a dye-manufacturing company in Germany. In the 1870s Hoffmann began to look for a compound that would relieve his father's painful rheumatism and be less upsetting to his digestive system than salicylic acid (a form of salicylate). Hoffmann developed acetylsalicylic acid. This compound became commonly known as aspirin. Other chemists in Europe developed similar products at the same time. Andermann describes the competition among chemists to control the patent on aspirin and to reap the benefits. She describes an alliance that developed between the medical profession and the emerging pharmaceutical industry, an association that Andermann says continues to this day.

Aspirin is a product of the late-nineteenth-century laboratory, pharmaceutical industry, and medical community. The prevailing scientific techniques, industrial approaches, and medical beliefs were instrumental in the development, promotion and reception of the drug. As a result, the present account does not extend further back than a few decades prior to the release of aspirin from the laboratories of Farbenfabriken vormals Friedrich Bayer & Co. in 1899. In contrast, much of the current literature on aspirin attempts to trace the compound back to antiquity through the Ebers papyrus, the Hippocratic [Hippocrates, 460–360 B.C.] writings, and the works of Galen [130–200 A.D.]. Such histories tell a simple linear tale of the numerous "discoveries" proposed to have led to the use of certain salicylate-containing plants, such as willow bark and wintergreen, or salicylate-related compounds, including salicilin and salicylic acid, as cures for a variety of ailments. Indeed, according to Mann [C.C.] and Plummer [M.L.]:

> Both [salicilin and salicylic acid] attacked fever and pain, and their partisans advocated the salicylates' use as antiseptics, mouthwashes, and water preservatives for ocean voyages; one important chemist further suggested (erroneously) that sodium salicylate, a chemical relative, would successfully treat scarlet fever, diphtheria, measles, syphilis, cholera, rabies and anthrax.

However, it is difficult to establish what effect, if any, these examples of the "historical" uses of "proto-aspirin" had on the impetus for and modes of developing and using the actual drug called aspirin. As a matter of course, aspirin is usually described as the natural descendant from these salicylate forefathers. However, the history of aspirin is not as straightforward a tale as conventional histories suggest, but rather is a complex narrative of the people and circumstances involved in transforming a simple chemical compound into a popular pharmaceutical product that has remained one of the most widely consumed drugs for almost a century.

### Drugs as Industrial Products

Bayer began in 1863 as Friedrich Bayer & Co., a dye-manufacturing plant in Germany. When the dye industry began to wane during the late 1880s, Bayer made the transition into the more active and lucrative sector of pharmaceuticals by developing, producing, and marketing phenacetin (acetophenetidin) from a dye-making by-product. The company's switch from dyes to pharmaceuticals was so rapid that the first lots of the drug were alkylated in make-shift containers—empty beer bottles wrapped in towels—before the company decided to invest in suitable equipment and proper facilities for its production. However, despite the change in the products being manufactured, Bayer retained many of the methods used previously in the sale of dyestuffs in highly competitive markets: sales representatives, advertisements in trade journals, and the use of patents and trade names. As [J.] McTavish, a noted medical historian, remarks:

> By restricting its market to the pharmaceutical and medical professions, the chemical industry avoided the unseemly trappings of the nostrum trade and established itself as a member of the 'ethical' fraternity.

From then on, McTavish affirms, "[drug production] took place in an industrial setting. Drugs were commodities similar in most respects to any other commodity: they were manufactured for profit." During the 1890's, Carl Duisberg and other key figures at Bayer were busily involved in reorganizing the company, in setting up pharmaceutical laboratories for the development and standardization of drugs, and, most importantly, in establishing links with the medical world.

The late nineteenth century saw an unprecedented rise in the number of new pharmaceutical products on the market. One physician in 1889 commented: "Every week, almost every day, brings its new drug, each in turn praised as being the greatest discovery of modern therapeutics." McTavish attributes this tremendous influx of new products to "the increasing industrial role of the laboratory, especially in the drug industry." However, the utility of these novel therapeutic products in medical practice was a source of great debate. Certain physicians staunchly opposed what they saw as "the growing tendency among German medical men to convert the 'Republic of Science' into a commercial oligarchy for the benefit of plutocrats at the expense of suffering humanity," [according to McTavish]. . . .

For those pharmaceutical companies that had managed to establish a place for themselves within the medical community, drug production became a legitimate science-based industry, whereby manufacturers and medics engaged in a profitable producer-consumer partnership. For instance, as written in the Lancet in August 1899, many new pharmaceuticals were the product of the increased attention paid "to the toleration of drugs and to the avoiding of effects which are undesirable." Furthermore:

> Modification of the salicylates and the introduction of new morphine derivatives [which were both activities carried out in the Bayer laboratories] occur as single examples. In these matters it is satisfactory to find that the pharmacist is guided by the medical man and not solely by a knowledge of the chemistry of the principles concerned.

Thus, the inspiration and drive to produce aspirin can be explained in terms of a medico-industrial relationship in which the pharmaceutical companies supplied products that interested the doctors, and the doctors, in turn, maintained an active interest in what the pharmaceutical companies had to offer.

During the 1880s and 1890s, when physicians became intensely interested in the possible adverse effects of fever on the human body, the use of antipyretics [antifever] became one of the hottest topics in therapeutic medicine. . . .

Until the fever fad ended at the turn of the century, most likely as a result of the increasing popularity of the germ theory, most physicians concentrated their efforts on treating pyrexia [fever]. The drug companies responded to the medical demands of the day by catering to, and perhaps even fueling the fires of, the antipyretic era. New antipyretics and analgesics [pain-relief medication]—most drugs in this class were believed to possess more or less of both properties—were introduced monthly: "those coal-tar crystalline products which have almost deluged the market as quinine substitutes, [were] being offered from time to time as analgesics, anodynes, antipyretics, as the case may be," [according to the British Medical Association]. Moreover, most of these new therapeutic compounds were commonly promoted as and subsequently referred to by catchy brand names such as malarin, pyrantin, cosaprin, phesin, eupyrine, and, of course, aspirin.

## Development of Aspirin

Still, it is not exactly clear how aspirin came to be. Many give the title of "discoverer of aspirin" to Felix Hoffmann, a chemist at Bayer whose father suffered from rheumatism. According to legend, Hoffmann's father was taking salicylic acid, already mass-produced, widely used, and highly profitable by the end of the 1870s, to treat his rheumatic condition. Unfortunately, the drug was terribly irritating to the stomach and was associated with other ill-effects: most notably, in addition to having an unpleasant, sometimes nauseating, taste, it was believed that salicylic acid disrupted digestion and had an enfeebling action on the heart. Therefore, the dutiful son took on the task of developing a less toxic replacement. However, acetylsalicylic acid (ASA)—the common chemical name of aspirin—may have already been produced by the French chemist Charles Frédéric Gerhardt [1816–1856] in 1853, although he called his compound acetosalicylic anhydride, which was not necessarily the same as ASA. The compound was synthesized in a purer form by Johann Kraut in 1869. Indeed, acetylsalicylic acid was already being manufactured by the Chemische Fabrik von Heyden Company in 1897, although without a brand name. Therefore, it is difficult to determine whether Hoffmann truly developed a new chemical compound or even a novel method of producing a known one, which could then have been patented in Germany.

In addition to the uncertainties regarding the chemical origins of ASA, the prevailing medical opinions concerning the widely-used salicylic acid and related compounds, including acetylsalicylic acid, were mixed. Similarly, there was a wide divergence in opinion within the Bayer pharmaceutical laboratories concerning the value of the work being done on ASA in 1897. According to [C.C.] Mann and [M.L.] Plummer, there was a certain degree of animosity between Arthur Eichengrün, who ran the research and development-based [Bayer] Pharmaceutical Division where Hoffmann worked, and Heinrich Dreser, who was in charge of testing and standardization in the Pharmacological Division. Eichengrün supported Hoffmann's chemical compound, whereas Dreser initially had no interest in even testing it as a potential new drug. Apparently, Eichengrün even went so far as to surreptitiously distribute the compound to physicians for trials. However, it was Dreser who eventually published the first article on aspirin. His change of heart regarding the value of this compound likely reflects his own financial interests, since, according to Mann and Plummer:

> "[Hoffmann and Eichengrün] had contracts with Bayer by which they would receive a royalty on any patentable product they invented. Since there was no patent, neither of them received any royalties from the sale of aspirin in Germany. However, Heinrich Dreser had an agreement with Bayer by which he would receive a royalty on any product that he introduced. Thus he received a very substantial royalty for aspirin and was able to retire early a very rich man.". . .

## Medical and Pharmaceutical Alliance

The elegance of the early medical and pharmaceutical reports lies in their ability to ally aspirin with the already widely accepted salicylic compounds, whilst concurrently presenting aspirin as distinct from them. Thus, the new drug possessed a certain familiarity, and more importantly, the manufacturers could then claim the proven medicinal properties of salicylic acid and related compounds by association. However, it was equally important to disassociate aspirin from the negative qualities that had been attributed to these products through the development of scientific truths in the laboratory which attested to such differences. In this way, a white powder that had spent many years collecting dust on a shelf along with hundreds of other chemical compounds stored at Bayer was transformed into a substantive pharmaceutical product. Since then, each new report by members of the medical community or pharmaceutical world has expanded and altered the ever-growing narrative on aspirin. . . .

Aspirin had quickly become a household name around the

world, finding its way even into literary works of the early twentieth century. For instance, when the young Lady Caroline Desta of Elizabeth von Arnim's 1922 novel *The Enchanted April* complained of a headache during a holiday in Italy, one of her companions asked, "Do you know what aspirin is in Italian?"—to which an erudite old Englishwoman interjected that "the proper remedy for headaches . . . is castor oil." In a similar vein, Franz Kafka [writer, 1883–1924] once explained to his fiancée Felice Bauer, in the course of their tormented relationship, that aspirin was one of the few things that eased the unbearable pain of being.

Aspirin has certainly been put to many different uses throughout the twentieth century, and serves as an example of one of many products of the novel and tenuous relationship that developed during the late nineteenth century between laboratory science, the manufacturing industry, and medical humanitarianism. Indeed, the early pharmaceutical industry's establishment of a close association with the medical community and its adoption of scientific techniques, or, at the very least, a scientific veneer, were instrumental in its success, "and changed the character of medical practice as much as it did the industry itself" [according to historian J.M. Liebenau]. Over the years, these medico-industrial connections have consolidated to form the modern pharmaceutical industry of today, an industry that has pervaded almost all aspects of medical science and practice.

# Fleming's Discovery of the Effects of Penicillin

Gladys L. Hobby

Alexander Fleming (1881–1955) was a Scottish bacteriologist interested in antiseptics that would defeat microorganisms. In this selection from her book on the discovery of penicillin, Gladys L. Hobby points out that Fleming's early career coincided with that period in medical history when great strides were being made in identifying organisms and determining their relationship to disease. Many scientists consider Fleming's discovery of lysozymes (enzymes in tears and saliva that attacks bacterial cell walls) to be his most significant scientific contribution. Fleming is best known, however, for discovering in 1928 that a colony of staphylococci bacteria in his lab was unable to grow in the presence of a mold that had contaminated the colony. The mold was *Penicillium notatum*. Fleming reported his findings a few months later and noted that penicillin could possibly be used to treat bacterial infections. He did little to publicize his discovery, according to Hobby, because of the strong division in those times between basic laboratory research and applied clinical work. Fleming was a basic researcher. More than ten years later, Howard Walter Florey (1898–1968) and Ernst Chain (1906–1979), uncovered Fleming's research findings and began looking for a way to apply the findings to a clinical setting. They proceeded to synthesize a concentrated, nontoxic form of penicillin useful in fighting infections. All three won the Nobel Prize in 1945 for their work with penicillin. Hobby was a microbiologist who helped to develop antibiotics, as well as a teacher at Cornell University. She was also the author of more than two hundred articles and the book *Penicillin: Meeting the Challenge*.

Alexander Fleming [1881–1955] discovered penicillin in 1928. He named it, described its properties, and suggested cautiously that the use of the substance as a laboratory tool might be secondary in importance to its possible use in the treatment of bacterial infections:

> Penicillin, in regard to infections with sensitive microbes appears to have some advantages over the well-known chemical antiseptics. . . . Experiments in connection with its value in the treatment of pyogenic infections are in progress. . . . In addition to its possible use in the treatment of bacterial infections penicillin is certainly useful to the bacteriologist for its power in inhibiting unwanted microbes in bacterial cultures.

Fleming, who was professor of bacteriology at St. Mary's Hospital Medical School in London, made his first observations on penicillin just six years after he had discovered another lytic [break down, destroy] agent to which he had given the Greek name *lysozyme* [enzyme that is found in tears and saliva that acts as an antiseptic]. Bacteriolytic agents are substances that act on the carbohydrate moiety of certain bacteria, causing their disintegration. The discovery of lysozyme is regarded by some as more fundamentally important than the discovery of penicillin.

## Fleming's Interest in Bacteriology

The discovery of penicillin was announced in the scientific literature in June 1929, nine months after the event, but the article aroused no special interest. Indeed, the discovery, regarded merely as an observation, remained virtually unknown outside scientific circles, for the scientific community at the time considered publicity to be unethical. Not until more than a decade later was penicillin rediscovered through a survey of the literature on microbial antagonisms made by Ernst Chain [1906–1979]. . . .

In the end of the nineteenth century and the beginning of the twentieth, the new branch of science called bacteriology began to develop. In 1881, Robert Koch [1843–1910] published his methods for the study of pathogenic microorganisms, and Louis Pasteur [1822–1895] reported the development of vaccines for the prevention of fowl cholera and anthrax. Three years later, Koch set down his famous postulates which continue to serve as a guide in establishing the etiology of infectious diseases. Lord Joseph Lister [1827–1912], professor of surgery at the University of Glasgow and later at the University of Edinburgh, had already successfully applied the principles of Pasteur's germ theory of disease to surgery, and Koch had shown that various infectious diseases could be produced by injecting "putrid" fluids into animals. Establishment of Pasteur's theory and the perfection of bacteriological techniques by Koch—the use of agar in culture media and staining techniques and oil immersion for the microscopic study of bacteria—opened the way for the rapid advances that were made early in the twentieth century. By the 1920s, bacteriology had become an important scientific discipline, and in time the term *microbiology* was introduced to connote the science that concerns viruses, protozoa, and fungi, as well as bacteria.

Because Alexander Fleming's early years in medicine coincided with this period of proliferating activity in the isolation and characterization of species of microorganisms and their relation to infectious diseases, it is not surprising that he chose the field as his life's work.

Born on a farm in Ayrshire in 1881, Fleming had followed one of his brothers into the study of medicine, entering St. Mary's Medical School in 1901. He accepted a post as medical bacteriologist at St. Mary's on the day he completed his courses and in 1906 joined the staff of the Inoculation Department under the direction of Sir Almroth Wright [1861–1947]. He qualified in surgery in 1908 and later became a Fellow of the Royal College of Surgery, but he never practiced as a surgeon to any great extent.

Fleming spent his entire professional career at St. Mary's. Upon the retirement of Sir Almroth in 1945, he was named principal (director) of what had become by then the Wright-Fleming Institute of Microbiology. He continued there until his retirement on January 15, 1955. Fleming died two months later on March 11 and was buried in the crypt of St. Paul's Cathedral in London, an honor conferred on only a few of the most illustrious Britons. He had been knighted in 1944 and received the Nobel Prize for Medicine the following year.

Fleming inherited from Sir Almroth a keen interest in the destruction of bacteria by leucocytes (white blood cells, also known as phagocytes). During World War I, he spent considerable time investigating problems associated with septic wounds. He was particularly impressed with the antibacterial power of the leucocytes contained in the pus exuded from wounds and also was impressed by the fact that the chemical antiseptics in common use were far more destructive to leucocytes than to bacteria. From his observations, he became convinced that the ideal antiseptic or antimicrobial agent must be highly active against microorganisms but harmless to leucocytes.

Fleming's work with antiseptics and leucocytes continued after World War I, and in 1922 he discovered a substance he regarded as approaching the ideal antiseptic—lysozyme. Two years later, he modified a technique first described by Sir Almroth in 1923, adapted it to the study of antiseptics [agents that destroy disease-causing organisms], and clearly established that only lysozyme (which was never of any therapeutic value) approached his concept of the ideal antiseptic. Later he showed with this technique that penicillin met the same criteria.

## Fleming's Discovery

In September 1928, Fleming was growing strains of staphylococci (organisms that cause boils as well as more serious infections) and noticed one day a contaminating colony growing on one of his plates. The contaminant was obviously a mold, and it seemed probable that a spore from the air circulating in the laboratory had lit upon the plate. Around the contaminating colony, the staphylococcus colonies appeared transparent, as if they were being lysed or dissolved. Fleming recognized that anything capable of dissolving staphylococci might be biologically important, so he isolated the contaminant for further study. Later he said, "I must have had an idea that this was of some importance, for I preserved the original culture plate."

In retrospect, we know that the contaminant must have

been producing penicillin which diffused out from the colony and acted on the surrounding staphylococci. Today, the action of penicillin usually is more easily detected by observing its ability to inhibit growth of susceptible microorganisms. Fleming, however, first detected the substance by observing its lytic action on organisms that had already grown enough to produce colonies.

For many years after his discovery, numerous photographs, many of them taken by Fleming, were stored in a cabinet in his laboratory. Among the photographs was the original agar plate itself, showing the lysis of staphylococci in the vicinity of the contaminating mold (originally designated *Penicillium rubrum*, later correctly identified as a strain of *Penicillium notatum*). That plate and a replica are now located in the British Library (London), Collection 56209, vol. CIV, Fleming 1928 (z.3.c.1.). The original shows only a thin, well-dried shell of what was the culture medium. The staphylococcal colonies are visible around the contaminant and appear flat and transparent. There is no indication of any inhibition of growth around the contaminant. Rather, all colonies on the plate (except that of the contaminant) appear to have been lysed, indicating that the penicillin had acted on mature organisms.

In contrast, the so-called replica shows around the contaminant a clear zone in which no growth occurred. This zone is surrounded by a second zone in which the staphylococcal colonies are smaller and lower in number than in the area farther removed from the contaminant. Growth inhibition, but not lysis, is readily apparent. Thus, the "replica" shows the growth-inhibitory action of penicillin, whereas the original plate shows penicillin's lytic action. (The difference between the "replica" and the original plate is unaccounted for.) Fleming apparently assumed, or knew, that the two effects were due to a single agent, for almost immediately he turned his attention to studies of its growth-inhibitory effects only.

Thus, Fleming's discovery of penicillin was not merely a fortuitous observation. It was a direct outgrowth of his discovery of lysozyme and his six years of study of its lytic action. If he had not already been interested in bacteriolysis, he might well in 1928 have discarded the contaminant that produced penicillin. . . .

The term *penicillin* first came into use on March 7, 1929.

## Diabetes and the Discovery of Insulin

*Diabetes is a serious and debilitating disease known from ancient times that, if left untreated, leads to gangrene, blindness, coma, and death. Sufferers of this disease have a pancreas that does not produce insulin, or they have cells that are unable to use insulin properly. Insulin is a hormone that makes it possible for the body's cells to convert the sugars in food into energy. Diabetes meant certain death until a team of Canadian researchers was able to isolate the hormone and produce a form of insulin that could be administered to diabetic patients. Insulin injections do not cure the illness but instead make it manageable.*

First recognized in ancient times, diabetes is characterized by an inability to convert sugar—or glucose—into energy. There actually are two distinguishable forms of diabetes: type 1 and type 2.

Many people think that diabetes results from eating too many sweets, but the truth is more complex. In type 1, or juvenile diabetes, the pancreas fails to produce insulin, the hormone that enables the cells to convert sugar into energy. The disease, which usually appears at an early age, results from the body's immune system attacking the insulin-producing cells in the pancreas.

Type 2 diabetes—also known as adult-onset diabetes—is characterized by "insulin resistance," or an inability of the cells to use insulin, sometimes accompanied by a deficiency in insulin production.

At least 16 million Americans suffer from diabetes, and the number has been increasing rapidly, according to the Centers for Disease Control and Prevention (CDC). Between 1990 and 1999, the prevalence of the disease jumped 41 percent nationwide. . . .

Physicians in India and Greece described the symptoms of diabetes more than 2,000 years ago. In about 400 B.C., Susruta [c 380–450 B.C.], the father of medicine in India, described patients with "honeyed urine." The Greek physician Aretaeus noted around 150 A.D. that the "remarkable disorder" was marked by

All prior experiments mentioned in Fleming's notebooks were conducted with "mould juice," "mould filtrate," or "mould fluid." Initially the new term was applied to the

"incessant" urination, a "rapid" wasting away of the body and a "speedy" death. Greeks called the syndrome diabetes: "dia" meaning "through," and "betes" meaning "to go.". . .

In 1788 English physician Thomas Cawley first found the link to the pancreas, after finding a shriveled pancreatic gland in a diabetic patient during autopsy. Then in 1869 Paul Langerhans [1847–1888], a Berlin medical student, discovered a previously unknown cell type within the pancreas. He was unable to identify its function, but the cell clusters today bear his name: the islets of Langerhans.

Twenty years later, the German physicians Joseph von Mering [1849–1908] and Oskar Minkowski [1858–1931] made a decisive advance in understanding diabetes by showing that the removal of the pancreas from a dog produced diabetes. The finding resulted in an intense search for an anti-diabetic agent. Physicians produced extracts from animal pancreases to treat diabetes in animals and humans; blood sugar levels were reduced, but impurities in the extracts produced fever. The not-yet-identified substance was termed "insulin."

A team of Canadian researchers finally isolated therapeutically active insulin in Toronto in the early 1920s. Surgeon Frederick Banting [1891–1941] and medical student Charles Best [1899–1978] reconfirmed that pancreatic extracts could be used to treat dogs after the removal of the pancreas, but again with toxic effects. Professor John Macleod [1876–1935], head of the University of Toronto's physiology department, added biochemist James Collip [1892–1965] to the team. He used beef pancreases to prepare a purer extract that was used successfully to treat dogs and then humans in 1922. Banting and Macleod were awarded the Nobel Prize in medicine in 1923 for their work; they divided their shares of the prize money with Best and Collip.

Kenneth Jost, "Diabetes Epidemic," *CQ Researcher*, vol. 11, no. 9, March 9, 2001, pp. 187–92.

penicillium culture fluids or "mould juices" with which Fleming worked. By common usage, however, *penicillin* came to refer to the active antibacterial substance(s) in the culture fluids. It is now used to refer specifically to certain antimicrobial substances derived as metabolic products of *Penicillium notatum* or *Penicillium chrysogenum.*

In the months immediately following his discovery, Fleming established that the antibacterial substance could be produced by certain strains of *Penicillium*, but not by all molds. He studied methods of producing it, established its presence in culture filtrates, determined its stability (lability) at various temperatures and its antimicrobial spectrum, and showed that it is nontoxic and nonirritating. He was most impressed with the fact that it did not interfere with leucocyte [white blood cell] function.

On May 10, 1929, he submitted to the *British Journal of Experimental Pathology* his first report on penicillin. . . .

Many have questioned why Fleming never tested the systemic chemotherapeutic activity of penicillin. It may be that he thought he had done so, for he believed strongly in the significance of the in vitro slide cell procedure he had developed. Moreover, his studies on chemical antiseptics and their use in the treatment of wounds (particularly during World War I) had conditioned him to think in terms only of topical therapy. More important, though, is the fact that in 1928–29, the worlds of basic research and applied research rarely conjoined. It was not considered important that basic research should lead to some practical application.

During the 1930s, Fleming received little credit for his discovery of penicillin. His associates in the Inoculation Department at St. Mary's continued to regard it as a substance of no real importance. Later they would credit the discovery to chance alone.

It is undeniable that the contaminating spore(s) lit upon the plate of staphylococci at just the time in their growth cycle when they were susceptible to the lytic action of the penicillin produced by the spores. As was shown in our laboratories in 1942 and has been shown repeatedly since, penicillin is active only when cell multiplication is taking place.

Any decrease in the rate of growth of microorganisms results in a decrease in the rate at which penicillin acts. Lysis does not occur routinely; the conditions required for growth inhibition and for lysis are not identical.

Nevertheless, Fleming was prepared for the fortuitous event. Because of his experience with lysozyme and the fact that lytic agents were much on his mind, he observed the contaminant, noted its lytic action, and preserved the plate. None of this was a matter of chance.

At the time of the discovery, Fleming was conducting a study of staphylococci and of mutants derived from them in preparation for a chapter he was writing for *A System of Bacteriology in Relation to Medicine*, to be published by the British Medical Research Council. During the course of this study, he observed and isolated the contaminant and noted its lytic activity. Unfortunately, he failed to record the culture medium employed in his experiments, its pH, and other cultural conditions that might have contributed to the appearance of bacterial lysis. Moreover, although he preserved the contaminant, he failed to preserve the susceptible staphylococcal mutant. In the light of recent studies, it seems possible that that strain of staphylococci may have been as important in its own way as the contaminant, for even now, after more than fifty years, there is inadequate understanding of the lytic phenomenon. . . .

Initially, Alexander Fleming observed, on his original plate, only lysis, the end stage of penicillin's action.

On balance, then, chance obviously contributed to the discovery of penicillin, but Fleming's experience, intuition, and keen powers of observation were all important to the discovery. As Ernst Chain commented in 1979 only a few months before his death on August 12:

> Fleming made a very important and very original new biological contribution towards the discovery of the curative properties of penicillin. He was certainly very much favoured by good luck, but this is the case in most important discoveries. . . . There is no doubt that this discovery, which has changed the history of medicine, has justly earned him a position of immortality.

# Medication for Mental Illness: Chlorpromazine

James Le Fanu

British physician James Le Fanu, who is the author of books and medical columns for London newspapers, describes the progress that was made in the 1950s with pharmaceutical drugs used to treat mental illness. He points out that chemical abnormalities in the brain can lead to mental disorders such as schizophrenia, and several generations of drugs have been developed to treat these disorders. Psychopharmacology, the use of drugs to treat psychiatric disorders, developed because physicians hoped to find alternatives to cruder treatments such as electric shock, insulin coma, and lobotomies (removing portions of the brain). A French physician, Henri Laborit, noticed in 1949 that the antihistamine promethazine produced a "euphoric quietude" in his patients. Researchers found that the drug chlorpromazine, which was from the same drug group as promethazine, had a positive effect when tested on mentally ill patients, and even acute schizophrenics could be helped with the new drug. From this, new, related drugs were developed to address specific forms of psychiatric disorders.

Serious psychiatric illnesses such as schizophrenia are usually perceived as having 'something to do' with the chemistry of the brain, an abnormality of one or other of the many chemicals (or neurotransmitters) that transfer 'messages' from one nerve to another, and some of whose names may be vaguely familiar—noradrenaline, acetylcholine and dopamine. Similarly modern drugs—such as chlorpromazine—are presumed to work by correcting these chemical abnormalities.

This schematic view of contemporary psychiatry is plausible enough but incorrect, and importantly so, for it conceals the truly extraordinary nature of the therapeutic revolution in psychiatry in the post-war years. In just over ten years—the decade of the 1950s—six entirely new types of drug were introduced into psychiatric practice and remain its mainstay today. But their discovery was not based on a scientific knowledge of brain chemicals, which was at the time extremely primitive. Rather the drugs came first, being discovered for the most part by chance, preceding by several years the identification of their effect on neurotransmitters.

But that is not all, for even though drugs like chlorpromazine and the antidepressants that followed soon after were subsequently found to alter the chemistry of the brain by boosting or blocking the action of different chemicals, the underlying 'problem'—what actually is happening in the brains of the mentally ill—remains, despite an extraordinary amount of research, unknown. Thus it subsequently became clear that chlorpromazine blocks the activity of the neurotransmitter dopamine, from which one might reasonably infer that, to have such a beneficial effect, schizophrenia must in some way be associated with an excess of dopamine in the brain. But as far as modern science can tell—and there are some fairly sophisticated ways of finding out—the dopamine systems in the brains of schizophrenics appear to be completely normal. The current state of medical knowledge about severe mental illness can thus be summarised as follows: we know that a handful of drugs discovered by accident almost fifty years ago are effective in relieving the symptoms of schizophrenia and depression—but why they work, the nature of the abnormal changes in the brain they correct and especially the causes of psychiatric illness remain a mystery. . . .

## Suffering of the Mentally Ill

[In 1953] in Birmingham's [England] Winson Green Hospital, Joel Elkes, Professor of Experimental Psychiatry, was studying the effect of a new drug, chlorpromazine, which had shown promising results in acute schizophrenia but whose effects up until this time had not been assessed in the chronic, 'burned-out', no-hope patients in the back wards. 'Our limited aim,' wrote Professor Elkes, was 'to determine the usefulness of chlorpromazine in the overactive chronic psychotic patient in the crowded disturbed wards of the mental hospital.' Among those given the new drug was a 32-year-old schizophrenic man who had been in hospital for six years:

"His behaviour was greatly disturbed by terrifying visual and auditory hallucinations. He referred to them as 'bogies' and, when present, they occupied his whole attention. He spent a great deal of time writing inconsequential sentences, or drawing to 'ward off the bogies', and he would often shout abuse at them, banging the furniture and marching about the ward. His sleep was disturbed and he required sedation nearly every night. Socially he was very withdrawn and solitary. After three weeks on chlorpromazine he gradually became more accessible and friendly. He worked on the ward and took charge of the Christmas decorations. Eventually he was able to attend occupational therapy for the first time since his admission, where he practiced his talents for painting. He received no medication apart from chlorpromazine and had only occasional restless nights despite this. Sporadically he would shout at his hallucinations but he said that 'the bogies do not worry him so much'. He relapsed when on placebo tablets.". . .

Chlorpromazine 'tore through the civilised world like a whirlwind and engulfed the whole treatment of psychiatric disorders', but to fully appreciate its impact it is first necessary to return to the 'dark before the dawn'.

Within the spectrum of psychiatric disorders it is customary to distinguish the neuroses, such as anxiety and hypochondriasis, from the psychoses, the severe mental illnesses in which consciousness and perception is impaired, such at schizophrenia and manic depression. It is this latter group who filled the mental hospitals in the 1930s and 1940s in their tens of thousands.

Grim the pre-war asylums certainly were, but it is important not to lose sight of the real misfortune of their inmates—the mental suffering caused by the illness for which they had been admitted. Thus the patient with schizophrenia is often fearful, persecuted by frightening hallucinations or the machinations of delusionary others: 'Fear comes suddenly, chilling and shocking and with it uncertainty and new shadows—shadows with movements and hidden life, the life of the small night-time enemies, rodents, insects, marauders, [one patient reported]. . . .

## Early Treatments for Mental Illness

It is only within this context of quite unimaginable mental suffering, where medicine had nothing to offer other than custodial care and sedation, that it is possible to understand the rise in popularity in the 1930s and 1940s of what now seem crude and often cruel treatments—insulin coma, electric shock (ECT) and psychosurgery. These became known as the 'physical therapies', for that is precisely what they were—physical assaults on the patient's brain in the hope that the trauma would somehow correct its malfunctioning.

The first was 'prolonged narcosis', introduced in 1920, where patients were put to sleep for several days with a combination of barbiturate drugs. The next, 'insulin coma', required patients to be given large doses of insulin which, by lowering the blood sugar, induced a comatose state from which they would be rescued by a large dose of glucose. Next they were given a drug, cardizol, that caused them to have epileptic fits, and this in turn was replaced by the use of electric shock therapy (ECT) pioneered by an Italian, Ugo Cerletti [1877–1963]. The last of the physical therapies—lobotomies, where the brain was cut with a knife—was pioneered by a Lisbon neurologist, Egas Moniz. The apparent effectiveness of the physical therapies in some patients generated an enormous enthusiasm 'untainted by the normal requirements of rational scientific scepticism'. But they were massively overused, frequently in patients who were quite unsuitable. . . .

## Chemicals as Treatment

The physical therapies (with the exception of ECT) were killed off not by a psychiatrist or a psychoanalyst or a brain chemist, but by a jobbing French naval surgeon with an inquisitive mind, Henri Laborit [1914–1995]. In 1949, while working at the Maritime Hospital in Tunisia, Laborit was investigating ways of treating patients in 'shock' who had low blood pressure. Shock may result from a variety of causes: severe blood loss, a failing heart, overwhelming blood infection or major surgery. The shock arising from blood loss can be counteracted with blood transfusion but the cause—and therefore the appropriate treatment—in other situations was at the time unknown. Laborit's hypothesis, shared by others, was that the trauma of a major operation or overwhelming infection might lead to the release from the cells of chemicals such as histamine (better known as being involved in allergic reactions like hayfever) and that this would produce the fall in blood pressure. If this hypothesis were correct—which it was not—then blocking the release of these chemicals should prevent the development of post-operative shock. Accordingly Laborit gave his patients before and during their operation a cocktail of drugs including the antihistamine promethazine, which blocks the action of histamine (and is similar to the drugs currently used in the treatment of hayfever). Laborit claimed in an article published in 1949—remarkable for its complete absence of any data—that with this combination 'we have been able to distinctly influence the development of post-operative problems'.

More importantly, though, he made an extraordinarily insightful clinical observation about the effects of the antihistamine promethazine. The main drawback of this group of drugs, recognised since their introduction in 1937, was that they caused drowsiness, so it was not surprising that he should note that they had 'an extremely powerful hypnotic effect', but he also observed that they had 'an appreciable analgesic property' such that he no longer found it necessary to give morphine to deaden the pain following operations: 'Antihistamines product a *euphoric quietude* . . . our patients are calm, with a restful and relaxed face.' In an interview several years later Henri Laborit elaborated on this observation of euphoric quietude, describing the action of promethazine on the brain as 'disconnecting' its functions, resulting in 'a state of complete calm and tranquillity without depression of mental faculties or clouding of consciousness'.

In 1950 the drug company Rhône-Poulenc, alerted to the possibility that promethazine might be useful in the treatment of psychiatric disorders, initiated a major research programme. The group of drugs to which promethazine belongs are known as the phenothiazines, and Paul Charpentier, the company's chief chemist, set out to synthesise as many variations of its molecular structure as possible in the hope of finding one which had the same, or greater, ability to create a sense of 'euphoric quietude'. The compounds he synthesised were then tested on rats that had learned to climb a rope to avoid an electric shock signalled by the ringing of a bell. One compound in particular, chlorpromazine, left the rats unmoved when the bell was rung.

Hearing of this, Jean Delay and Pierre Deniker, two leading Parisian psychiatrists, were the first to treat a schizophrenic patient, a 57-year-old labourer, Giovanni A., who had been admitted to hospital for 'making improvised speeches in cafés, becoming involved in fights with strangers, and walking around the street with a pot of flowers on his head proclaiming his love of liberty'. After nine days on chlorpromazine he was able to have a normal conversation and after three weeks he was ready to be discharged. This was much better, much quicker, much safer than any response that had been obtained by the physical therapies such as ECT and insulin coma. The news then spread to Britain, where Joel Elkes at Birmingham's Winson Green Hospital— as already described—started to give chlorpromazine to the 'burned-out' cases on the long-stay wards on whom at the time no treatment availed.

Across the Atlantic the experience of another psychiatrist, Heinz Lehman [1911–1999] of the Verdun Boston Hospital in Montreal, a refugee from Nazi Germany, exemplified the difference that chlorpromazine made. When Lehman had first arrived in Montreal Hospital before the war it was 'a pretty horrible place . . . I was always convinced that psychotic conditions had some sort of biological cause so . . . I kept experimenting with all kinds of drugs including very large doses of caffeine, in one or two stuporose schizo-phrenics—of course with no results'. He injected sulphur suspended in oil into his patients, 'which was painful', and typhoid antitoxins to produce a fever. 'Nothing helped, I even injected turpentine into the abdominal muscles which produced a huge sterile abscess and marked raising of the white count. None of this had any effect, but all this had been proposed as being of help in schizophrenia.' Then, in May 1953, Lehman managed to lay his hands on a supply of chlorpromazine:

"Two or three acute schizophrenics became symptom-free. Now I had never seen that happen before. I thought it was a fluke—something that would never happen again, but any-how there they were. At the end of four or five weeks there were a lot of symptom-free patients. By this I mean that a lot of hallucinations, delusions and thought disorders had disap-peared. In 1953 there just wasn't anything that ever pro-duced something like this—a remission from schizophrenia in weeks."

Chlorpromazine was the first swallow, and in rapid suc-cession over the next few years four other major groups of drugs applicable to the whole spectrum of psychiatric ill-ness—depression, mania and anxiety states—were intro-duced in exactly the same way, through a combination of chance, shrewd observation and the screening of chemical compounds. Nor indeed could it have been otherwise, for at the time there was simply no perception of how the brain functioned, nor even an inkling of what abnormalities lay behind mental illness and consequently no idea of how these drugs—which appeared to work so well—worked at all.

Thus in 1955 the Parisian psychiatrists Delay and Deniker, when summarising their experience of treating 1,000 patients, clearly had not the slightest idea of its mode of action. They suggested variously that it might stimulate the sympathetic nervous system, or reduce oxygen metabo-lism in the brain, or alter the pattern of the brain waves in the same way that occurs during sleep. It was not until 1963—eleven years after Giovanni A. had first been given chlorpromazine—that it was shown to interfere with the action of the neurotransmitter dopamine. It was thus only natural to infer that the underlying problem in patients with schizophrenia was a neurochemical one. Perhaps their brain contained too much dopamine or dopamine in the wrong place, or the receptors to dopamine in the brain were oversensitive. But this obvious explanation turned out to be incorrect. Neither autopsy studies nor sophisticated scanning techniques have been able to identify or demonstrate any single abnormality of dopamine biochemistry in the brain of schizophrenics (or indeed that of any of the other neurotransmitters).

Similarly, the mechanism of the antidepressant drug, imipramine, led to the hypothesis that depression was caused by an abnormality of adrenaline in the brain. But even though these drugs are certainly highly effective in treating depressed patients, the question of 'what is wrong' remains as unanswered as it is for schizophrenia.

# The Women Behind "the Pill"

Lara V. Marks

The process of developing an oral contraceptive, which came to be known as "the Pill," can be attributed to the vision and support of two women: Margaret Sanger (1879–1966) and Katherine Dexter McCormick (1875–1967). In this selection from her comprehensive book on oral contraceptives, *Sexual Chemistry*, author Lara V. Marks writes that it was Sanger's concern for the situation of women, especially poor women, and McCormick's knowledge, money, and desire to contribute to social progress that made possible a marketable contraceptive pill. Marks points out that Sanger devoted her life to helping free women from unwanted pregnancies, poverty, and disease. Sanger was a long-standing advocate of birth control for women and had even been arrested and jailed in 1915 and 1916 for sending birth control information through the mail and for opening a birth control clinic—both illegal activities at the time. Sanger became convinced that a birth control pill was the answer to the problem of unwanted pregnancy.

Katherine McCormick, a trained biologist, came into money when she married into a wealthy family. Concerned about the condition of women, she wrote Sanger and asked how she could help. McCormick took Sanger's suggestion and began funding the work of Gregory Pincus (1903– ), a chemist who was researching chemical methods of suppressing female ovulation and conception in the 1950s. Pincus's work developing and testing an oral contraceptive was made possible by McCormick and Sanger's support. Marks is a medical historian at the University of London and has written several books on the history of medical developments.

While it is clear that researchers were conducting tests to discover an oral contraceptive from the late 1940s into the 1950s, many found it difficult to obtain money to do such research. The hesitation of the MRC [Medical Research Council, Britain] indicates the general difficulties investigators faced during this period. Although research money existed for basic scientific research into endocrinology and reproductive physiology through philanthropic organizations such as the Rockefeller Foundation, little investment was available for exploring how this research might be applied to practical contraceptive technology.

Significantly it had been an individual American philanthropist, Clarence Gamble (1894–1966), and not a government body, who had initiated and funded the clinical trials with the Indian field pea, *Pisum sativum linn* [thought to be a natural contraceptive]. Inheriting a fortune from Proctor and Gamble Company, the manufacturer of Ivory soap, Gamble had little to fear in terms of his social status. Originally trained as a physician, from 1925 he began to deploy his money in testing the efficacy of new contraceptives around the world. From his perspective, such research was crucial for making birth control medically and socially respectable. His sponsorship of the trials in India was one of many initiatives he undertook in the contraceptive field.

## Margaret Sanger

It was to be the enthusiasm and drive of Margaret Sanger [1879–1966] which proved critical to the development of the first marketable pill. As early as 1912 Sanger had expressed the hope of finding a 'magic pill' for contraception. This was part of her long-term strategy to improve access to birth control. Sanger's zeal for this quest had been awakened by her own personal experiences. The sixth of eleven children, she was born in Corning, New York in 1879. Her parents were first generation Irish-American Catholics, who had been uprooted from County Cork by the great famine. She had grown up in the midst of a large and devout Catholic Irish immigrant community, and was baptised at the age of 13. Her first real friendships were formed with churchgoing Catholic girls who, even as they attended Mass every Sunday, would ridicule the frocked parish priests. Her father Michael Higgins, a stonemason by trade, preached socialism and was contemptuous of religious authority, and he had a continuous struggle to gain work given that most of it depended on cutting gravestones for church cemeteries. By contrast her mother, born Anne Purcell, was a pious Catholic, whose religious faith helped her keep the family together in the face of eviction and deprivation. Margaret remembered her mother constantly coughing in terrible pain because of chronic tuberculosis and wasting away as a result of constant pregnancies that weakened her resistance to the disease. She died at the age of 50. Later on Margaret was to blame her parents' ignorance about contraception for the harsh life her mother had experienced, as well as her premature death. Margaret dedicated her first book to the memory of her mother, 'who gave birth to eleven living children'.

Originally wishing to be a doctor but finding it difficult to enter medical school because of sexual discrimination and educational and financial constraints, Sanger enrolled in training to be a nurse shortly after her mother's death in 1899. Married in 1902, Margaret soon experienced some of the health problems she had witnessed in her mother. Having suffered tuberculosis herself, and pregnant within six months of marriage, she quickly deteriorated physically and mentally. Advised against a further pregnancy on health grounds, Margaret and her husband faced the dilemma encountered by young and passionate couples at a time when access to reliable contraception was still limited. Her distaste for condoms and the withdrawal method in later years might indeed have come from the personal frustrations she experienced during this time. After she bore two more children in 1908 and 1909 Margaret and her husband soon faced the financial hardships that forced her to take up nursing again to support the family. Working on the Lower East Side of New York, where she witnessed the ill-health and deaths of many women who resorted to illegal abortion to cope with constant childbearing, she became even more resolved in her fight for greater access to contraception and began to envisage a contraceptive pill. In mounting this campaign, she argued against the Catholic doctrine forbidding contraception, charging the church with aligning itself 'on the side of ignorance against knowledge, of darkness against light'.

By the end of her life Sanger had married twice and openly admitted to having had at least four lovers. Her diary entry of 1914 captures her delight in and enjoyment of sex: 'I love being ravaged by romances.' Years later a friend, Mabel Dodge, recalled that Sanger was 'the first person I ever knew who was openly an ardent propagandist for the joys of the flesh'. Sanger's campaign for contraception, therefore, was not only bound with up with a fight to improve women's health, but also to give women the sexual freedom already enjoyed by men. Despite facing a jail sentence in the early 1900s, and a great deal of opposition throughout the early twentieth century, by the time of her death Sanger had established a number of birth control clinics in the United States and an international organization, together with several journals, to promote scientific efforts to improve contraceptive methods. Moreover, it was Sanger who provided the impetus for developing the first contraceptive pill.

For Sanger it was vital to find a contraceptive technique that would grant women full control over their fertility without the cooperation of the male as was necessitated by barrier contraceptive methods. Ideally she saw this as something that could be taken by mouth and not at the moment of intercourse. Writing to a friend in 1946, she summed up the strength of her feelings on the matter: 'I was feeling more and more despondent as I saw and realized more than ever the inadequacy of the diaphragm reaching millions of women who need and should have something as simple as a birth control pill.

## Katherine Dexter McCormick

In looking to boost contraceptive research, Sanger found a powerful ally in Katherine Dexter McCormick [1875–1967]. Born into an aristocratic family in Michigan in 1875, Katherine was the second of two children of Writ Dexter, one of Chicago's most successful lawyers, and came from a family which had long ties with Harvard and Harvard Law School. In 1904 she became the second woman ever to graduate from Massachusetts Institute of Technology, majoring in biology. That same year she married Stanley McCormick, heir to the fortune of Cyrus McCormick, inventor of the reaper and founder of the International Harvester Company. Having married into wealth, however, Katherine found herself trapped with a man who, within two years, turned out to suffer from schizophrenia. In 1909 she won legal control of her husband's estate when Stanley was declared legally insane, and she began to immerse herself into the woman's suffrage issue, becoming the vicepresident and treasurer of the National American Woman's Suffrage Association, an organization which in 1919 helped to secure women's right to vote in the United States.

*birth control advocate*
*Margaret Sanger*

After meeting Sanger in 1917, Katherine Dexter McCormick also began to invest some of her time in birth control issues, becoming one of the European travellers who smuggled diaphragms into the United States during the 1920s in order to supply Sanger's contraceptive clinics. Like Sanger, McCormick saw contraception as the key to improving women's position. Part of her interest in contraception might have stemmed from her own marriage and a desire to prevent conception of children who risked inheriting the same affliction as her husband. . . .

Like Sanger, McCormick saw a 'fool-proof' contraceptive as an important weapon in the fight against population growth.

For twenty years McCormick corresponded with Sanger about furthering contraceptive research. Since she was trained in biology, McCormick had the necessary scientific background for understanding the research needed to achieve a contraceptive pill. Her marriage to Stanley Mc-Cormick also provided her with vast financial resources. In the words of John Rock, the obstetrician who planned the human trials of the first marketable pill, McCormick was 'as rich as Croesus. She had a *vast* fortune . . . she couldn't even spend the interest on her *interest*.' Prior to her husband's death in 1947, however, McCormick was restricted in the amount she could devote to contraceptive research because much of her fortune was invested in neuropsychiatric investigations in an effort to find a cure for schizophrenia to help her husband.

## Gregory Goodwin Pincus

In 1950 McCormick began to consult Sanger in earnest about the best way to invest her money in contraceptive research. Sanger recommended the distribution of $100,000 a year to several university laboratories to promote contraceptive projects. Bureaucratic procedures involved in settling her late husband's estate, however, temporarily prevented McCormick from pursuing this line. In March 1952 Sanger alerted McCormick to the possibilities of funding a new avenue of research. This was the work of Gregory Goodwin Pincus [1903– ]. Sanger had met Pincus through Abraham Stone, an associate of the Planned Parenthood Federation of America [PPFA] and director of the Margaret Sanger Research Bureau in New York. During this meeting she had managed to persuade Pincus to consider directing his work towards contraception. Pincus was later to acknowledge that he 'invented the pill at the request of a woman'. . . .

By the time Sanger met Pincus in 1950 he had managed to co-found and become co-director of the Worcester Foundation for Experimental Biology. Established in 1944, and based in Worcester, Massachusetts, this institution specialized in steroidal research and was a key clearing centre for testing the physiological effects of new steroidal compounds produced by pharmaceutical companies. Pincus himself had become a consultant for several of the pharmaceutical companies, including G.D. Searle in Chicago and Syntex in Mexico. Much of the investigation into the compounds sent by the pharmaceutical firms was to see whether they could be used to treat diseases such as cancer and arthritis, and other nervous and mental conditions such as schizophrenia. Under the direction of Pincus, investigations were also conducted on the process of fertilization in order to find ways of preventing spontaneous abortion and menstrual disorders.

Pincus thus had access to many of the latest discoveries in steroid chemistry, placing him in an ideal position to carry out the hormonal contraceptive research proposed by Sanger. Moreover, the fact that the Worcester Foundation was an independent, non-profit, tax-privileged educational and research institution allowed him much greater freedom to explore the controversial issue of contraception—as we have seen, it would not have been so easy had he been based within a university or government-sponsored establishment. For Pincus, Sanger's contraceptive project also represented a potentially lucrative source of funding for the Foundation.

Spurred on by Sanger, Pincus managed to get $6,500 (equivalent to $43,000 today) from the PPFA between 1951 and 1952 to study hormonal contraception. This allowed Pincus and his colleagues to study the oral administration of progesterone in animals. From these studies it seemed feasible that Pincus could develop an oral contraceptive. Despite its promising results, however, the PPFA was reluctant to fund the project further. From their perspective the research did not differ from animal experiments being conducted elsewhere, such as those at the National Drug Company in Philadelphia. Within the PPFA Pincus's work was also viewed with suspicion because it did not conform to the organization's 'accepted social code', which involved research into existing methods of birth control or projects undertaken by medical doctors in clinical settings. In the eyes of PPFA officials, the development of a pill was too risky in terms of its potential side-effects and ineffectiveness. Any flaw in the project would, they feared, backfire badly on the organization and the family planning movement as a whole.

While the PPFA was reluctant to fund Pincus further, McCormick was excited about his work. She had never met Pincus, but was familiar with the Worcester Foundation, having collaborated with its other co-director, Hudson Hoagland, through her sponsorship of research into schizophrenia. In May 1952 McCormick, then aged 76, moved from Santa Barbara to Boston with the intention of following Pincus's work. By June 1953 she had agreed to pay $10,000 a year towards the pill project. This sum was subsequently increased to meet whatever expenses Pincus incurred, including $50,000 to build a new animal house and funds for extra building space to expedite the human trials. McCormick saw this money as crucial in freeing Pincus from what she saw as the frustratingly bureaucratic red-tape of the PPFA. By 1960 McCormick had provided over $1 million for clinically testing the drug. Data from these trials provided the basis on which the US Food and Drug Administration (FDA) approved the first pill. McCormick's funds were not only vital to the development of the pill, but also necessary to the overall financial well-being of the Worcester Foundation. For the remainder of her life McCormick gave the foundation donations of between $150,000 and $180,000 a year. She also left the foundation $1 million in her will. Overall, her contribution to the pill project amounted to over $2 million (equivalent to $12 million today).

# Chapter 5

# Medical Tools

Turning|Points
IN WORLD HISTORY

# Röntgen Retrospective: One Hundred Years of a Revolutionary Technology

Ronald G. Evens

Physician Ronald G. Evens reviews the discovery of X rays made by German physicist Wilhelm Conrad Röntgen (1845–1943) in his laboratory in 1895 as well as the development of radiography based on X rays in the subsequent one hundred years. Röntgen's discovery was accidental, but he saw immediately that the mysterious "X" rays had tremendous potential. His first photograph of an X-ray image was of his wife's hand, showing her bones and wedding ring. The scientific community and the public took to the new invention immediately, and it became popular to have "bone portraits" made in special studios. A new medical specialty, radiology, emerged, and new technologies involving medical imaging developed over the course of time. Evens also discusses the impact of the new technology on the medical profession. He is associated with the Washington University School of Medicine in St. Louis, Missouri.

One hundred years ago, on November 8, 1895, Wilhelm Conrad Rontgen [1845–1943] made a startling discovery in his laboratory in Wurzburg, Germany. The physics professor was experimenting with the action of electric energy in partially evacuated glass tubes—a popular scientific activity in the last quarter of the 19th century. Meticulously laboring in a darkened laboratory with the electrically charged tube, he noticed a glow from the far corner of the room. This observation led to a series of experiments, and while passing his

Ronald G. Evens, "Rontgen Retrospective: One Hundred Years of a Revolutionary Technology," *JAMA*, vol. 274, September 20, 1995, p. 912. Copyright © 1995 by American Medical Association. Reproduced by permission.

hand between a fluorescing screen and the tube, he was astonished to see what appeared to be the shadows of his bones.

It is impossible to know exactly what Rontgen thought at that moment. Most of the great technological inventions have been foreseen by "dreamers" who anticipated the discovery by prediction or fantasy. For example, people have always thought about flying—the airplane made these dreams reality. Physicians had long speculated on the possibility of a "miracle pill" to cure all infection, and the discovery of penicillin in 1927 would take medical science part of the way to that goal. But who could have predicted that it would be possible for a machine to see through the living flesh of the human body to the structure and function beneath. Over the course of the next few weeks, working in guarded privacy, Rontgen verified his observations by recording the bone shadows on photographic plates. On January 23, 1896, he presented his findings on "A New Kind of Ray" ("Eine Neue Arte von Strahlen") to the Physico-Medical Society of Wurzburg, using as partial evidence the now-famous radiograph of a human hand (either the hand of Mrs. Rontgen, his wife, or Professor Killiken, his colleague). His findings were also published earlier in the proceedings of the Wurzburg Physico-Medical society (December 1895), and also published in a Vienna, Austria, newspaper on January 8, 1896, 2 weeks before his official presentation. Within a few days, journals and newspapers around the world were spreading the amazing story of the new rays.

## The Early Years

The public and professional excitement that immediately ensued was fueled in part by the ready availability of apparatus for generating the rays. A simple experimental glass tube of the type first used by Sir William Crookes [1832–1919] in physics laboratories, a fluorescent screen or photographic plate, and a reliable generator (static electricity or coil) were the only tools that the legion of amateur scientists in the United States and Europe needed to produce radiographs, called at that time "shadow pictures," skiagrams," or "Rontgen (or Roentgen) pictures." By the middle of January 1896 the *New York Times* would trumpet "Hidden Solids Revealed" in a series of articles that explained in detail how the new technology worked and how the correct apparatus should be configured for reproducing Rontgen's results. "X-ray pictures" appeared in popular magazines, scientific journals, and medical offerings. Popular publications as diverse as *Scientific American, The Electrical World, Appleton's Popular Science Monthly*, and *Century Magazine* devoted substantial articles and attention to the new phenomenon in the spring of 1896. For the most part, these early images were of foreign bodies (generally in the extremities, since these most easily yield a clear picture), of normal anatomy (feet in shoes, hands with rings), or of novelty arrangements (coins in purses, lead weights in wooden boxes).

By the time of the appearance of the first American clinical diagnostic radiograph, made at Dartmouth College by Dr Edwin Frost on February 3, 1896, physicians were becoming increasingly aware of the extraordinary potential for the new discovery. By April, "X-ray mania" had seized the United States. X-ray studios had opened for "bone portraits," and countless photographers and electricians had set up shop as "skiagraphers."

Events in the early history of radiology have been told in several published histories and doubtless will be told and retold during this centennial year [1995] of Rontgen's discovery. Rontgen's discovery was more than a technological event (or even a breakthrough). It not only changed medical practice, but dramatically transformed the philosophy and culture of medical science in several fundamental ways. The advent of the X-ray posed questions completely new to medicine at the turn of the century—questions that would set the tone for other medical specialties in the years to come. In looking at the advent of the X-ray, we can see the radical reorientation of thought and practice that inevitably accompanies the introduction of a new and groundbreaking technology. But in a more fundamental way the X-ray profoundly altered the course of medicine, and a closer look at these changes can reveal much about our own reactions in the final years of the twentieth century where innovations and breakthroughs seem daily occurrences.

## Control of X-Rays

Despite the obvious medical benefits of Rontgen's magical rays, in 1895 the physician was not the clear and obvious choice to make the radiographic image or to interpret its meaning. Electricians, photographers, and other technical specialists hurried to open facilities to serve the needs of neighboring physicians. In Chicago, Ill, in 1896, for instance, the bustling "X-ray Laboratory" of electrician Wolfram Fuchs received patients on gurneys from nearby hospitals and produced what are, even today, stunning sepiatoned radiographic prints of foreign bodies, calculi, and fractures. (Many of Fuchs' original radiographic prints can be seen at the Center for the American History of Radiology at the American College of Radiology in Reston, Va.) In San Francisco, Calif, photographer Elizabeth Fleischman bought the proper equipment and enjoyed great success in radiographing Spanish-American War casualties at the Presidio. Soon special training courses were offered in radiography, and advertisements emphasized the ease with which anyone could acquire the skills to take X-ray pictures. Electrotherapists, who for years had practiced at the margins of traditional medicine applying static electricity to a variety of aches and pains, suddenly found themselves with the right electrical apparatus and a base of patients. Many of these early technically skilled X-ray workers availed themselves of the less-than-orthodox medical degrees offered by correspondence schools and loosely organized "medical schools," so that by the end of 1896 a number of new "Physicians" appeared with varying and often unpredictable medical capabilities.

Even in the sphere of traditionally legitimized medical practice there was no clear-cut definition of a "roentgenologist." The new technology leapt almost full-blown into hospital and clinical use, and there was little agreement on who should take the pictures, how they should be interpreted, which conditions required radiographic diagnosis—or even who should pay for the service. In many hospitals, an adventuresome physician with an interest in the physical sciences took on the task of running the Rontgen room—most often in the far reaches of the basement. The rooms were noisy, overheated, and festooned with uninsulated live wires, and were made even more uncomfortable by the noxious photographic developing fumes. In some hospitals, reluctant staff or medical students were "volunteered" to run the X-ray operations. At Philadelphia (PA) General Hospital, young George Pfahler was "dragooned" in 1899 into heading up the "X-ray rooms"—a 12 × 15-foot area cordoned off into a machine room, an examining area, and a darkroom. Pfahler himself was skeptical that there was any future in the endeavor, noting, "I can see no future in the field. All of the bones of the body and foreign bodies have been demonstrated."

Many department heads in hospitals saw this effort as the equivalent of any other hospital technical service—requiring only a technician working away to provide the raw materials from which surgeons, internists, and other specialists could make their diagnoses. Despite a growing number of specialized journals on radiography (the earliest journals included the *Archives of Clinical Skiagraphy* [April/May 1896] in London, later the British *Journal of Radiology*, and the *American X-ray Journal*, which began publication in 1897) and a growing rank of physicians working exclusively in the field, there was substantial tension between those in the hospital who believed that the images "spoke for themselves" and fledgling radiologists who maintained that radiographic interpretation required new and specialized skills. The American Roentgen Ray Society was founded in 1900 in an effort to give cohesion to the growing numbers of persons calling themselves "roentgenologists." By 1903, however, it had become apparent that very specialized medical skills and training were necessary, and nonphysicians (as well as those with degrees of dubious origin) were asked to leave the organization.

## Role of Physicians

Not only was there a period of adjustment in settling the question of which physicians should use and interpret the X-ray pictures, there was a pervasive sense that perhaps the miraculous new invention would eliminate the need for physicians entirely. The X-ray apparatus was the first widely used machine to interrupt the traditionally sacred relationship between physician and patient. No longer were history, inspection, touch, percussion, and auscultation the major means of confirming the nature of disease, but an energy-generating electrical machine—the sine qua non of achievement to Americans at the turn of the century—appeared to be a dramatic advance for the physician. Thomas Edison's [1847–1931] early enthusiasms for the X-ray, capped off by a riotous series of performances in which he attempted to radiograph the human brain "at work," and by his more serious contribution of a working handheld fluoroscope, were based on his notion that someday this technology might be in every home. For many observers it was not difficult to imagine domestic X-ray machines taking pictures of every broken bone, major injury, or minor discomfort. The resulting picture would show the "obvious" to even the untrained eye, and the sufferer could then obtain the medication or rehabilitative treatments needed. To a population regularly poked, prodded, and dosed with alcohol- and narcotic-based medications, the notion of eliminating the diagnostic physician from the scene was not without its appeal. And the idea that the radiographic image existed as concrete self-evident proof, not subject to interpretation or multiple meanings, soon made it a favorite of attorneys and patients in malpractice suits.

## A New Specialty

In fact, both physicians and patients soon learned that these new images were not as easy to obtain or interpret as photographs. In these earliest years even the range of normal radiographic anatomy was completely undefined, and exploration of the meaning and types of structural and functional variations had only begun. The advent of contrast imaging, first with postmortem injections of mercury compounds or the insertion of metal styluses, would reveal new areas of radiographic analysis. It became clear that the new technology would be the basis for a new medical specialty, with skilled practitioners and auxiliary personnel, rather than as a service adjunct to already extant hospital departments. The birth of a new medical specialty can be a difficult and torturous labor, involving as it does the inevitable ceding of turf from established fields to the newcomer. Radiology and anesthesiology were the first specialties to emerge directly from inventions. Anesthesiology, with a limited and highly focused sphere of action in the operating room, achieved departmental status in hospitals without tremendous difficulty. But the early roentgenologist seemed to be all over the hospital—presenting his or her diagnoses to surgeons and internists who felt their seniority and experience made them more than qualified to read films without assistance.

The resulting tensions would prevent some major hospitals from establishing true radiology departments until well into the 20th century. The first department head was not named at Johns Hopkins University until Russell Morgan was appointed in 1946, despite a fine tradition of radiology at the institution. The American College of Radiology, founded in 1923, and the American Board of Radiology, first convened in 1934, were two organizations started in an effort to establish firmly that the applications of Rontgen's rays were a specialty requiring specific and exacting standards and practice.

At the end of the 19th century Americans were enchanted with scientific progress and invention. Homes and cities were being changed forever by the introduction of electric lights, telephones, subway systems, and 1001 smaller inventions that promised to make life easier and more pleasant. Medicine, though, seemed stubbornly set in its ways, immune to the benefits of inventions and innovations revolutionizing other scientific fields. In 1894, a writer for the Smithsonian Institution marveled at the immediate possibilities for air and sea travel, but saw little hope for change in medicine or biology.

## Excitement About X-Rays

The impact of the announcement in December 1895 that a machine had been invented to see through the living body was, to say the least, electrifying. When, in February and March of that year, it became clear that the rays also had undefined therapeutic effects, public and professional excitement reached a fever pitch. The possibility that the X-ray could actually cure cancer (before the end of the century,

Francis Williams had shown to the Boston City Medical Society cases of carcinoma of the skin and lip healed by Rontgentherapy), a disease for which there was no hope except for limited surgical intervention, must have seemed truly miraculous to physicians and patients alike. And if the X-ray could diagnose any illness and cure others—what else could it do? To a population ready for a "miracle machine," the possibilities seemed endless.

Tempering and directing enthusiasm for new technologies would become an ongoing problem in medicine, but in 1896 there were no constraints. Each new "miracle" observation became a promise of cure. For example, numerous researchers attempted to apply the rays (both in vitro and in vivo) to the tubercle bacillus, often seeing positive results when there actually were none. Others went further afield in their work, claiming X-rays could transmit thoughts, restore vision to the blind—even raise the dead!

The public response to reports of these efforts was predictable. Not only did everyone expect access to the new technology—whether to identify long-embedded foreign bodies or to verify their self-made diagnoses—they expected the new machines to deliver easy answers to even the most difficult clinical questions. Soon the appearance of X-ray machines in general practitioners' offices across the United States would underline the notion that the new technology was available to diagnose any and every ailment. Some physicians even thought it would eliminate the need for laboratory analysis in medicine. Moreover, in an age in which people had come to believe there would be a "pill for every ill," many thought there would soon be a machine for every disease. Numerous new "rays" to cure everything from smallpox to insanity were announced by both deceptive and well-intentioned practitioners after Rontgen's discovery.

The hope, sincerity, and occasional unfortunate results of this enthusiasm cannot be discounted. The years immediately after Rontgen's announcement saw a marked shift from a general preoccupation with improvements in sanitation and public health as the media for medical advancement, to a notion that miracles lay just ahead ready to revolutionize medicine overnight. To sufferers this brought comfort; every physician has dealt with terminal patients who hold out hopes that "any day now some cure may be discovered." New treatments and innovations would be given charmed popular titles; [Paul, 1854–1915] Ehrlich's introduction of salvarsan for the treatment of venereal disease would be called the magic bullet. But magic and miracles lead not only to unfulfilled expectations—often they lead to the undervaluation of the less exciting aspects of medicine. If a miracle cure is just around the corner, why devote money and effort to studying and evaluating diseases that might just go away entirely? Such reasoning has often been just below the surface of public discourse on the direction of progress and was first seen in the years immediately following Rontgen's discovery. Editors of *Scientific American*, only weeks after the announcement of the new rays, noted that the possibilities were so astonishing that they "almost dangerously increase our powers of belief." In fact, the diagnostic and therapeutic applications of the X-ray would begin a tradition in which these powers of belief would often be stretched beyond the powers of the new technology to contain them.

Unfortunately, hope did not become reality. Not only were diagnosis and therapy by X-ray imperfect, the rays were associated with risk. In fact, many of the pioneering radiologists became victims of radiation injury and radiation-induced cancer.

## Technology in Medicine

The advent of the X-ray into the medical picture changed more than our expectations of medicine. For physicians it marked the beginning of a most profound revolution in practice: the need for continual adaptation to new and changing technologies. Physicians at work in 1890 experienced incremental advances in the knowledge and tools necessary to diagnose and treat patients: a new discovery about contagion, a more convenient surgical instrument, a clearer auscultation device. In hospitals, new purchases were generally limited to replacing those items that had broken or worn out: linen, labware, wheelchairs.

The impact of the X-ray in this relatively static medical setting would set the scene for a century of innovation. Imagine the difficult position of a young radiologist who, having convinced his institution to pay $200 or $300 for an X-ray machine in 1897, turned up in 1900 announcing that the hospital must have the newer, better model for $500? At the 1902 meeting of the American Roentgen Ray Society a number of manufacturers displayed and demonstrated their apparatus for physicians who had traveled long distances to make difficult purchase decisions. This modest display was the first true medical trade show in America, inaugurating a tradition of technological innovation that would prove a central focus of clinical, political, and financial debate throughout the century.

For the radiologist, as for all other physicians, this tradition of technical innovation has dictated a constant readjustment in expectations—both in terms of skills and in the direction of practice. Most physicians who trained even 50 years ago envisioned a world in which their medical lives would stay more or less the same—where keeping up involved staying informed about the latest medications and new treatment methods. Today's young physicians know they will spend their professional lives working with diagnostic and therapeutic technologies of ever-increasing complexity—and that they will be trained and retrained throughout their practices. Moreover, they will be surrounded by auxiliary and ancillary personnel undergoing the same continuous processes of reevaluation and reeducation. And just as hospital boards questioned the need for new X-ray machines in 1900, the choices and directions implicit in these new technologies will be under ever more vigilant scrutiny from governmental and organizational health planners.

Rontgen's discovery was clearly revolutionary and worthy of high honor, including the first Nobel Prize in physics in 1901. The X-ray encouraged a series of associated advances that created medical imaging (including ultrasonography, nuclear medicine, magnetic resonance imaging), radiation therapy, and several new medical subspecialties. It encouraged investment in a variety of medical technologies that have become the scientific basis of medical practice. But technology is not a cure-all, the dream of a magic bullet is still a dream, we certainly need physicians and their colleagues, and we continue to have turf battles and other political distractions from our clear goal of improving the health of our patients and society. Rontgen's discovery was a beginning, but there remains much to be done.

# Modern Medical Imaging: CTs and MRIs

Bettyann Holtzmann Kevles

Wilhelm Röntgen's (1845–1943) discovery of X rays opened the door to the new field of medical imaging, or using images to diagnose a patient's injury or illness. In her book *Naked to the Bone: Medical Imaging in the Twentieth Century*, from which this passage is excerpted, Bettyann Holtzmann Kevles brings medical imaging technology into modern times, and she reviews the imaging descendants of X rays. She explains the development and use of computerized tomography (CT) and magnetic resonance imaging (MRI), both of which rely heavily on computers. She reviews how these technologies are affecting law as well as medicine. Kevles has published many articles on medicine and science, and she is the author of *Female of the Species: Sex and Survival in the Animal Kingdom* as well as her book on medical imaging.

Ronald Reagan had been president of the United States for just over two months when he left the White House at 1:45 P.M. on March 30, 1981, to talk to the AFL-CIO's Building and Construction Workers Union. He was only going up the road to the Washington Hilton, but he went in full presidential style: a three-car motorcade including the White House physician and the press secretary, James S. Brady.

At 2:20 the president finished speaking to the generally unresponsive audience and stepped outside with his bodyguard. He was still wearing his trademark grin when the television cameras caught a change of expression. Seconds later he disappeared from view as he was pushed into a waiting limousine, which sped off.

Left behind, James Brady collapsed, his head bloodied. He had caught the first of six exploding "devastator" bullets that twenty-six-year-old John W. Hinckley, Jr., had just fired. The second bullet went astray; a third and fourth hit a D.C. police officer in the back, a fifth struck the chest and liver of a Secret Service agent, and the last ricocheted off the limousine and caught the president under his left armpit.

Unlike his predecessors, Garfield and McKinley, Reagan survived the assassin's attack, and the public was confident that his doctors could see exactly where the bullet was. There was plenty of X-ray apparatus in the emergency room at the George Washington Medical Center where the president had been rushed. Once they had located the bullet near the heart, the surgeon, Benjamin Aaron, operated and retrieved the dime-shaped fragment, which he displayed to the press. In the days that followed, no one marveled at the daily X-rays. They were as integral to his care as the antibiotics that saved him from the infections that had killed his predecessors.

James Brady's shattered brain was a different matter. Traditional X-rays were not much better at probing the brain in 1981 than they were in 1896, but the CT scanner in the emergency room was, and its use in 1981 signaled the acceptance of a new kind of image—a new way of seeing— into popular consciousness. This new instrument used X-ray beams to capture cross-sectional images beneath the skull and a computer to construct an image from the data. Like the tomographs of the 1930s, CT obtained images of slices inside the body, but unlike the old tomographs, the CT slice was not blurred by the intermediary bones. CT produces crisp, detailed pictures of bones and cartilage, and, most importantly, incredibly precise images of the brain itself.

When Brady arrived at the trauma unit minutes after Reagan, and lay bleeding on a gurney only a curtain away from his boss, Arthur Kobrine, the neurosurgeon on duty, saw immediately that the bullet had wreaked enormous damage as it blasted through. Wasting no time, he ordered a CT scan.

In 1981 there were more than thirteen hundred CT scanners in the United States. The National Institutes of Health would soon pronounce them "safe, powerful and cost-effective." CT was then called "CAT," the "A" standing for either "assisted" or "axial," depending on who was doing the explaining. It was shortened to CT by the end of the 1980s in medical circles, though it is still called CAT by much of the public. At the time of the shootings, scanners had been on the market for nine years and emergency room physicians had come to depend on the black and white cross-sectional slices of the interior of the body. David Davis, chief of neuroradiology, showed Kobrine the CT image of Brady's brain, with a huge blood clot. Recalling the scan as "fantastically useful," Davis says it showed exactly where Kobrine had to operate in order to pop the clot immediately. Without the CT scan they would not have seen the clot in time and Brady would have died.

The entire operation—clearing away pieces of bone and tissue and parts of the shattered bullet—took almost seven hours. Kobrine could not predict the extent of the damage or the success of his repairs and was relieved on April 1 to see Brady tossing cotton balls with his wife and hear him pronounce her name and count from one to ten. Though Brady was never able to resume work, his humor and personality survived the assault. He was able to appreciate the role of the new CT scanner as well as his wife's campaign for gun control in a bill bearing his name.

In the nine years that CT machines had been available, they had become clinical fixtures, and "scan" had joined international medical terminology. The verb, which had once meant a superficial once-over, became a way of describing the meticulous gathering of data from computer-controlled sensors and its display on a screen.

From the crude instrument first demonstrated in London in 1971, CT scanners had evolved through four generations into a streamlined, swift, efficient machine. This was in large part the result of American medicine's response with open checkbooks—the machines started out at about half a million dollars apiece, including installation. Not every hospital could afford one, but every major research hospital could as well as large trauma centers. The CT scan enabled almost every kind of doctor, from brain specialist to pediatrician, to look deep within the patient without inflicting pain. It helped make "exploratory surgery" an increasingly rare event. Not only could CT spot tumors, but the scans enabled surgeons to save lives through rapid diagnoses of organ trauma, fractures, internal bleeding, masses, and swelling.

## Relationship of CT to X-Rays

In 1981 Americans were used to watching computerized reconstructed images from NASA's planetary probes and did not question the provenance of the images on their doctor's computer screen. Most people knew that CT scans were produced by X-rays, but few understood that the X-rays in CT scanners do not make any initial picture, much less an image on film. Instead, CT scanners send collimated beams of X-rays through the body to an array of detectors that send signals to a computer for processing. The computer's program turns the signals into pixels on the video monitor. The image can then be "enhanced," colored, or made larger or smaller by the computer. The system works in two ways: it can reveal an anatomical slice by mathematically reconstructing the data the computer has received, and it can take a weak image and clean it up—the equivalent of retouching a photograph.

This new machine, like the ancestral, noncomputerized versions manufactured in the 1930s, was conceived at almost the same time by a handful of people in different areas of science and in different parts of the world. Each had the impression that he was alone in stating the problem and suggesting the solution. That problem had arisen more than once in the history of science—how to make a two- or three-dimensional image of an *interior* slice of an object by reconstructing data from a large number of projections *through* the object. The theoretical problem suggested many approaches, but the amount of mathematical processing needed to solve it was daunting, even with the computers that were just becoming available. Computers in the early 1970s had limited data storage capacity which restricted the scope of problems they could solve and the resolution of the images they could project from the CT scan. Engineers had to take into consideration these limits. As computers became faster and added memory, the range of what the new scanners could do also expanded. . . .

## The CT in Court

The scanner that helped save James Brady's life also saved the life of the man who shot him. John Hinckley, though obviously disturbed, had never before used a gun to shoot anyone. Caught with the weapon in his hand, his defense team needed to prove he was not responsible for his actions. They turned to psychiatric experts, who sought evidence in a CT image.

First they had to establish that Hinckley had a disease with a label. This was achieved by psychiatrist David Bear who, on his first day of testimony, lectured the court on "schizophrenia spectrum disorder," a condition he described as a progressive illness that produces depressive episodes. It was exacerbated on the day of the shooting by Hinckley's ingestion of Valium. To prove Hinckley's impoverished ability to reason, Bear introduced a CT scan—the first time that a CT scan had been admitted as evidence in an American court.

Judge Barrington D. Parker wanted to know how this new kind of image could help the case. Bear responded that "there is overwhelming evidence that the brain's physiology related to a person's emotions and that an abnormal appearance of the brain relates to schizophrenia." Bear was specifically referring to a study from St. Elizabeth's Hospital in Washington that showed that, in the brains of one-third of the schizophrenics autopsied, the sulci (the folds and ridges on the surface of the brain) are more shallow than in normal people. He had a radiologist show the court a scan of Hinckley's brain and pointed to the widened sulci. He was saying that Hinckley's diminished brain was part of "a statistical fact." He did not say that the widened sulci caused schizophrenia, but he said the image indicated a good chance that Hinckley was suffering from the disease.

A witness for the prosecution testified that the degeneration of some of Hinckley's brain tissue, as revealed "on a device known as a CAT-scan—was the same as that found in half the nation's adult population." He did not add that most of the human brain had not been mapped and the causes of schizophrenia are unknown so that reading the scan was akin to reading the entrails of a slaughtered eagle.

The judge pondered the problem, rejected the admissibility of the CT scan evidence, and then, nine days later, reversed his decision, adding a new legal precedent to the already unusual trial. The jury seemed to accept the meaning of the scan as the defense portrayed it and declared Hinckley not guilty by virtue of insanity. He was sent to St. Elizabeth's Hospital for an indefinite length of time in June 1982. The CT scan began a career as a staple in insanity pleas.

CT scans were already part of the coroner's toolbox. Like skeletal and dental X-rays, CT images of the brain are an excellent way of identifying otherwise unidentifiable corpses. When fingerprints are hard to read, or when there are no fingers to print from (canny murderers often remove them), final identification can be made from the shape of the frontal sinuses, if there is a CT on file. Sinuses are as individual to humans as nose prints are to gorillas. No two are the same, not even in the case of identical twins. . . .

## Magnetic Resonance Imaging (MRI)

The particles inside an atom's nucleus can be manipulated beyond what was the realm of fantasy a century ago. Then scientists held the atom to be both indestructible and homogeneous, and the word *nucleus* had no meaning beyond the central structure in a plant or animal cell. Within the single generation between the wars, physicists probed the atom, discovered its cloud of electrons surrounding a nucleus containing other particles, and posited the possibility of tapping the energy inside. The next generation would discover how to manipulate these particles to obtain remarkable images of interior spaces in a procedure now known as magnetic resonance imaging, or more commonly, MRI.

CT images bone, cartilage, and calcium deposits extremely well, but has difficulty imaging soft tissue surrounded by bone or cartilage. MRI does to bones what X-rays do to skin: in an MRI, bones disappear from view. The skeleton, the symbol of X-rays, dissolves completely. Without the carapace of bone, soft tissues are visible in all their complexity. The black negative spaces on an MRI are comparable to the black space on an X-ray or CT scan—they denote the places where no signal is picked up. On an X-ray or CT image, the tissue that does not absorb radiation is black. But in MR, bones are black and everything else is revealed in detail. The act of visual penetration no longer carries the association of stark white skeletons, and death.

A decade after MR machines entered the clinic, their images would be accepted as evidence in court. MRI pictures provided dramatic corroboration of the beating, fortuitously videotaped, of an African-American, Rodney G. King, by four white policemen in Los Angeles on March 3, 1991. The acquittal of those policemen on charges of police brutality sparked three days of riots the following May, but the images produced by magnetized hydrogen protons in King's bruised head convinced another jury in a civil trial to award King 3.8 million dollars in compensatory damages.

The second jury saw pictures akin to, yet qualitatively different from, the CT scans that the Hinckley jury had seen a decade earlier. Both images show slices of the interior of the targeted organ, but only MRI can produce an image of organic tissue wherever there is a trace of water, as there was in the swollen tissue inside Rodney King's scalp and right temporalis muscles. The MRI showed the jury where cerebral spinal fluid had leaked through multiple skull fractures (seen on accompanying CT images) into King's right maxillary sinus. Three years after the beating, physicians would attribute King's continued complaints of headaches, visual problems, numbness along the right side of his face, and memory loss to these injuries.

## MRIs with X-Rays and CTs

When MRI images are used as evidence, they invariably appear as part of a triptych with the two earlier kinds of images—X-ray and CT. King's victory in his civil suit was a victory for the use of MRI in court. MRI has had to overcome an obstacle that did not exist when X-rays were first accepted in the courtroom, and which CT avoided by being accepted as a version of X-ray radiographs. This obstacle was the Frye rule, a legal test of the scientific validity of a new technique. King's lawyers had to convince the court that an MRI of the inside of his head was a scientifically accepted procedure that would show damage, otherwise invisible, that the police had inflicted that night.

Magnetic resonance imaging is inconceivable without computers. MRI benefited from the struggles CT developers had gone through a few years earlier to find the mathematics to reconstruct images. Although the nature of the signals differ, the human body remains the same, and the problem of reconstructing an image from a mass of data from within the body is essentially the same. In the few years separating the development of the two imaging technologies, the mathematics had been figured out. These algorithms were a major gift from CT.

In every other way, however, MRI has different scientific roots from CT—and its heroes began by exploring quite different problems. The two kinds of anatomical images meet often in the courtroom and on computer screens and today give the impression of being partners. But this was not always the case. Without CT's dramatic entry into the medical marketplace, it is hard to imagine how MRI would have gotten the kind of support it needed to trigger its own revolution, coming, as it happened, from a specialized area of particle physics.

# Genetic Analysis and Testing

Neil Campbell, Jane B. Reece, and Lawrence G. Mitchell

Gregor Mendel's (1822–1884) discovery that the patterns of inheritance follow mathematical laws made it possible to predict human genetic traits, including the inheritance of genetic disorders. In this selection from their book, biology professors Neil Campbell, Jane B. Reece, and Lawrence G. Mitchell discuss the analysis of a human family pedigree based on Mendelian patterns to determine the mathematical probability that certain disorders will appear in a family. They review some important genetic disorders in humans and discuss the technology that makes it possible to test a fetus for genetic disorders. Newborn screening and treatment for the genetic disorder phenylketonuria are also discussed.

Whereas peas are convenient subjects for genetic research, humans are not. The human generation span is about 20 years, and human parents produce relatively few offspring compared to peas and most other species. Furthermore, well-planned breeding experiments like the ones Mendel [Gregor, 1822–1884] performed are impossible (or at least socially unacceptable) with humans. In spite of these difficulties, the study of human genetics continues to advance, powered by the incentive to understand our own inheritance. New techniques in molecular biology have led to many breakthrough discoveries, but basic Mendelism endures as the foundation of human genetics.

## Pedigree Analysis

Unable to manipulate the mating patterns of people, geneticists must analyze the results of matings that have already occurred. As much information as possible is collected about a family's history for a particular trait, and this information is assembled into a family tree describing the interrelationships of parents and children across the generations—the family *pedigree*. . . .

Pedigree analysis is a more serious matter when the alleles [alternate forms of genes] in question cause disabling or deadly hereditary diseases instead of innocuous human variations such as hairline or earlobe configuration. However, for disorders that are inherited as simple Mendelian traits, these same techniques of pedigree analysis apply.

## Genetic Disorders

Thousands of genetic disorders are known to be inherited as simple recessive traits. These disorders range in severity from traits that are relatively harmless, such as albinism (lack of skin pigmentation), to life-threatening conditions, such as cystic fibrosis. . . .

In general, a genetic disorder is not evenly distributed among all groups of humans. These disparities result from the different genetic histories of the world's peoples during less technological times, when populations were more geographically, hence genetically, isolated. We will now examine three examples of recessively inherited disorders.

The most common lethal genetic disease in the United States is cystic fibrosis, which strikes one out of every 2500 whites of European descent but is much rarer in other groups. One out of 25 whites (4%) is a carrier. The normal allele, for this gene codes for a membrane protein that functions in chloride ion transport between certain cells and the extracellular fluid. These chloride channels are defective or absent in the plasma membranes of children who have inherited two of the recessive alleles that cause cystic fibrosis. The result is an abnormally high concentration of extracellular chloride, which causes the mucus that coats certain cells to become thicker and stickier than normal. The mucus builds up in the pancreas, lungs, digestive tract, and other organs, a condition that favors bacterial infections. Recent research indicates that the extracellular chloride also contributes to infection by disabling a natural antibiotic made by some body cells. When immune cells come to the rescue, their remains add to the mucus—creating a vicious cycle. Untreated, most children with cystic fibrosis die before their fifth birthday. Gentle pounding on the chest to clear mucus from clogged airways, daily doses of antibiotics to prevent infection, and other preventive treatments can prolong life. In the United States, more than half of the people with cystic fibrosis now survive into their late twenties or beyond.

Another lethal disorder inherited as a recessive allele is Tay-Sachs disease. The disease is caused by a dysfunctional enzyme that fails to break down brain lipids of a certain class. The symptoms of Tay-Sachs disease usually become manifest a few months after birth. The infant begins to suffer seizures, blindness, and degeneration of motor and mental performance. Inevitably the child dies within a few years. There is a disproportionately high incidence of Tay-Sachs disease among Ashkenazic Jews, Jewish people whose ancestors lived in central Europe. In that population, the frequency of Tay-Sachs disease is one case of the disease out of 3600 births, about 100 times greater than the incidence among non-Jews or Mediterranean (Sephardic) Jews.

The most common inherited disease among blacks is sickle-cell disease, which affects one out of 400 African-Americans. Sickle-cell disease is caused by the substitution of a single amino acid in the hemoglobin protein of red blood cells. When the oxygen content of an affected individual's blood is low (at high altitudes or under physical stress, for instance), the sickle-cell hemoglobin deforms the red cells to a sickle shape. Sickling of the cells, in turn, can lead to other symptoms. The multiple effects of a double dose of the sickle-cell allele exemplify pleiotropy [ability of one gene to have multiple effects]. Doctors now use regular blood transfusions to ward off brain damage in children with sickle-cell disease, and new drugs can help prevent or treat other problems, but there is no cure. . . .

Although it is relatively unlikely that two carriers of the same rare harmful allele will meet and mate, the probability increases greatly if the man and woman are close relatives (for example, siblings or first cousins). These are called consanguineous ("same blood") matings, and they are indicated in pedigrees by double lines. Because people with recent common ancestors are more likely to carry the same recessive alleles than are unrelated people, it is more likely that a mating of close relatives will produce offspring homozygous for a harmful recessive trait. Such effects can be observed in many types of domesticated and zoo animals that have become inbred.

There is debate among geneticists about the extent to which human consanguinity increases the risk of inherited diseases. Many deleterious alleles have such severe effects that a homozygous embryo spontaneously aborts long before birth. Most societies and cultures have laws or taboos forbidding marriages between close relatives. These rules may have evolved out of empirical observation that in most populations, stillbirths and birth defects are more common when parents are closely related. But social and economic factors have also influenced the development of customs and laws against consanguineous marriages.

## Dominantly Inherited Disorders

Although most harmful alleles are recessive, many human disorders are due to dominant alleles. One example is achondroplasia, a form of dwarfism with an incidence of one case among every 10,000 people. . . .

A lethal dominant allele can escape elimination if it is late-acting, causing death at a relatively advanced age. By the time the symptoms become evident, the individual may have already transmitted the lethal allele to his or her children. For example, Huntington's disease, a degenerative disease of the nervous system, is caused by a lethal dominant allele that has no obvious phenotypic effect until the individual is about 35 to 45 years old. Once the deterioration of the nervous system begins, it is irreversible and inevitably fatal. Any child born to a parent who has the allele for Huntington's disease has a 50% chance of inheriting the allele and the disorder. . . .

The hereditary diseases we have discussed so far are sometimes described as simple Mendelian disorders because they result from certain alleles at a single genetic locus. Many more people are susceptible to diseases that have a multifactorial basis—a genetic component plus a significant environmental influence. The long list of multifactorial diseases includes heart disease, diabetes, cancer, alcoholism,

---

## Polymerase Chain Reaction

*An essential tool for many tests involving identification of DNA (deoxyribonucleic acid) is polymerase chain reaction (PCR). This technique amplifies very small amounts of DNA, such as DNA retrieved from a crime scene or from a patient ill with a mysterious disease. Once amplified, scientists can proceed with additional tests for identifying the organism from which the original DNA came. PCR makes possible the Southern blotting method of identifying DNA. Kary Mullis won a Nobel Prize in 1993 for inventing the polymerase chain reaction technique.*

Southern blotting is used in a method of identification known as *DNA fingerprinting.* The DNA of every organism is unique; DNA fingerprinting can be used to identify bacterial or viral pathogens, but its primary application is in forensic medicine. Probes constructed from variable regions in human DNA can be used in Southern blotting to compare DNA from hair, blood, or semen left at the scene of a crime with that of suspects. In a recent application of this new forensic technique, DNA fingerprints were used as evidence that the blood found on a murder suspect's clothes came from the murder victim. . . .

Southern blotting requires substantial amounts of DNA, much more than is available from a crime scene sample. Small samples of DNA can be quickly *amplified*—increased to quantities large enough for analysis—with a method called the *polymerase chain reaction* (PCR). This procedure was originally developed by Kary Mullis in 1986; he received the Nobel Prize for this work in 1993.

Starting with just one gene-sized piece of DNA, PCR can be used to make literally billions of copies in only a few hours. In the PCR technique, 1. a solution containing the piece of DNA

and certain mental illnesses, such as schizophrenia and manic-depressive disorder. In many cases the hereditary component is polygenic [many genes]. For example, many genes affect our cardiovascular health, making some of us more prone than others to heart attacks and strokes. But our

---

to be amplified is first heated to 98°C in a test tube to separate the two strands of DNA, which will serve as the initial templates for DNA synthesis. 2. To this DNA is added a supply of the four nucleotides (for assembly into new DNA) and the enzyme for catalyzing the synthesis, DNA polymerase. Short pieces of nucleic acid called primers are also added to help start the reaction. 3. Then, during a period of incubation at 60°C, the primers hybridize to the ends of the fragments to be amplified, and the polymerase synthesizes new complementary strands. 4. After each cycle of synthesis, the DNA is heated to convert all the new DNA into single strands. Each newly synthesized DNA strand serves in turn as a template for more new DNA. As a result, the process proceeds exponentially. PCR is made possible by the use of DNA polymerase taken from a thermophilic bacterium such as *Thermus aquaticus*; the enzyme from such organisms can survive the heating phase without being destroyed. Thirty cycles, completed in just a few hours, will increase the amount of target DNA by more than a billion times.

PCR can be applied to any situation that requires the amplification of DNA. Especially noteworthy are diagnostic tests that use PCR to detect the presence of infectious agents, such as the AIDS virus, in situations in which they would otherwise be undetectable. In one dramatic case, PCR was used to amplify DNA of the AIDS virus in tissue samples from a British sailor who died in 1959 of a then-mysterious cause. Thus, PCR was used over 30 years after his death to establish that this sailor had the earliest documented case of AIDS. Because of the usefulness of the PCR technique, machines that perform it automatically are becoming common fixtures in research laboratories.

Gerard J. Tortora, Berdell R. Funke, and Christine L. Case, *Microbiology: An Introduction.* 5th ed. Menlo Park, CA: Benjamin/Cummings, 1995, pp. 241–42.

lifestyle intervenes tremendously between genotype and phenotype for cardiovascular health and other multifactorial characters. Exercise, a healthful diet, abstinence from smoking, and an ability to put stressful situations in perspective all reduce our risk of heart disease and some types of cancer.

At present, so little is understood about the genetic contributions to most multifactorial diseases that the best public-health strategy is to educate people about the importance of environmental factors and to promote healthful behavior.

## Genetic Testing and Counseling

A preventive approach to simple Mendelian disorders is sometimes possible, because in some cases the risk that a particular genetic disorder will occur can be assessed before a child is conceived or in the early stages of the pregnancy. Many hospitals have genetic counselors who can provide information to prospective parents concerned about a family history for a specific disease.

Let's consider the example of an imaginary couple, John and Carol, who are planning to have their first child and are seeking genetic counseling because of family histories of a lethal disease known to be recessively inherited. John and Carol each had a brother who died of the disorder, so they want to determine the risk of their having a child with the disease. From the information about their brothers, we know that both parents of John and both parents of Carol must have been carriers of the recessive allele. Thus, John and Carol are both products of $Aa$ and $Aa$ crosses, where $a$ symbolizes the allele that causes this particular disease. We also know that John and Carol are not homozygous recessive ($aa$) because they do not have the disease. Therefore, their genotypes are either $AA$ or $Aa$. Given a genotypic ratio of $1AA:2Aa:1aa$ for offspring of an $Aa \times Aa$ cross, John and Carol each have a ⅔ chance of being carriers ($Aa$). Using the rule of multiplication [one of Mendel's mathematical laws], we can determine that the overall probability of their first-born having the disorder is ⅔ (the chance that John is a carrier) multiplied by ⅔ (the chance that Carol is a carrier) multiplied by ¼ (the chance of two carriers having a child with the disease), which equals ⅑. Suppose that Carol and John decide to take the risk and have a child—after all, there is an ⁸⁄₉ chance that their baby will not have the disorder—but their child is born with the disease. We no longer have to guess about John's and Carol's genotypes. We now know that both John and Carol are, in fact, carriers. If the couple decides to have another child, they now know there is a ¼ chance that the second child will have the disease.

When we use Mendel's laws to predict possible outcomes of matings, it is important to keep in mind that chance has no memory: Each child represents an independent event in the sense that its genotype is unaffected by the genotypes of older siblings. Suppose that John and Carol have three more children, and *all three* have the hypothetical hereditary disease. This is an unfortunate family, for there is only one chance in 64 (¼ × ¼ × ¼) that such an outcome will occur. But this run of misfortune will in no way affect the result if John and Carol decide to have still another child. There is still a ¼ chance that the additional child will have the disease and a ¾ chance that it will not. Mendel's laws, remember, are simply rules of probability applied to heredity.

## Carrier Recognition

Because most children with recessive disorders are born to parents with normal phenotypes, the key to assessing the genetic risk for a particular disease is determining whether the prospective parents are heterozygous carriers of the recessive trait. For some heritable disorders, there are now tests that can distinguish individuals of normal phenotype who are dominant homozygotes from those who are heterozygotes, and the number of such tests increases each year. Examples are tests that can identify carriers of the alleles for Tay-Sachs disease, sickle-cell disease, and the most common form of cystic fibrosis. On one hand, these tests enable people with family histories of genetic disorders to make informed decisions about having children. On the other hand, these new methods for genetic screening could be abused. If confidentiality is breached, will carriers be stigmatized? Will they be denied health or life insurance, even though they are themselves healthy? Will misinformed employers equate "carrier" with disease? And will sufficient genetic counseling be available to help a large number of individuals understand their test results?

New biotechnology offers possibilities of reducing human suffering, but not before key ethical issues are resolved. . . .

## Fetal Testing

Suppose a couple learns that they are both Tay-Sachs carriers, but they decide to have a child anyway. Tests performed in conjunction with a technique known as amniocentesis can determine, beginning at the fourteenth to sixteenth week of pregnancy, whether the developing fetus has Tay-Sachs disease. To perform this procedure, a physician inserts a needle into the uterus and extracts about 10 milliliters of amniotic fluid, the liquid that bathes the fetus. Some genetic disorders can be detected from the presence of certain chemicals in the amniotic fluid itself. Tests for other disorders, including Tay-Sachs disease, are performed on cells grown in the laboratory from the fetal cells that had been sloughed off into the amniotic fluid. These cultured cells can also be used for karyotyping to identify certain chromosomal defects.

In an alternative technique called chorionic villus sampling (CVS), the physician suctions off a small amount of fetal tissue from the placenta. Because the cells of the chorionic villi are proliferating rapidly, enough cells are undergoing mitosis to allow karyotyping to be carried out immediately, giving results within 24 hours. This is an advantage over amniocentesis, in which the cells must be cultured for several weeks before karyotyping. Another advantage of CVS is that it can be performed as early as the eighth to tenth week of pregnancy.

Other techniques allow a physician to examine a fetus directly for major abnormalities. One such technique is ultrasound, which uses sound waves to produce an image of the fetus by a simple noninvasive procedure. This procedure has no known risk to either fetus or mother. With another technique, fetoscopy, a needle-thin tube containing a viewing scope and fiber optics (to transmit light) is inserted into the uterus. Fetoscopy enables the physician to examine the fetus for certain anatomical deformities.

In about 1% of the cases, amniocentesis or fetoscopy causes complications, such as maternal bleeding or fetal death. Thus, these techniques are usually reserved for cases in which the risk of a genetic disorder or other type of birth defect is relatively great. If the fetal tests reveal a serious disorder, the parents face the difficult choice of terminating the pregnancy or preparing to care for a child with a genetic disorder.

## Newborn Screening

Some genetic disorders can be detected at birth by simple tests that are now routinely performed in most hospitals in the United States. One screening program is for the recessively inherited disorder called phenylketonuria (PKU), which occurs in about one out of every 10,000 births in the United States. Children with this disease cannot properly break down the amino acid phenylalanine. This compound and its byproduct, phenylpyruvate, can accumulate to toxic levels in the blood, causing mental retardation. However, if the deficiency is detected in the newborn, retardation can usually be prevented with a special diet, low in phenylalanine, that allows normal development. Thus, screening newborns for PKU and other treatable disorders is vitally important. Unfortunately, very few genetic disorders are treatable at the present time. . . .

We owe the "gene idea," the concept of heritable factors that are transmitted according to simple rules of chance, to the elegant experiments of Gregor Mendel. Mendel's quantitative approach was foreign to the biology of his era, and even the few biologists who read his papers apparently missed the importance of his discoveries. It wasn't until the beginning of the twentieth century that Mendelian genetics was rediscovered by biologists who studied the role of chromosomes in inheritance.

# Chapter 6

# The Social Impact of Great Medical Discoveries

Turning | Points

IN WORLD HISTORY

# Modernization Brings a Change in Disease Patterns

Gregory L. Weiss and Lynne E. Lonnquist

*Epidemiological transition* refers to the shift in patterns of human disease within a given society from predominately acute, infectious disease to mostly chronic, degenerative diseases. The transition is usually associated with economic development, modernization, improved public health and sanitation measures, and higher standards of living. In this selection from their book on the sociology of health, the authors discuss the impact that the epidemiological transition has had on the United States and what it means for the next generation. They also point out that infectious diseases continue to be a problem, especially as bacteria and viruses become increasingly resistant to antibiotics. Gregory L. Weiss teaches at Roanoke College and Lynne E. Lonnquist is at Mary Baldwin College. Each is the author of several scholarly articles on health-related topics.

As societies develop and modernize, the patterns of morbidity [disease] and mortality [death] change systematically. Early stages of development are characterized by high risks of death at relatively young ages from acute, infectious diseases. As societies advance, there is a greater likelihood of dying at older ages from chronic, degenerative diseases. To capture this epidemiological transition, [A.] Omran divided the mortality experience of humankind into three stages: the Age of Pestilence and Famine, The Age of Receding Pandemics, and the Age of Degenerative and Human-made Diseases.

The Age of Pestilence and Famine dominated throughout the world for thousands of years and still exists today in many of the world's developing countries. Factors including lack of proper nutrition, poor sanitation, and unclean drinking water lead to almost unceasing epidemics of infectious and parasitic diseases such as influenza, pneumonia, diarrhea, smallpox, and tuberculosis.

Infants, children, and women of reproductive age are at particularly high risk during this era and are often the victims of nutrition-related diseases or other diseases to which they are more susceptible because of continuing inadequate

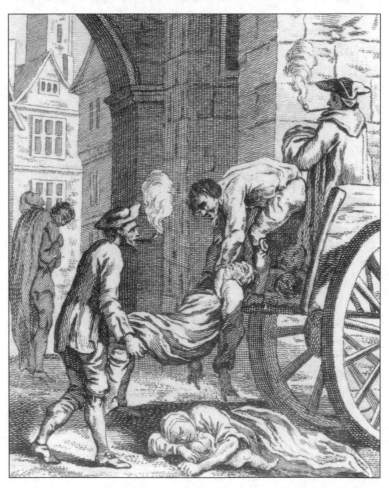

*Bubonic plague epidemics caused widespread devastation between 1340 and 1370.*

nourishment. Infant mortality rates remain very high today in many developing countries in which more than one baby in every ten dies in the first year of life. Moreover, adult health in developing countries is a serious and continuing problem. Data reveal that in industrialized market-based economies, the risk of death between the ages of 15 and 60 is 12 percent for males and 5 percent for females. The corresponding figures in sub-Saharan Africa, a developing area, are 38 percent for males and 32 percent for females. Historically, life expectancy during this period was between 20 and 40 years, though in most of the world's developing countries today, it has reached at least the mid-forties.

## Age of Receding Pandemics

As today's modern countries progressed through The Age of Receding Pandemics, improvements were made in sanitation and standard of living, and advances in medical knowledge and public health led to a decline in the number of people dying from infectious and parasitic diseases. The development process for every country has some features particular to that country, but many epidemiologists believe that there is a standard progression of changes in disease patterns as modernization occurs. In response to their own efforts and, in some cases, from technical assistance (e.g., in agricultural or industrial techniques) provided by the United States and other modern countries, many developing countries today are lowering their mortality rates. As the frequency of acute, infectious diseases declines, people begin to survive into older age when they are more likely to experience and to die from chronic, degenerative diseases like heart disease and cancer. Historically, during this stage, life expectancy was about 50 years.

## Degenerative and Chronic Disease

As mortality from acute, infectious diseases stabilizes at a relatively low level, and the most common causes of death become chronic, degenerative diseases, The Age of Degenerative and Human-made Diseases arrives. Mortality rates drop considerably from earlier times, and life expectancy reaches approximately 70 years.

At one time, it was generally believed that the decline in morality experienced during the third period put life expectancy at about its biological limit. However, in the mid-1960s, an unexpected and rapid decline in deaths from major degenerative diseases such as heart disease occurred. These declines first affected middle-aged people, but today the lives of older people are being extended as well.

[S.] Olshansky and [A.] Ault (1986) suggest that highly developed societies have entered a fourth period of epidemiological history, which they label The Age of Delayed Degenerative Diseases. While the major degenerative causes of death that prevailed during the previous stage remain, the risk of dying from these diseases is pushed back to older ages. Both reduction in behavioral risk factors (e.g., a decline in cigarette smoking) and recent advances in medical tech-

## Disillusionment with Western Medicine

*People in Western societies have become increasingly disillusioned with their medical care systems for two reasons, according to Stephen Lock: the rising cost of health care and the sense that disease has become more important to physicians than their patients.*

The onset of Western society's disillusion with modern medicine came in the 1960s. Several causes were self-evident. First were the ever-increasing costs, whether to governments or to individuals. Health care came to be funded in two major ways, neither of which fulfilled the ideal of countrywide high-quality treatment available immediately to all on demand. Countries, such as the UK and the Nordic states, where funding was largely provided by the State, had to contain costs by covert rationing: using the family doctor as a gatekeeper to the hospital, long hospital waiting lists, and even not offering certain procedures at all (such as advanced treatments for infertility). Countries, such as the USA, where care was funded by the individual, usually through insurance, might have the highest standards of medical care available immediately regardless of need. The

nology are responsible for this shift.

The Age of Delayed Degenerative Diseases raises new questions about the health of the population. First, will prolonging life result in additional years of health or additional years of disability? Will healthier lifestyles and the postponement of chronic disease retard the aging process? Will death increase from other diseases? Will there be continued outbreaks of epidemic disease (e.g., AIDS and the recent increases in rates of tuberculosis) that represent an inconsistency in this fourth period? . . .

One thing is certain: during the period of Delayed Degenerative Diseases, all segments of the elderly population are expected to increase dramatically in absolute numbers. The Bureau of the Census has projected that the U.S. population aged 65 and over will increase to 65 million in 2030 (having been only 16.7 million in 1960 and 30 million in 1990).

---

other side was that not everybody was covered (in the USA, for instance, an estimated 15 per cent of the population had no insurance whatsoever) [U.S. Census Bureau reports the same percentage, 15, in 2000], complex procedures such as intensive care might exhaust the insurance available and bankrupt the patient, and long-term care posed particular problems in geriatrics and psychiatry. . . .

The second factor in the disillusion was the feeling that health professionals were no longer interested in patients as people, but only in diseases. The Victorian physician in Luke Fildes's famous painting had been powerless; all he could do was to sit by the dying child's bedside, chin cupped in his hand—but at least he had exuded concern and compassion. In the era of safe effective surgery and the therapeutic revolution, many thought that doctors had lost their humanity. The more they could do for individual patients, seemingly the less they cared about them as fellow human beings.

Stephen Lock, "Medicine in the Second Half of the Twentieth Century," in *Western Medicine: An Illustrated History.* Ed. Irvine Loudon. Oxford, UK: Oxford University Press, 1997, pp. 135–36.

## Resistance of Diseases to Antibiotics

In the last few years, epidemiologists have discovered a pattern that could be tremendously disruptive to the epidemiological transition: several diseases, including tuberculosis, syphilis, gonorrhea, and bacterial pneumonia, are becoming increasingly resistant to the antibiotics that have been so successful in defeating them. Malaria (spread by a parasite) was all but eradicated in the world in 1965; today, it infects an estimated 270 million people annually and kills up to 2 million. Diphtheria is very rare in the United States, but in the mid-1990s it was affecting more than 50,000 Russians each year. Tuberculosis, the most common, fatal infectious disease in the world (a death toll of 2.5 million per year), has re-emerged in the United States after a 30-year decline. In the early 1990s, more than 25,000 cases of TB were being reported annually in this country. About 9 percent of these cases are considered to be "multi-drug resistant." Both the Centers for Disease Control and Prevention and the World Health Organization are on record that the state of preparedness for outbreaks of disease epidemics is inadequate. . . .

## Life Expectancy

Based on current mortality data and projections, life expectancy rates reflect the average number of years that a person born in a given year can expect to live. Due to variations in rates among segments of the population, life expectancy typically is calculated separately for males and females and according to race or ethnic background.

Trends. Life expectancy has increased more in the twentieth century than in all prior human history. Since 1900, life expectancy in the United States has increased approximately 29 years from 47 to 76 (in 1995). However, this increase does not mean that a significant increase has occurred in the life span (the maximum biological age). In the early part of the century, death for males and females often occurred in the first year of life and often during childbirth in females. These deaths significantly reduced average life expectancy. Males and females who survived these stages could expect to live on average almost as long as males and females do today. . . .

Greater life expectancy together with a lower fertility rate (i.e., the rate of reproduction of women in their most fertile years—age 15 to 44) has resulted in a larger proportion of the United States population being over 65 years of age. While just 4 percent of the population was 65 or older in 1900, more than 13 percent will be in this category by the year 2000.

This "aging" of the American population has many implications. The greater number of elderly persons will require significant increases in the supply of ambulatory health care, short-term hospitalization, and extended care. Their number will also provide a formidable voting bloc and lobbying force to ensure that their needs will not be overlooked. Because extended care can be very expensive, increasing numbers of the elderly may need to reside with their adult children, thus requiring a family member to take on a full-time caregiving role, or necessitating the use of home health care services. Many elderly persons and their families will be faced with having to determine the relative value of quality versus quantity of life and the extent to which high technology medicine will be employed.

## Mortality

Mortality refers to the number of deaths in a population. While death itself is easy to document, determination of the actual cause can be problematic because death may result from a combination of many factors. In the United States, an attempt is made to classify each death according to the International Statistical Classification of Diseases, Injuries, and Causes of Death, which consists of a detailed list of categories of diseases and injuries. While this system is valuable, it is not totally reliable due to the problems in diagnosing the actual underlying cause of death—something that is especially difficult for some chronic diseases.

Measurement. Mortality rates are reported in ratios such as the crude death rate (CDR). To calculate the CDR, the number of deaths in a designated population during a given year is divided by the population size. This figure is then multiplied by a standard number (usually 1,000 or 100,000). The formula for crude death rate is:

$$\frac{\text{Total number of deaths in specified population in a given year}}{\text{Total population of the group at mid-year}} \times 100,000$$

In 1991, the CDR for the United States was 859 per 100,000 population. However, this rate varies considerably among age groups, racial and ethnic groups, and between males and females. A more useful measure for sociologists who are interested in the effects of specific social characteristics on death within a population is an "age-specific" or other "characteristic-specific" rate. To determine the death rate for a particular group, a Specific Rate (SR) is calculated by confining the number of deaths and the population size to that given segment of the population. By using this measure, for example, we learn that for white males, ages 5–14, the death rate is 27 per 100,000 population, while the rate for black males in the same age group is 42. This information shows the large discrepancy in death rates between young blacks and whites, whereas the overall population rate of 29 for this age group does not illuminate the disadvantage young black males experience.

Trends. The crude death rate in the United States has declined by almost 50 percent since 1900 and continues to drop each year. The largest reduction has been for females, both black and white, while the least reduction has been for black males. In addition, the major causes of death have changed substantially. Today, death is much more likely than ever before to result from a chronic, degenerative disease. Almost three-fourths of deaths in the United States are due to heart disease, cancer, stroke, diabetes, chronic obstructive pulmonary disease, and cirrhosis, while in 1900, the major killers were acute, infectious diseases such as influenza and pneumonia, infectious gastrointestinal diseases, and tuberculosis. To an increasing extent, people are now dying of multiple system diseases—being afflicted with more than one fatal disease.

# Bacterial Resistance to Antibiotics

Mark Nichols

Journalist Mark Nichols describes the outbreak of antibiotic-resistant bacteria in a Saskatoon, Canada, hospital in 1996 and goes on to discuss the growing problem of microorganisms that are resistant to antibiotic drugs. Penicillin, discovered by Alexander Fleming (1881–1955), and other antibiotics have been wildly successful in controlling bacteria-caused diseases in the twentieth century, but researchers warn that those easy successes have come to an end. Nichols points out that although the growth in drug-resistant microorganisms has several causes, one of the greatest is the irresponsible overuse of antibiotics. Overuse and improper use (not finishing the entire prescription) of antibiotics have facilitated the mutation and growing resistance of bacteria. The problem is worse today than when Nichols first wrote his article in 1996. In 2002 doctors began reporting resistance to the main class of antibiotics now in use, the most popular of which is ciprofloxacin, or Cipro.

Medical staff and visitors entering the area wear gloves and full-length gowns. When they leave, they take off the protective clothing for washing, and scrub their hands carefully. The reason for the precautions last week on the fifth floor of Saskatoon's [Canada] St. Paul's Hospital: [a 1996] outbreak of a mutant microbe called VRE that is resistant to just about every commonly used antibiotic. June, twenty-one patients with a mix of medical problems—some with kidney failure, others recovering from surgery of one kind or an-

other—were kept in strict isolation from other patients in
the 130-bed hospital. Most of them were merely carrying
VRE; only one was mildly infected with the potentially
deadly bug, and doctors thought that it would clear up by itself. But VRE is a frightening example of a rapidly growing
trend: many common infectious agents are becoming resistant to antibiotics. The epidemic of drug-resistant bacteria,
warns Dr. Julian Davies, head of microbiology and immunology at the University of British Columbia in Vancouver, "should be recognized as a crisis, because unless we do
something now it's going to get worse."

## Drug-Resistant Bacteria

How bad could it get? Terrifyingly bad, if the rapidly reproducing and mutating microbes continue to find ways of out-
foxing medicine's battery of antibiotics. There would be
nothing to stop some children's ear infections, for instance,
from turning into life-threatening meningitis, and cases of
pneumonia that are now routinely treated could instead become routinely fatal. Already, drug resistance is plaguing
North American hospitals and the new bugs are making it
harder for doctors to treat once easy-to-cure infections.
Globally, drug resistance has aided the resurgence of such
diseases as dysentery and gonorrhea—and helped turn tuberculosis into the world's biggest bacterial killer. If the
number and variety of drug-resistant bacteria continue to
proliferate, warns Dr. Stephen Vas, a University of Toronto
microbiologist, "running out of antibiotics could become a
real possibility."

As the mutants have gained ground, outbreaks of the so-
called superbug VRE and of MRSA, a drug-resistant form of
a bacterium called staphylococcus aureus, have become almost endemic in some American hospitals—and the mutant
bugs increasingly are infiltrating Canadian institutions.
Over the past five years, hospitals in almost every part of the
country have confronted outbreaks of drug-resistant bacteria. In Ontario, which appears to be more severely affected
than the rest of the country, the number of hospital-based
MRSA cases has more than tripled since 1993—to 1,112

known cases [in 1995]. "This problem is like a grass fire," says Dr. Donald Low, the Toronto microbiologist who is one of Canada's leading authorities on bacterial problems. "It's popping up everywhere."

Drug-resistant bacteria are already killing people, though precise figures are hard to come by. In Ottawa, federal officials are currently carrying out their first study of VRE and MRSA, but the results will not be available until next year. As it is, Dr. Andrew Simor, head of microbiology at Toronto's Sunnybrook Health Science Centre, says that he is aware of five or six deaths in Canada during the past decade that were caused by drug-resistant bugs. In the United States—where hospital-based drug-resistance problems have made far heavier inroads than in Canada—officials at the Centres for Disease Control and Prevention in Atlanta say that at least 10,000 hospital patients probably die each year while infected with drug-resistant bacteria. "The problem is that people with VRE or MRSA infections are usually seriously ill to begin with," says Dr. Wendy Johnson, chief of Health Canada's national bacteriology laboratory. "So it's often difficult to decide what exactly caused death."

## Multiple Causes

The invasion of the world by bacteria that can outsmart antibiotics has resulted from a combination of factors. Confident in the 1980s that sophisticated antibacterial drugs had all but won the war on microbes, many of the big multinational drug companies shelved costly research that could have produced new classes of antibiotics. In the meantime, profligate use of antibiotics has created an environment that gives the versatile microbes constant opportunities to come up with drug-resistant mutations.

In North America, drug resistance is showing up with alarming frequency in the form of middle-ear infections in young children. The problem can often be traced to day care centres, where kids pick up viruses that cause colds and flu. Those viral illnesses can, in turn, set the stage for bacterial ear infections, usually involving a bug called streptococcus pneumoniae, which is becoming increasingly resistant to penicillin. Because of that, doctors are often forced to turn to expensive drugs like cefaclor, which costs $1.02 per capsule, compared with amoxicillin, a form of penicillin, which costs only about 10 cents per capsule. The same bug is a common cause of pneumonia. If drug resistance continues to grow, says Dr. Kelly S. MacDonald, associate microbiologist at Toronto's Mount Sinai Hospital, paying for costly alternatives to penicillin-type drugs "will break hospital antibiotic budgets. And a whole generation of general practitioners will need training in which antibiotics to use. It's a really difficult situation."

Some experts think that the growing microbial menace is part of a broader phenomenon, in which humanity's bruising collision with the natural world is creating new dangers, including those posed by viruses, a class of microbes that are fundamentally different from bacteria—but no less threatening. The so-called emerging viruses including Africa's deadly Ebola virus, are believed to have been unleashed as a result of industrial development in the Third World and whisked to the industrialized nations by jet-borne travellers. In the same way, a mutated bacterium that emerges anywhere in the interconnected modern world can soon be infecting victims thousands of miles away. . . .

## Overuse of Antibiotics

What is clear is that widespread overuse of antibiotics provides an ideal breeding ground for mutant bacteria that can threaten human life: the more antibiotics are used, the more opportunity the bacteria have to develop invulnerability—and pass that talent on to other bugs. Boston's Levy [Stuart] cites a widely accepted estimate that "more than half of the prescriptions written for antibiotics in the United States are either not needed, or are for the wrong drug." Adds UBC's Davies: "Patients say, 'Give me an antibiotic, Doc.' And if you don't, they go somewhere else and get one." Experts say that prescribing antibiotics has become so automatic that many doctors do not even bother to determine first if an illness is viral—in which case antibiotics are ineffective—or bacterial in origin. Last year, doctors in Canada alone wrote more than 26 million prescriptions for oral antibiotics.

The thinking in North America, says Toronto's Low, is, "'Well, it can't do any harm—might as well start them on antibiotics.' Now, we're seeing the consequences of this." Mississauga, Ont., pediatrician Peter Strachan says that about 70 per cent of childhood ear infections will clear up without antibiotic treatment. In some European countries, drugs are used "only on the most severe ear infections," he notes. "That is probably better than our approach, which is to use antibiotics for almost any ear infection."

Today's crisis over drug resistance is the product of a competition that has raged for the past half-century between disease-causing bacteria and the modern, manmade agents designed to combat them. It began with the birth of the antibiotic era in the early 1940s, when British doctors first treated patients with a drug based on a naturally occurring mould called penicillin. The new drug had a remarkable ability to tame infection-causing bacteria. But within a few years, penicillin-resistant forms of staphylococcus—the drug's principal target—had begun to appear. Over the years, the process has been repeated with the introduction of almost every new antibiotic—methicillin (a semi-synthetic form of penicillin introduced in the early 1960s), the cephalosporins (a family of penicillin-like drugs), ampicillin, amoxicillin, tetracycline, and vancomycin, a drug first introduced 38 years ago and increasingly used today when other drugs fail.

## Rapidly Mutating Bacteria

What enables bacteria to gain the upper hand is their ability to spawn a new generation every 15 or 20 minutes—a rate conducive to a relatively rapid appearance of mutations. Sooner or later, one of those mutants will have characteristics that enable it to thumb its nose at the latest antibiotic. What follows is a classic example of the Darwinian law of the survival of the fittest: as an antibiotic in a patient's body wipes out one strain of bacteria, the drug-resistant version thrives, with successive generations of the bug producing millions of offspring a day.

Moreover, bacteria have a remarkable ability to hand on their most useful genes to other bugs—so that drug resistance developed by one microbe can easily be bestowed on others. Just how the microbes manage this feat can baffle even the experts. Biochemist Gerry Wright of McMaster University in Hamilton cites the case of enterococcus, a bowel-inhabiting bacterium that became resistant to vancomycin by somehow acquiring five new genes. It was "a very sophisticated process," says Wright, which allowed the enterococcus to alter its cell wall so that vancomycin could no longer bind to it and kill the bug. Where did the five genes come from? One possibility, says Wright, is the original source of vancomycin itself—a family of soil bacteria called actinomycetes. Those bacteria secrete a vancomycin-like substance, which is toxic to other microbes—and possesses genes that protect it from its own deadly secretions. "Somehow," says Wright, "the enterococcus bacterium may have acquired those genes."

For a number of reasons, drug resistance in Canada is less of a problem—so far—than in the United States. That is partly due to differences between the U.S. and Canadian health-care systems. Because most medical services in Canada are publicly funded, hospitals, and to a lesser extent community-based physicians, face more stringent limitations than many of their American counterparts in prescribing expensive antibiotics. Moreover, experts say that since significant drug-resistance problems first surfaced during the 1980s, Canadian hospitals have routinely taken tougher action to contain outbreaks than American institutions. "Canadian hospitals took drug resistance very seriously from the start," says Sunnybrook's Simor. "I don't believe infection-control measures in many U.S. hospitals are nearly as stringent."

# Sexual Liberation and the Pill

Suzanne White Junod

Suzanne White Junod discusses the social impact of the first oral contraceptive, which was introduced in 1960 after approval by the Food and Drug Administration (FDA). She describes the discomfort that the idea of "sexual liberation" produced in several sectors of U.S. society. Despite this, women adopted the new drug enthusiastically and took control of their reproductive capability for the first time. Oral contraceptives turned out to have health risks associated with them for certain populations of women, but the clock could not be turned back. Junod, a historian at the FDA, says that oral contraceptives unleashed energies that fueled social movements of the 1960s. Junod and coauthor Lara Marks won the 2003 Charles Thompson Prize awarded by the Society for History in the Federal Government for their April 2002 article in *Journal of the History of Medicine and Allied Sciences* entitled "Women's Trials: The Approval of the First Oral Contraceptive Pill in the United States and Britain."

This summer [2000] marks the fortieth anniversary of the day the Food and Drug Administration approved, on June 23, 1960, the first oral contraceptive, Enovid by G.D. Searle. It may not have rocked the ground like the 1945 detonation of the first atomic bomb or energized an industry, like the first time current flowed through a transistor in 1947, but Enovid did more than just provide a technological tour de force. It transformed the very fabric of modern society.

Physiologically, the birth control pill simply prevents ovulation. Though an important scientific achievement, the real

Suzanne White Junod, "The Pill at 40," *FDA Consumer*, vol. 34, July/August 2000, p. 36.

revolution began when millions of young women began to use it.

Searle's first marketing campaign showed its understanding of the Pill's revolutionary potential. One marketing logo featured the dramatic, colorful image of a sensuous Greek goddess freed from her bondage. This concept, however, proved too potent for the general public. Marketing for the Pill quickly switched to themes of domestic tranquility, portraying cozy couples, newly married and merely wishing to postpone their children.

Sexual liberation did not appeal to the U.S. government, either. When the Eisenhower administration released a report suggesting that family planning be included in a European aid program, opposition by Catholic bishops killed the plan. The government thereafter said little about the Pill. It was treated as merely another drug, its approval deemed a medical decision best dealt with by the pharmacology experts. So it was sent to the bureaucratic hinterlands, to a smallish agency just refining its scientific foundation: The Food and Drug Administration.

## Health Concerns

The Pill presented FDA with several dilemmas. Commissioner George Larrick, the last agency commissioner to rise up through the ranks, worried about potentially medicating half the population for something that wasn't a disease. What would its side effects be in healthy women? Some experts feared that it might cause cancers, which might not be seen for decades. This proved not to be the case, and, in fact, the Pill has proven to protect women from certain kinds of reproductive cancers. More significantly, however, some women developed severe blood clots while on the Pill and died. It took a decade to conclusively link the Pill with these adverse events, but early reductions in the drug's estrogen component substantially cut the risk.

Commissioner Larrick pondered the medical pros and cons, and according to witnesses, finally concluded that young couples might benefit from the ability to plan their families more carefully. But, the agency remained cautious.

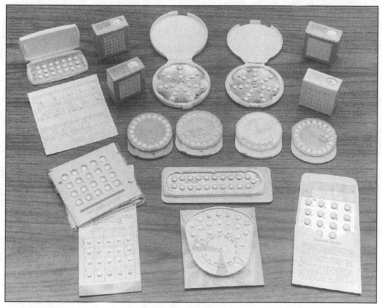

*The development of the birth control pill empowered women, giving them more control over their bodies.*

The Pill was the first and only drug approved with an imposed time limit. Women were not to be prescribed the Pill for more than two years until more data came in showing that it was safe to take it for longer periods. Many women, though, skated around the time limit by changing doctors and contraceptive brands. The restriction proved unenforceable.

## Social Changes

Whatever its scientific issues, the Pill took the country by storm. Its extreme efficacy in preventing pregnancy opened up many new worlds. Young women with access to the Pill experimented with sex on college campuses. Mothers limited their families, both with and without their husbands' approval. Catholics in the United States, who were largely expected to reject the Pill, split with Rome over the issue.

A physician friend credits the Pill, in fact, with paving the way for many of the advances in late 20th century medicine. He vividly recalls that almost all of the physicians in the class ahead of him in medical school already had children by the time they graduated. They hurried into practice to support them. His class, however, was the first whose wives had access to the Pill, and virtually none of them had children at graduation. This allowed some to pursue advanced training and altered the very course of their careers.

New reproductive choices unleashed not only new professional energies, but new social energies as well. The women's movement and even the civil rights movement were fueled by some of these new energies.

# Social Responsibility in Genetics

Jon Beckwith

Jon Beckwith, a professor of microbiology and molecular genetics at Harvard University Medical School, discusses the double-edged sword that genetics presents to society. He reviews the U.S. eugenics movement in the early twentieth century in which information from the emerging science of genetics was used to falsely characterize and classify races and ethnic groups. He finds some interesting parallels between the early eugenics movement and contemporary genetics. He warns against reducing each human life to an analysis of one's genes, a mindset that Beckwith labels "biological determinism." Beckwith argues that the "overextension of the applications of genetics" can lead to discrimination and unjust categorization of a person based on his or her genetic makeup. Beckwith is a member of the Work Group on Ethical, Legal, and Social Implications of the Human Genome Project and is a member of the Genetic Screening Study Group that is researching genetic discrimination.

Today, as reflected in *Jurassic Park* and other works of science fiction, the science of genetics most prominently presents society with a double-edged sword. Fortunately, there is the opportunity for geneticists to become sensitized to these problems through a study of a time past when genetic science played a large social role.

With regard to genetics, there are striking parallels between conditions today and in the early part of this century in the United States. In both periods, dramatic breakthroughs generated highly productive periods in genetics research. In 1900, the rediscovery of Mendel's laws opened up

Jon Beckwith, "A Historical Review of Social Responsibility in Genetics," *Bioscience*, vol. 32, May 1993, p. 327. Copyright © 1993 by *Bioscience*. Reproduced by permission of Copyright Clearance Center, Inc.

the field of genetics as we now know it. Today, we see an era in which technical developments ranging from recombinant DNA to DNA sequencing to the polymerase chain reaction have produced a revolution in the ease with which genetic problems can be addressed. In the early 1900s, the new era in genetics was accompanied by a powerful eugenics movement that influenced social policy. Today, the increasing focus on genetics both within biology and in the media is beginning to shift public attention to genetic explanations and genetic solutions to health problems and social problems. . . .

## The Eugenics Movement in the United States

In the early 1900s, the burgeoning field of genetics was quickly incorporated into the eugenics movement. The origins of this movement are complex, evolving in part from a cattle breeding association and led by a number of men from the upper social classes. Prominent aristocratic figures in the eugenics movement such as Madison Grant [1865–1937], author of the popular eugenics book *The Passing of the Great Race* (1916), and Robert DeCourcy Ward [1867–1931], a leader of the Immigration Restriction League, used the new concepts of genetics to support their claims for the inferiority of certain ethnic groups and of the lower social classes. But, more important for our purposes, many of the leading geneticists supported the eugenicists or even became active in the enterprise. According to Kenneth Ludmerer, in the early days (1906–1915) of this movement most of the leading geneticists were seduced by or promoted eugenic theory. . . .

Yet, the new so-called science of eugenics, was, in retrospect at least, based on shoddy and primitive scientific analysis. For instance, Charles Davenport [1866–1944], who had done impressive scientific work in showing that Huntington's Disease was inherited as a dominant Mendelian trait, also argued that social phenomena such as criminality, poverty, intelligence, and even seafaringness could be attributed to single genes. These conclusions were often based on nothing more than crude family studies or population-based use of IQ tests. Even less evidence was used to argue that reproductive intermingling of different racial and ethnic groups would lead to inferior progeny. . . .

By the time the eugenics movement had reached its peak, many of the geneticists had withdrawn their backing. This falling off of scientific support, however, had little effect on the implementation of eugenics policies. Geneticists generally stayed away from the fray, even though they recognized the harm that was being done. They rarely spoke out against these policies, and, by the time they did, it was essentially too late. [Geneticists Edward M.] East, [William E.] Castle, and [Herbert S.] Jennings began to criticize the eugenically based Immigration Restriction Act and the arguments that had been put forth for many years only at about the time the act was being passed by Congress.

The studies and proclamations of the U.S. eugenicists were also closely followed in Germany in the 1920s and 1930s. The perhaps most widely used text in human genetics during this period was by the prominent German geneticists Fritz Lenz and Erwin Baur and German anthropologist Eugen Fischer. This book, which used data and conclusions from U.S. mental testers such as L. Terman and E.L. Thorndike and U.S. eugenicists such as Davenport, was a eugenics and biological determinist text. It contained characterizations of races and ethnic groups as exhibiting certain genetically based personality traits:

"Fraud and the use of insulting language are commoner among Jews"

"In general, a Negro is not inclined to work hard . . ."

[T]he Mongolian character . . . inclines to petrifaction in the traditional". . .

## Rejection and Return

The universal revulsion at the Nazi eugenics policies after World War II led to a rejection of many of the general claims of the eugenics movement. In particular, the position that human behavioral traits and social problems had their origins in genetics was replaced by the position that environment was the determining factor in such issues. Some of these positions are reflected in two statements issued by UNESCO [United Nations Educational, Scientific, and Cultural Organization] in the early 1950s. One of these, prepared by leading physical anthropologists and geneticists (several of them from the group that wrote the 1939 statement [statement issued by geneticists that criticized Nazi German genetic claims and programs]), criticized the concept of race and argued that differences in culture, intellectual achievement, and behavior between ethnic groups were not genetic in origin.

However, beginning in the late 1960s, scientific arguments for a genetic basis for various behavioral traits began to attract increasing attention. One of the earliest and most dramatic of such claims was the proposal that males with an extra Y chromosome (XYY males) are more aggressive than the average male and exhibit a susceptibility to lead criminal lives. Despite the weakness of the initial evidence, the myth of the "criminal chromosome" took hold of the public imagination. Within a few years of the first findings, it became clear that XYY males were neither hyperaggressive nor doomed to lives of criminality. But by the time these conclusions were reached, the XYY myth was already being presented as fact in everything from high school biology texts to medical school psychiatry texts.

There followed other controversial claims of evidence for a genetic basis for black-white differences in performance on IQ tests, for boy-girl differences in performance on mathematical examinations, and for a host of human behavioral traits including male dominance, xenophobia, religiosity, and shyness. The XYY research was carried out for the most part by geneticists, but the remaining studies were the work of psychologists or students of animal behavior. Thus, there was little involvement of the genetics community in the resurgence of interest in genetic explanations of human social behavior and aptitudes.

## The Recombinant DNA Era and the Human Genome Project

Although it is possible that the molecular biology of the 1950s and 1960s generated an environment in which reductionist approaches to a wide range of problems seemed appropriate, the breakthroughs in genetics in the 1970s have even more clearly created such an environment. The improvements in DNA sequencing techniques, the development of recombinant DNA approaches to gene cloning and manipulation, and a host of further advances have made simpler the genetic approaches to biological problems in any organism, including humans. The successes in biology based on this progress have been extraordinary. A partial list of such achievements include mapping and characterization of genes involved in numerous genetic diseases, working out of developmental pathways at the genetic level in several organisms, refinement of evolutionary trees based on DNA sequence homology, and an extraordinary increase in the understanding of the development and functioning of the immune system.

As a result of the technological breakthroughs, biology's focus has shifted dramatically to the analysis of genes. This shift has been extraordinarily productive and exciting. The reductionist approach of focusing on genes has worked for a host of previously intractable biological problems. However, accompanying this transformation of biology has been a strengthening of an extreme reductionist position toward both the science itself and its social applications. As with the period that initiated genetics at the turn of the century, the successes of the science have been translated into a world view. First, some molecular biologists have implied that essentially all biological problems are best approached by studying genes. For instance, according to Walter Gilbert, "To identify a relevant region of DNA, a gene, and then to clone and sequence it is now the underpinning of all biological science."

Second, many leaders of the revolution in molecular biology have publicly claimed a nearly all-explanatory role for genetics. Many of these claims have been associated with the initiation of the Human Genome Project. James Watson was quoted in *Time* magazine, "We used to think our fate was in our stars. Now we know, in large measure, our fate is in our genes." Norton Zinder calls the human genome sequence a "Rosetta Stone", whereas Walter Gilbert termed it the "Holy Grail of genetics." Gilbert also stated that from the sequence "we can have the ultimate explanation for a human being."

Robert Sinsheimer says that the sequence is what "defines a human being." Charles DeLisi entitled a subsection of his article on the Human Genome Project "The blue print for life." Paul Berg stated at a recent Stanford conference, "Many if not most human diseases are clearly the result of inherited mutations." Frances Collins suggests that "[The Human Genome Initiative] will likely transform medicine in the twenty-first century into a preventive mode, where genetic predispositions are identified and treated before the onset of illness rather than after illness is under way."

In an editorial in *Science* magazine and elsewhere, Daniel Koshland argued that the Human Genome Project will provide solutions to many of our social problems, including homelessness. "The homeless problem is tractable. One

---

### The Promises and Pitfalls of Genetics

*Genetic therapies promise to cure human disease, but author Philip J. Boyle warns about the dangers of unrealistic expectations of this changing science. People frequently misunderstand the meaning of genetic information, and Boyle warns that genetic information must be used with caution.*

Opportunities to predict, cure, and prevent disease with genetic technology seem limitless. Preimplantation genetic testing will offer future parents the opportunity to evaluate embryos so that they may transfer to the prospective mother's uterus only the ones they deem desirable and discard those they find undesirable for whatever reason. Prenatal genetic testing will enable parents to prepare for the birth of a child with particular genetic characteristics or to avoid it. Each of us will be able to be tested for, or to test our children for, conditions well before their onset, information that may help us prepare for the onset of the condition by adjusting life styles or seeking prophylactic therapies. And the development of new genetic therapies holds out the promise of effective treatment for many hitherto intractable diseases. . . .

The number of potential abuses of genetic information—de-

third of homeless are mentally ill—some say 50%. These are the ones who will most benefit from the Genome Project." Koshland's rationale is that mental illness has a genetic basis and that finding the postulated genes for mental illness will allow cures to be developed. . . .

## Additional Approaches

There are many complex basic and applied problems that require approaches other than genetics. Although the improvement in genetic techniques has occurred at an incredibly rapid pace, comparable improvement in techniques of cell biology have been neglected. The greatest rewards in biology today come for those working in the areas of DNA and gene manipulation.

---

nial of medical insurance or discrimination in employment, to name but two—should urge caution. So should the recognition that many find it morally unacceptable to preselect and dispose of embryos, manipulate germline cells, or genetically enhance persons who have no disease condition. Complicating matters even further, we tend to hold unrealistic expectations about the accuracy and certainty of genetic information. People will be tested for conditions that might never fully express themselves as a disease, or only express themselves in a mild form. For example, nearly 20 percent of persons who carry the gene for fragile-X, the most common form of inherited mental retardation (affecting one in every 2,500 live births), will never express any form of mental retardation. Yet if parents knew their children's genetic status, they might treat unaffected children as if they were mentally disabled. Other markers for which there will be tests will provide information about multifactorial conditions in which environment, other genes, or both interact in determining just how—or if—the condition will be expressed. Genetic information must be interpreted with caution if it is to serve as a basis for action.

Philip J. Boyle, "Shaping Priorities in Genetic Medicine," *Hastings Center Report*, vol. 25, no. 3, May/June 1995, p. S2.

The devaluing of descriptive biological work and of technical innovations in such areas as electron microscopy could ultimately lead to a drying up of the source of the very information that is needed to make sense of genetic studies or even to stimulate new areas of genetic research. The training of students in the latest technological developments to the detriment of broader biological training could also contribute to an impoverishment of the field. Molecular biologists should not be blinded by the dazzling successes of genetics to the balance in approaches that are required for future progress.

The translation of the reductionist approach to an analysis of everything from human health to the human condition is also problematic. The arguments about health are based, in part, on the finding that some instances of susceptibility to common diseases such as heart disease or cancer are correlated with the inheritance of an altered gene. It is likely that more such instances will be found. However, such findings do not imply that most cancer or most heart disease is related to such susceptibility genes. Further, in those cases where there is a susceptibility, it is usually only a susceptibility. The actual development of cancer will be due to many factors, including other genes and the environment. It is not at all clear that the best way to approach cures or prevention of cancer is a study of a cancer gene, as opposed to systematic analysis of environmental factors and the many other approaches that are currently employed in studying this problem.

This area is full of uncertainty. There are few examples that would give us confidence that gene characterization will lead to solutions to health problems. For instance, researchers have understood the molecular basis of sickle-cell anemia in terms of the amino acid change in the hemoglobin protein for more than three decades, but it has been continuing medical studies on the progress of the disease rather than genetic knowledge that has contributed to the significant improvements there have been in survival and health of those suffering from the condition. It is only quite recently that the molecular genetic studies have begun to bear fruit in this area.

## Social Problems and Genetics

Of even more concern are the claims concerning genetics and social problems such as homelessness. It is useful to analyze the content of such claims. First, a social problem is relegated to the realm of medicine or biology when the roots are often in failings of the society itself. Clearly, some of the homeless do have severe mental problems, but much homelessness has its roots in economic deprivation. Second, the reliance on genetics to account for mental disorders exaggerates and distorts what we know. There is relatively convincing evidence that, for example, some cases of manic depressive illness have a heritable component, although a gene has yet to be discovered; but this evidence does not mean that all manic depressive illness can be traced to genes and certainly not that all depression has a genetic basis. Furthermore, even in those cases where there is substantial evidence for manic depressive illness having a genetic correlate in certain families, it is clear that not everyone who inherits the susceptibility develops the disorder. It seems likely that environmental factors are also important and should be explored in considering how to deal with the disorder.

Third, the fact that a gene plays a role in a particular disease does not necessarily imply that genetics will provide solutions. As discussed above, although finding a gene for a particular condition will certainly promote better understanding of that condition, there is no certainty that cures or treatments will be generated. Finally, the recent molecular genetic searches for genes related to such conditions as manic depressive illness, schizophrenia, and alcoholism have suffered from much of the same hastiness and overconfidence that characterized the behavior genetics of the eugenics era. Fortunately, molecular genetic studies are more easily replicable, and, as a result, mistaken conclusions have been rapidly picked up. The problems with the current attempts to discover genes for these complex behavioral traits has led to suggestions that the search will be long and arduous and to restoring of some balance in examining genetic and environmental contributors.

## Consequences of Biological Determinism

In the last 15 years, the public has not only witnessed an explosion of genetic information but also has been deluged with reports of the discovery of genes for everything from cystic fibrosis to alcoholism. These are exciting times, and the publicity for the achievements of genetics is warranted. But, what kind of environment is now being generated by the publicity that genetics has achieved with the grandiose claims that accompany it? One effect of this publicity has been to promote the conception that genetics is all-explanatory. Reductionist statements from scientists of the sort quoted above only reinforce a distorted perception of the basis of the human condition. Genes are used in the popular media more and more to explain social phenomena. Everything from the attitudes of TV critics to the basis of violence among soccer fans in Great Britain to presidential candidate Ross Perot's frugality are ascribed to genes. As in the early part of this century, the media is serving as a means of transmission of the perspective of scientists and, thus, helping form public opinion that can influence social policy.

It may be that the increased attention to genetics in society will give greater courage to those who argue that our social problems and social inequities are genetic in origin. For example, recent reports of gene discoveries have been used to support the arguments made by proponents of human sociobiology in the 1970s. A number of sociobiologists received considerable public attention for their suggestions that such social characteristics as xenophobia, male dominance, and class structure were genetically based. In 1988, Melvin Konner, one of the contributors to this field, referred to the mapping of genes for Huntington's disease and manic depressive illness as a refutation of the critics of sociobiology. (The report of the mapping of the manic-depressive-illness gene was later retracted.) These discoveries were seen by Konner as showing that human behavior was strongly influenced by genes, and thus, by inference, providing greater support for sociobiological theories of human behavior.

The reawakened interest in issues of genetics, human behaviors, and social policy is also reflected in the resurgence of academic controversy over arguments that blacks are genetically inferior to whites in intelligence. It may be that the reappearance of this controversy is facilitated by the climate in which genetics is made to appear more and more important. Of course, racism is not generated by genetics, and an important source of the renewed interest in these issues arises out of the political climate, including the debate over affirmative action. But, historically, arguments from the scientific community have provided important support for racist ideology and political action.

Overall, then, overextension of the applications of genetics can have profound effects on society. In general, the focus on genetics alone as explanatory of disease and of social problems tends to direct society's attention away from other means of dealing with such problems. At its extreme, a false hope of cures for disease distorts the distribution of resources. Genetic explanations for intelligence, sex role differences, or aggression lead to an absolving of society of any responsibility for its inequities, thus providing support for those who have interest in maintaining these inequities. They can influence the development of social policy in such areas as education. In the early 1970s, arguments for genetically based racial differences in intelligence were used as a justification for the dismantling of compensatory education programs and in school desegregation controversies. Claims for women's inferiority in mathematics ability influenced the attitudes of both female students and their parents.

Genetics has also intruded into discussions of the problem of crime in the United States. The temporary ado about XYY males led to screening programs of both newborns and juvenile delinquents in some states. We may not have to worry about a eugenics program in this country in the foreseeable future, but the other consequences of misguided biological determinist claims are severe enough. (It should be noted that eugenics programs are in effect in some societies such as Singapore, where scientific studies from the United States are marshaled in support of the policy.)

An examination of the history of genetics and its relationship to social issues holds many lessons. First, the work of geneticists can ultimately be translated into social policy, sometimes with deleterious consequences. These consequences may occur with the active participation of scientists themselves. In the eugenics movement of the early part of the twentieth century, geneticists played a significant role. But even geneticists who are not committed to a public role in influencing social policy may still contribute to the potential repercussions by their public statements.

Second, statements by geneticists, with or without their active participation, are rapidly translated for the public. This translation occurs, in part, by the popular media's representation of scientific advances and scientists' views. Today's geneticists, caught up in the enthusiasm of the successes of the new molecular biology, are contributing to an unbalanced view of the role of genetics and environment. A climate is being created in which social policy and individual attitudes may be formulated on the basis of incomplete or incorrect views of the human condition. Care for the way in which genetics is presented to the public and involvement in countering any misrepresentations is a responsibility of the genetics community.

Finally, the history of eugenics and its disastrous consequences raises the question of the role of the genetics community in dealing with the social impact of its field. Even after they became disaffected from the science and politics of the eugenics movement, geneticists did little to blunt its effects. It seems likely to me that if geneticists such as [T.H.] Morgan and [William E.] Castle had spoken out loud and often of their disdain for eugenic science, the outcome might well have been different.

Today, dealing with the concerns about the social consequences of the new genetics and the Human Genome Project is being relegated, for the most part, to ethicists, social scientists, lawyers, and other nonscientists. Yet, those involved in the science have a key role to play and a responsibility to ensure that progress in their field is not used to harm rather than benefit people. This role calls for more knowledge of history and less hubris.

# Discussion Questions

## Chapter 1: Human Body Structure and Function

1. According to John Galbraith Simmons, Andreas Vesalius challenged the traditional teachings of the Greek physician Galen concerning the structure of the human body. In so doing, Vesalius revolutionized the study of anatomy. What methods did Vesalius use to learn about the human body?

2. Like Vesalius, English physician William Harvey challenged Galen's teachings on human structure, according to Farokh Erach Udwadia. How were his findings different from those taught by Galen?

3. What new field of anatomical study did Ramón y Cajal establish by studying the anatomy of nerves?

4. Over several generations in his experiments, Gregor Johann Mendel was able to document important patterns. What were these patterns and what field of science developed from Mendel's discoveries?

5. According to Michael D. Lemonick, a race developed in the mid-twentieth century to discover the structure of DNA? How were James Watson and Francis Crick able to accurately model DNA for the first time? What were the roles of Linus Pauling and Rosalind Franklin in this race?

## Chapter 2: Disease and Disease Prevention

1. Dutch merchant Antoni van Leeuwenhoek had an intense interest in microscopy that he loved to practice in his free time, according to William Bullock. In what way did Leeuwenhoek's observations lay the foundation for later efforts to control disease in humans?

2. What was the awful discovery made by physician Ignaz Semmelweis about the death rates of women giving birth in hospitals compared to those of women giving birth at home? Can you think of other health problems that have been caused by medical ignorance?

3. Louis Pasteur and Robert Koch are key figures in the field of bacteriology, according to John R. Green. What theory of dis-

ease did Pasteur introduce and how did he prove the validity of his theory? What are Koch's Postulates and how are they used?

4. Ralph H. Major describes the problems physicians encountered when attempting to conquer the tropical diseases malaria and yellow fever. Who proved that mosquitoes carry the malarial parasite, and how did he make this discovery?

5. According to Christine Gorman and Alice Park, American physician David Ho overturned conventional medical wisdom concerning HIV and AIDS. What did he discover about the infection process that led to a complete change in the way that AIDS patients were treated?

## Chapter 3: Medical Procedures

1. The ancient surgical procedure known as trepanation was practiced around the world in Neolithic times. What are some possible reasons, according to Charlotte Roberts and Keith Manchester, that ancient people may have practiced the medical procedure of trepanation?

2. A competition developed in nineteenth century America to be the first credited with using surgical anesthesia, according to Meyer Friedman and Gerald W. Friedland. Do you think some historians are correct when they credit William Morton as the first to use anesthesia? Why or why not?

3. Why were twins chosen to be the first donor and recipient of a kidney transplant? Why does the human body reject a donated organ? How did doctors overcome this problem?

## Chapter 4: Pharmaceuticals

1. The ability of certain chemical compounds found in plants to reduce pain and fever were known for centuries, according to Anne Adina Judith Andermann. What role did Felix Hoffmann play in synthesizing the compound from plants?

2. What important observation did Alexander Fleming make when viewing his laboratory bacteria samples?

3. What were some of the treatment methods for mentally ill patients prior to the discovery of chemical therapy? Do you think mentally ill people should be required by law to take medications for their illness? Why or why not?

4. Oral contraceptives ("The Pill") would not have become avail-

able had it not been for the vision of two women, according to Lara V. Marks. Who were these women and in what way did each woman support the development of the pill? Do you think researchers should put more emphasis now on finding a contraceptive pill for males? Explain.

## Chapter 5: Medical Tools

1. How did Wilhelm Röntgen discover the X ray? How was his discovery received by the medical community?

2. How are CT scans now being used in court cases? Do you think CT and MRI images provide irrefutable proof of guilt or innocence in a court trial, or should these images be viewed as only one part of a body of evidence? Explain your answer.

3. Do you think every fetus should be tested for genetic defects during pregnancy? Why or why not? What should be done, if anything, about a fetus that has a genetic defect?

## Chapter 6: The Social Impact of Great Medical Discoveries

1. What is the difference between an acute, infectious disease and a chronic, degenerative disease? Do you think that infectious disease or chronic disease will be humanity's biggest problem in the next fifty years? Explain your answer.

2. According to Mark Nichols, what are some reasons that bacteria are becoming resistant to antibiotics? What can be done about this problem?

3. Oral contraceptives, first introduced in the 1960s, created a type of social revolution, according to Suzanne White Junod. Do you think the overall impact of oral contraceptives has been good or bad? Defend your answer with examples.

4. What are some of the social and political problems that could occur from misuse of genetic information? Do you think a person should be denied medical insurance if that person is a member of a family that is known to carry a genetic disorder? Why or why not?

# Appendix of Documents

## Document 1: Leeuwenhoek Describes the "Little Animals"

*Antoni van Leeuwenhoek carefully described the creatures living in a drop of rainwater that he viewed with one of his microscopes. He referred to these microorganisms as "animalcules."*

In the year 1675, about half-way through September (being busy with studying air, when I had much compressed it by means of water), I discovered living creatures in rain, which had stood but a few days in a new tub, that was painted blue within. This observation provoked me to investigate this water more narrowly; and especially because these little animals were, to my eye, more than ten thousand times smaller than the animalcule which Swammerdam [Jan, 1637–1680] has portrayed, and called by the name of Water-flea, or Water-louse, which you can see alive and moving in water with the bare eye.

Of the first sort that I discovered in the said water, I saw, after divers observations, that the bodies consisted of 5, 6, 7, or 8 very clear globules, but without being able to discern any membrane or skin that held these globules together, or in which they were inclosed. When these animalcules bestirred 'emselves, they sometimes stuck out two little horns, which were continually moved, after the fashion of a horse's ears. The part between these little horns was flat, their body else being roundish, save only that it ran somewhat to a point at the hind end; at which pointed end it had a tail, near four times as long as the whole body, and looking as thick, when viewed through my microscope, as a spider's web. At the end of this tail there was a pellet, of the bigness of one of the globules of the body; and this tail I could not perceive to be used by them for their movements in very clear water. These little animals were the most wretched creatures that I have ever seen; for when, with the pellet, they did but hit on any particles or little filaments (of which there are many in water, especially if it hath but stood some days), they stuck intangled in them; and then pulled their body out into an oval, and did struggle, by strongly stretching themselves, to get their tail loose; whereby their whole body then sprang back towards the pellet of the tail, and their tails then coiled up serpent-wise, after the fashion of a copper or iron wire that, having been wound close about a round stick, and then taken off, kept all its windings. This motion, of stretching out and pulling together the tail, continued; and I have seen several hundred animalcules, caught fast by one another in a few filaments, lying within the compass of a coarse grain of sand.

Antony van Leeuwenhoek, in Clifford Dobell, *Antony van Leeuwenhoek and His "Little Animals."* New York: Dover, 1932.

## Document 2: Insulin and Treatment for Diabetes

*Canadian researcher Frederick Grant Banting joined J.J.R. MacLeod, Charles Best, and J.B. Collip in winning the Nobel Prize in 1923 for their discovery of insulin. In this excerpt from his Nobel acceptance speech, Banting describes their tests on experimentally induced diabetes in dogs that led to the use of insulin for treatment of diabetic patients.*

Our first step was to tie the pancreatic ducts in a number of dogs. At the end of seven weeks these dogs were chloroformed. The pancreas of each dog was removed and all were found to be shrivelled, fibrotic, and about one-third the original size. Histological examination showed that there were no healthy acinus cells. This material was cut into small pieces, ground with sand, extracted with normal saline. This extract was tested on a dog rendered diabetic by the removal of the pancreas. Following the intravenous injection the blood sugars of the depancreatized dogs were reduced to a normal or subnormal level, and the urine became sugar free. There was a marked improvement in the general clinical condition as evidenced by the fact that the animals became stronger and more lively, the broken down wounds healed more kindly, and the life of the animal was undoubtedly prolonged. . . .

"The second type of extract was made from the pancreas of dogs in which acinus cells had been exhausted of trypsin by the long continued injection of secretin.

"The third type of extract used in this series of experiments was made from the pancreas of foetal calves of less than four months development. . . .

"The extracts prepared in this way were tried on depancreatized dogs and in all cases the blood sugar was lowered. . . . Diabetic dogs seldom live more than 12 to 14 days. But with the daily administration of this whole gland extract we were able to keep a depancreatized dog alive and healthy for ten weeks.

"The extract at this time was sufficiently purified to be tested on three cases of diabetes mellitus in the wards of the Toronto

General Hospital. There was a marked reduction in blood sugar and the urine was rendered sugar free . . . ."

Frederick Grant Banting, "Description of the Prize-Winning Work," in *Nobel Prize Winners in Medicine and Physiology, 1901–1965.* Ed. Theodore L. Sourkes. London: Abelard-Schuman, 1953, pp. 113–14.

## Document 3: The Yellow Emperor and Acupuncture

*The ancient healing art of acupuncture is said to date back to the first emperor of China, Qin Shi (the Yellow Emperor), in 221 B.C. Here are instructions from his book on Chinese medicine on the proper technique for inserting acupuncture needles.*

HUANG DI asked, "Could you please tell me the important principles of acupuncture?"

Qi Bo answered, "In disease one must differentiate between the external and the internal location of the pathogen. In acupuncture there are differentiations of deep or shallow insertion. If the illness is on the biao, or external, level, one should insert superficially; if on the internal level, one should insert more deeply. The location of the illness must be reached; but it is important not to insert too deeply so as to not injure the five zang organs. Inserting too shallowly, however, will not allow the physician to reach the area of illness, and the qi and blood can be disrupted, which allows an opportunity for pathogens to enter. Acupuncture performed without a guiding principle can be dangerous or damaging.

"It is said that illness may be on the hair level, the skin level, the muscle or flesh level, the level of the channels, the tendon level, the bone level, or the marrow level. When treating illness on the hair level with acupuncture, do not damage the skill level, as this will affect the health of the lungs. When the lung function is disrupted, by autumn one may become susceptible to malarial diseases. Gradually this may grow into a fear of chills. If the illness is at the skin level, one must take care not to damage the muscle level so as not to impact the spleen function. If the spleen function is damaged, during the last eighteen days of each season the patient will manifest distension, fullness, and loss of appetite. In illness at the muscle level, needling too deeply will damage the channel level. In this case the heart function will be disrupted; chest pain or angina will manifest by summer. In illness of the channels and vessels, needling too deeply will damage the tendon level. This will impact the liver function; by spring, one will manifest febrile disease or a flaccidity of the ligaments and tendons. In illness of the tendons, needling too deeply will damage the bone level. This will impact the kidney function. In this case, during the winter one will experience back pain and distension of the abdomen. Finally, in illness of the bones, needling too deeply will damage the marrow. The marrow then gradually depletes, causing soreness, tiredness, and weakness in the extremities, leading to disability."

Maoshing Ni, *The Yellow Emperor's Classic of Medicine*. Boston: Shambala, 1995, pp. 184–85.

## Document 4: Preparing the Human Body for Dissection

*Andreas Vesalius dissected the human body and, in so doing, established anatomy as a field of study. Here he gives explicit instructions on how to prepare a corpse so that the bones and cartilage can be inspected.*

Those physicians who were not born to prescribe syrups and impose upon mankind, but who are worthy devotees of the Hippocratic art, have been accustomed, although with no little effort, to collect bones for instruction, sometimes joined together, sometimes separated. Usually they have freed the cadaver, whether one dead from hanging or from some other cause, from most of its flesh and cut out the viscera without destruction of any of the joints. Then the body so dissected was placed in a long box filled up with lime and sprinkled with water. After the box had been kept in this way for a week, many small holes were drilled into it, and it was placed in a rapidly flowing stream of water so that in the course of time the lime with the macerated remains of the flesh might flow away and so be removed from the bones. Several days later, after the cadaver had been removed, it was cleaned all over with knives, but carefully so that none of the connections of the bones was destroyed, that the ligaments by which the bones are connected were preserved, and finally that everything except the joints of the bones glistened. The cleansed cadaver was then exposed to the sun so that the ligaments, dried by the heat of the sun, might hold the joints of the bones in that position in which it was desired that it be seen, posed sitting or standing.

This method of preparation, in addition to being troublesome, dirty, and difficult, displays almost none of the bony processes, epiphyses, heads, sinuses, and other things of that sort that ought especially to be seen, because all of them are covered by very dark ligaments. Hence this method of cleaning the bones is wholly unsuited to instruction, just as similarly the ridiculous method of observing the muscles, tendons, ligaments, nerves, veins, and arteries—which the professors of our art have hitherto imposed upon the students of medicine—has no value but merely blunts the minds of the students so that they will not seek from those Rabbins a demonstration of the organs I have now mentioned. These last assert that those things must be learned from bodies wasted away in streams of water—if it please the Gods—but not from the recently dead. However, nothing of value can be learned from bodies prepared, or rather corrupted, in this way, and all these things can be demonstrated to us much better in a recently dead body than by their usual and superficial method of demonstrating the liver, intestines, or heart to the students, in fact demonstrating these very ineptly and not dealing with the other parts of the body.

Andreas Vesalius, in C.D. O'Malley, *Andreas Vesalius of Brussels: 1514–1564.* Berkeley and Los Angeles: University of California Press, 1964, p. 327.

## Document 5: Observations of a Dying Heart

*William Harvey is credited with discovering the workings of the heart and the circulation of blood. Here he describes experiments conducted on living animals that demonstrate how the heart functions and how it behaves as it begins to die.*

In the first place, then, when the chest of a living animal is laid open and the capsule that immediately surrounds the heart is slit up or removed, the organ is seen now to move, now to be at rest; there is a time when it moves, and a time when it is motionless.

These things are more obvious in the colder animals, such as toads, frogs, serpents, small fishes, crabs, shrimps, snails, and shellfish. They also become more distinct in warm-blooded animals, such as the dog and hog, if they be attentively noted when the heart begins to flag, to move more slowly, and, as it were, to die: the movements then become slower and rarer, the pauses longer, by which it is made much more easy to perceive and unravel what the motions really are, and how they are performed. In the pause, as in death, the heart is soft, flaccid, exhausted, lying, as it were, at rest.

In the motion, and interval in which this is accomplished, three principal circumstances are to be noted:

1. That the heart is erected, and rises upwards to a point, so that at this time it strikes against the breast and the pulse is felt externally.

2. That it is everywhere contracted, but more especially towards the sides so that it looks narrower, relatively longer, more drawn together. The heart of an eel taken out of the body of the animal and placed upon the table or the hand, shows these particulars; but the same things are manifest in the hearts of all small fishes and of those colder animals where the organ is more conical or elongated.

3. The heart being grasped in the hand, is felt to become harder during its action. Now this hardness proceeds from tension, precisely as when the forearm is grasped, its tendons are perceived to become tense and resilient when the fingers are moved.

4. It may further be observed in fishes, and the colder blooded animals, such as frogs, serpents, etc., that the heart, when it moves, becomes of a paler color, when quiescent of a deeper blood-red colour.

From these particulars it appears evident to me that the motion of the heart consists in a certain universal tension—both contraction in the line of its fibres, and constriction in every sense. It becomes erect, hard, and of diminished size during its action; the motion is plainly of the same nature as that of the muscles when they contract in the line of their sinews and fibres; for the muscles, when in action, acquire vigor and tenseness, and from soft become hard, prominent, and thickened: and in the same manner the heart.

We are therefore authorized to conclude that the heart, at the moment of its action, is at once constricted on all sides, rendered thicker in its parietes and smaller in its ventricles, and so made apt to project or expel its charge of blood. This, indeed, is made sufficiently manifest by the preceding fourth observation in which we have seen that the heart, by squeezing out the blood that it contains, becomes paler, and then when it sinks into repose and the ventricle is filled anew with blood, that the deeper crimson colour returns. But no one need remain in doubt of the fact, for if the ventricle be pierced the blood will be seen to be forcibly projected outwards upon each motion or pulsation when the heart is tense.

These things, therefore, happen together or at the same instant: the tension of the heart, the pulse of its apex, which is felt externally by its striking against the chest, the thickening of its parietes, and the forcible expulsion of the blood it contains by the constriction of its ventricles.

William Harvey, in *Classics of Medicine and Surgery.* Comp. C.N.B. Camac. 1909. Reprint, New York: Dover, 1936, pp. 45–47.

## Document 6: Jenner's Vaccination Experiments

*English physician Edward Jenner developed a method to protect his patients from smallpox by vaccinating them with the far less serious disease cowpox. Here he describes an experiment he conducted to test the efficacy of his vaccination. He compared his cowpox-vaccinated patients to a patient he intentionally infected with smallpox—conduct that would be considered unethical today.*

After the many fruitless attempts to give the smallpox to those who had had the cow-pox, it did not appear necessary, nor was it convenient to me, to inoculate the whole of those who had been the subjects of these late trials; yet I thought it right to see the effects of variolous matter on some of them, particularly William Summers, the first of these patients who had been infected with matter taken from the cow. He was, therefore, inoculated with variolous matter from a fresh pustule; but, as in the preceding cases, the system did not feel the effects of it in the smallest degree. I had an opportunity also of having this boy and William Pead inoculated by my nephew, Mr. Henry Jenner, whose report to me is as follows: "I have inoculated Pead and Barge, two of the boys whom you lately infected with the cow-pox. On the second day the incisions were inflamed and there was a pale inflammatory stain around them. On the third day these appearances were still increasing and their arms itched considerably. On the fourth day the inflammation was evidently subsiding, and on the sixth day it was scarcely perceptible. No symptom of indisposition followed.

"To convince myself that the variolous matter made use of was in a perfect state I at the same time inoculated a patient with some of it who never had gone through the cow-pox, and it produced the smallpox in the usual regular manner."

Edward Jenner, in *Classics of Medicine and Surgery*. Comp. C.N.P. Camac. 1909. Reprint, New York: Dover, 1936, p. 229.

## Document 7: Using the Stethoscope

*French physician René-Théophile-Hyacinthe Laënnec describes the best method of using his invention, the stethoscope, to listen to sounds in the chests of his patients.*

The signs afforded by mediate auscultation [listening to organs] in the diseases of the lungs and pleura are derived from the changes presented by the sound of respiration, by that of the voice and coughing, within the chest, and also by the *rhonchus* [rattle] as well as certain other sounds which occasionally are heard in the same situation. Of these signs we shall now proceed to give some account. The notice of those which refer to the diseases of the heart will be deferred until we come to treat of the affections of this organ.

The general precautions which the practice of auscultation requires are the following: 1. The stethoscope must be applied very exactly and perpendicularly to the surface on which it rests, so as to leave no interval between the skin and any part of the extremity applied. 2. We must be careful not to produce pain by too strong pressure; this precaution is most necessary when the instrument is used without the stopper, and when the person is lean. 3. Although it is not necessary that the chest should be uncovered,—as all the positive stethoscopic signs, and frequently also the negative ones, may be perceived through clothes of considerable thickness, provided they are applied closely to the body,—still it is better that the clothing should only be light; for example, a flannel waistcoat and shirt. Silks and also woollen stuffs are often inadmissible on account of the noise occasioned by their friction against the instrument. The examiner ought to be careful, above all things, not to place himself in an uncomfortable posture, nor yet to stoop too much, nor turn his head backwards by a forced extension of the neck. These positions determine the blood to the head and thus obscure the sense of hearing: they may sometimes be properly avoided by kneeling on one knee. In examining the fore parts of the chest we ought to place the patient on his back in a recumbent position, or in a chair, and gently reclining backwards. When we examine the back, we cause the patient to lean forwards and to keep his arms forcibly crossed in front; and when we examine the side, we cause him to lean gently to the opposite one and to place the forearm on the head.

René-Théophile-Hyacinthe Laënnec, in *Classics of Medicine and Surgery.* Comp. C.N.B. Camac. 1909. Reprint, New York: Dover, 1936, pp. 167–68.

## Document 8: Surgical Anesthesia

*Georgia doctor Crawford Long was likely the first to use ether as a surgical anesthesia. Here he describes the effective use of the drug to painlessly perform two surgical procedures.*

The first person to whom I administered ether in a surgical operation was Mr. James M. Venable, who then resided within two miles of Jefferson, and at the present time in Cobb county, Ga. Mr. Venable consulted me on several occasions as to the propriety of removing two small tumors on the back part of his neck, but would postpone from time to time having the operation performed from dread of pain. At length I mentioned to him the fact of my receiving bruises while under the influence of the vapor of ether, without suffering, and, as I knew him to be fond of and accustomed to inhale ether, I suggested to him the probability that the operation might be performed without pain, and suggested to him operating while he was under its influence. He consented to have one tumor removed and the operation was performed the same evening. The ether was given to Mr. Venable on a towel and fully under its influence, I extirpated the tumor. It was encysted and about one-half an inch in diameter. The patient continued to inhale ether during the time of the operation, and seemed incredulous until the tumor was shown to him. He gave no evidence of pain during the operation and assured me after it was over that he did not experience the least degree of pain from its performance. . . .

My third case was a negro boy who had a disease of the toe which rendered amputation necessary, and the operation was performed July 3, 1842, without the boy evincing the slightest degree of pain.

These were all the surgical operations performed by me in the year 1842 upon patients etherized, no other cases occurring in which I believed the inhalation of ether applicable. Since 1842, I have performed one or more operations, annually, on patients in a state of etherization. I procured some certificates in regard to these operations, but not with the same particularity as in regard to the first operations, my sole object being to establish my claim to priority of discovery of the power of ether to produce anaesthesia. However, these certificates can be examined.

Crawford Williamson Long, in *Source Book of Medical History*. Comp. Logan Clendening. New York: Dover, 1942, pp. 356–57.

## Document 9: Applying Anesthesia

*William Morton experimented with the best way to apply ether as an anesthetic. He discovered that a sponge was the simplest method and the least likely to cause breathing problems for the patient.*

It was found that, if a sponge well saturated with ether was placed over the nose and mouth of a patient, so that all the air which he breathes must necessarily pass through it, he was brought as completely under the influence of the ether, and in about as short a time, as if he breathed it from the apparatus. Further experience having fully established this fact, and, as that which will produce a desired effect in the simplest and cheapest manner is always to be preferred, the sponge will, probably, before long, be in general use, in preference to any "inhalers," however ingeniously contrived.

Although it may excite some surprise that I thus unceremoniously dispose of instruments, many of which evince much care and ingenuity, a little consideration of the facts of the case will show that there is good ground for my assertions. The vapor of sulphuric ether, as is well known, will not support life in its pure and unmixed state, being destitute of oxygen; and fears were entertained, when it was first applied to its present use, that, unless extreme care was taken to supply the patient with a large amount of atmospheric air, not enough oxygen would enter the lungs to decarbonize the blood and change if from venous to arterial; venous blood would then be sent to the brain, and the patient die from asphyxia, in the same manner as when deprived of oxygen by immersion in water, or from any other cause. Attention was immediately turned to this point, and, in all the inhalers which have been constructed, apertures of greater or less size have been left for the admission of external air. There is, however, one fact which renders it a matter of extreme difficulty so to arrange the apertures that a sufficient supply of atmospheric air shall, in every case, be afforded to the patient. . . .

This danger is completely obviated by using the sponge; for, however high the temperature may be, and however great the consequent evaporation of ether, the patient has always a full allowance of atmospheric air; as the ethereal vapor, instead of being confined in the reservoir of the apparatus with no outlet but the air-hole and the mouth-piece, escapes freely into the room, and the patient breathes but little, if any, more of it than under ordinary circumstances. The sponge, too, has another advantage which, practically speaking, is of no small importance. This is, that, when the ether is given by a sponge, there is much less disposition to cough on the part of the patient than when it is given by the apparatus. This is owing to two circumstances: one, that ether inhaled from a sponge reaches the lungs mixed with a larger portion of atmospheric air than when it is inhaled from the apparatus; the other, that the sponge can be, at first, held at a little distance from the patient's mouth, and the ether thus entering the throat and lungs largely diluted with atmospheric air, the parts become gradually accustomed to the irritation which it produces, there is much less disposition to cough on the part of the patient, and less danger of producing spasm of the glottis, by which the wind-pipe might be closed. It can, too, be given more easily from the sponge than the apparatus where the patient is unwilling, or unable, to assist in the process, as in the case of operations on young children, and on the inferior animals in veterinary surgery. The simple sponge can also be easily cleansed, while that which remains in the apparatus must be frequently removed at the expense of considerable trouble, or there is danger of its becoming musty and offensive.

Inhaling ether from a sponge, therefore, may be considered as the most convenient, safest, and best method of taking it.

William T.G. Morton, in *Classics of Medicine and Surgery.* Comp. C.N.B. Camac. 1909. Reprint, New York: Dover, 1936, pp. 317–19.

## Document 10: Lister's Antiseptic Practices

*Joseph Lister, profoundly influenced by the finding of Louis Pasteur that air carries many "minute organisms," came to believe that these microorganisms were causing infection in wounds. He describes here his method of using antiseptic practices when treating wounds and injuries and the positive results.*

To prevent the occurrence of suppuration [pus discharge, a sign of infection] with all its attendant risks was an object manifestly desirable, but till lately apparently unattainable, since it seemed hopeless to attempt to exclude the oxygen which was universally regarded as the agent by which putrefaction was effected. But when it had been shown by the researches of Pasteur [Louis, 1822–1895] that the septic properties of the atmosphere depended not on the oxygen, or any gaseous constituent, but on minute organisms suspended in it, which owed their energy to their vitality, it occurred to me that decomposition in the injured part might be avoided without excluding the air, by applying as a dressing some material capable of destroying the life of the floating particles. Upon this principle I have based a practice of which I will now attempt to give a short account.

The material which I have employed is carbolic or phenic acid, a volatile organic compound, which appears to exercise a peculiarly destructive influence upon low forms of life, and hence is the most powerful antiseptic with which we are at present acquainted.

The first class of cases to which I applied it was that of compound fractures, in which the effects of decomposition in the injured part were especially striking and pernicious. The results have been such as to establish conclusively the great principle that all local inflammatory mischief and general febrile disturbances which follow severe injuries are due to the irritating and poisonous influence of decomposing blood or sloughs. For these evils are entirely avoided by the antiseptic treatment, so that limbs which would otherwise be unhesitatingly condemned to amputation may be retained, with confidence of the best results.

In conducting the treatment, the first object must be the destruction of any septic germs which may have been introduced into the wounds, either at the moment of the accident or during the time which has since elapsed. This is done by introducing the acid of full strength into all accessible recesses of the would by means of a piece of rag held in dressing forceps and dipped into the liquid. This I did not venture to do in the earlier cases; but experience has shown that the compound which carbolic acid forms with the blood, and also any portions of tissue killed by its caustic action, including even parts of the bone, are disposed of by absorption and organisation, provided they are afterwards kept from decomposing. We are thus enabled to employ the antiseptic treatment efficiently at a period after the occurrence of the injury at which it would otherwise probably fail. Thus I have now under my care, in Glasgow Infirmary, a boy who was admitted with compound fracture of the leg as late as eight and one-half hours after the accident, in whom, nevertheless, all local and constitutional disturbance was avoided by means of carbolic acid, and the bones were soundly united five weeks after his admission.

Joseph Lister, in *Classics of Medicine and Surgery*. Comp. C.N.B. Camac. 1909. Reprint, New York: Dover, 1936, pp. 9–10.

## Document 11: Learning More About X Rays

*After Wilhelm Röntgen's accidental discovery of X-ray images while working on another project in his laboratory, he began to experiment with the new rays. He tried to determine which substances could block X rays. Here are some of his laboratory notes.*

The most striking feature of this phenomenon is the fact that an active agent here passes through a black cardboard envelope, which is opaque to the visible and the ultraviolet rays of the sun or of the electric arc; an agent, too, which has the power of producing active fluorescence, Hence we may first investigate the question whether other bodies also possess this property.

We soon discover that all bodies are transparent to this agent, though in very different degrees. I proceed to give a few examples: Paper is very transparent; behind a bound book of about one thousand pages I saw the fluorescent screen light up brightly, the printer's ink offering scarcely a noticeable hindrance. In the same way the fluorescence appeared behind a double pack of cards; a single card held between the apparatus and the screen being almost unnoticeable to the eye. A single sheet of tinfoil is also scarcely perceptible, it is only after several layers have been placed over one another that their shadow is distinctly seen on the screen. Thick blocks of wood are also transparent, pine boards 2 or 3 cm.

thick absorbing only slightly. A plate of aluminium about 15 mm. thick, though it enfeebled the action seriously did not cause the fluorescence to disappear entirely. Sheets of hard rubber several centimetres thick still permit the rays to pass through them. Glass plates of equal thickness behave quite differently, according as they contain lead (flint-glass) or not; the former are much less transparent than the latter. If the hand be held between the discharge-tube and the screen, the darker shadow of the bones is seen within the slightly dark shadow-image of the hand itself.

Wilhelm Conrad Röntgen, in *Source Book of Medical History*. Comp. Logan Clendening. New York: Dover, 1942, p. 667.

## Document 12: The Future of AIDS Therapies

*David Ho, an AIDS researcher and physician, reveals his hopes for improved therapies for his AIDS patients, including the long-term possibility of a cure, in this 2001 interview with Phill Wilson, founder and executive director of the African Americans AIDS Policy and Training Institute.*

Wilson: From where you sit, where do you see the future of AIDS therapies going?

Ho: We now have 15 licensed drugs, basically. If we think back to the discovery of HIV as the start of this age, then it's almost one per year. Of course, most of them have been in the past five years or so, and I see that there are many more coming down the pipeline. I see a great deal of promise. I think there's no doubt people will continue to develop good drugs—and the drugs will have fewer side effects, will be easier to take, and hopefully will be cheaper. And as we do research in this area we see a lot of promising new agents much earlier than a typical patient might.

Ultimately, on the treatment side, we have to see if a cure is feasible. We don't know the answer to that; that's part of our research agenda—to address that issue, if it's even remotely possible. If it is, we ought to go all out for it.

Wilson: Actually, mentioning the word "cure" brings up a whole series of questions. One thing that comes to mind is the notion of "suppression." What does that mean—particularly to a person living with HIV?

Ho: Well, to me, suppression means using drugs to help control HIV replication so that we can bring it down to very low levels, so that the virus is no longer replicating at a rate that is damaging the immune system—that we halt the disease progression and in fact maybe even reverse the disease process. Not completely, but partially. That's what we have in some people today.

We want to get to, perhaps, a state where we could call it remission, where you control the virus so well that the remaining virus could be further controlled by the immune system. That's also a pretty noble objective. In such a state, if you were to stop the medication, the virus would not necessarily rebound right back. We [would] know it's still there, but it's there at very low levels—a low enough level that the immune system could handle it. That's a goal.

A cure would mean the virus is gone, period, and you could definitely stop the medication. The problem with this virus is that it integrates its way into the host, and therefore you have to wait until certain cells die off before you could have the cure. And all the lymphocytes that carry HIV are long-lived. The cure would require a long period of time—there's no doubt about that.

David Ho, interviewed by Phill Wilson, "Interview with Dr. David Ho," 2001. www.blackaids. org.

## Document 13: Learning About Human Genes

*Actor, writer, and director Alan Alda interviews Eric Lander, director of the Whitehead Institute for Genome Research in Cambridge, Massachusetts, about the potentials and challenges of studying the human genome. A genome is an organism's entire complement of genetic material. Lander describes how scientists collect and study human DNA in the hopes of unraveling its mysteries.*

LANDER: The sensible way to read a book is, you sit down at the beginning and you read sentence by sentence from chapter one to the end. I wish we could do that with the human genome. We can't come close. So instead, the nutty way that you read a genome is, you take the book, you tear it up into lots of pieces, you read the sentences, and then you paste them back together.

ALAN ALDA: But how do you know you've got it in some kind of logical sequence?

LANDER: Well, that's the challenge. You use a lot of information about the letters themselves, so you use a computer to put together sentences that could fit only with each other. But, half of the human genome is repeat sequences. This is the bane of our existence in putting it together. So we use only the unique bits. If you like jigsaw puzzles, you'll like the human genome. This is the world's top jigsaw puzzle with about 70 million pieces. And our goal is to get every one of the 3–5 billion letters right.

AA: Let me go back to the very beginning. What do you start with?

LANDER: The first thing you do is, you start with informed consent from the patient. That's very important. . . .

LANDER: Then you might take a blood sample. In your blood, there'll be lots of white blood cells that have DNA in them. There's DNA in every other cell in your body, but you're probably a little more willing to give blood up than a chunk of muscle or a hunk of brain or something like that. So, you take maybe 20 mils of blood out of somebody and you then spin the white blood cells down in a centrifuge, crack them open, and purify the DNA out of the blood cells. That gives you total human DNA. All 3 billion letters of the human genome are there. But we want to read each letter multiple times to be sure we get it right. Maybe 10 times? So we actually collect about 30 billion letters. We're reading about 60 million per day, just in this facility here. It's just a stunning rate. You could read the entire genetic code of some fungus like brewer's yeast in the course of a day here. You can read the bacteria in your gut in the course of a couple of hours here.

AA: Even the so-called "junk DNA." Everything gets read?

LANDER: Well, we had no good technical way to pick out the part of the DNA that contained the important information. More importantly, who's to say we knew what was the important information? It turns out to be far better to read it all. After all, evolution has spent 3.5 billion years getting this code together—who am I to say it's not worth reading the end of chromosome 16? So we're going to collect the whole thing, we read the whole thing, and make sense of it. It's going to take, I think, decades to make full sense out of the novel, but that's the case with any classic. You still read Shakespeare, and you get new meanings out of it. We're going to get a first pass read of the thing now, but I'm sure there are glosses on the text that are going to emerge over the course of the next centuries, and somebody's going to come back and recognize something in a sentence, and say, "we never realized it was telling us that!" It is text, it's great. And it is historical text.

Eric Lander, interviewed by Alan Alda, "The Gene Hunters," 2001. www.pbs.org.

## Document 14: Kary Mullis Invents the Polymerase Chain Reaction Technique

*In this interview from* Omni *magazine, scientist Kary Mullis describes how he was driving down the road when a flash of inspiration came to him. He envisioned a process by which he could amplify DNA sequences.*

*He won the Nobel Prize in 1993 for his technique, known as the polymerase chain reaction (PCR).*

*Omni:* What inspired PCR?

*Mullis:* I wasn't developing a way to amplify DNA at all. It was like I was randomly putting Tinkertoys together and finally made a structure and said, "You know what? If I turn this toy wheel over there, that damn thing would wind string." Driving up to Mendocino and thinking about an experiment to look at one particular letter of the genetic code, I designed a system in my mind. As I repaired the things I thought could go wrong with it, suddenly I generated something that If I did it over and over again would be PCR. It would go 2, 4, 8, 16, 32 . . . in 30 cycles make as many base pairs from one little region as I had in the whole genome! That was the eureka point. I said holy shit! By putting the triphosphates [DNA building blocks] in there myself, I could do this process over and over and amplify the DNA.

I slammed on the brakes and stopped by the side of the road to calculate it out. . . .

*Omni:* How does PCR work, starting with one oligonucleotide?

*Mullis:* I have suggested dropping that clumsy word from the dictionary. An oligonucleotide is a short piece of several nucleotides, of single-stranded DNA. In PCR it acts as a primer, anchoring itself onto a long, single strand of DNA and getting elongated by the polymerase, the enzyme molecule. The polymerase copies the DNA by snatching these little monomers [DNA constituents) out of the solution and stuffing them in at the right place on the oligonucleotide. The polymerase copies down the information from the long strand. With PCR, the first copy you make has one end defined, so it can't get elongated. During the next cycle, the other end is closed off, too, so the polymerase just copies the target section of DNA you want. Then in cycles after that, only the defined DNA piece will be copied. It can be copied forever.

PCR detects a very, very small amount of some sequence interspersed in a whole bunch of similar sequences. Then PCR makes so much of the sequence, you end up with something that is almost all what you're interested in. It purifies as it amplifies because it only amplifies one thing. It's like a radio amplifying only one wavelength amid all that are coming in.

A. Liversidge, and F. Collin, "Kary Mullis," *Omni*, vol. 14, no. 7, April 1992.

# Glossary

**acupuncture:** Ancient Chinese medical practice involving insertion of hair-thin needles into select points in the human body.

**acute, infectious disease:** Diseases that are infectious and that can occur as epidemics and are often associated with poverty, poor living conditions, and inadequate medical care. Examples are cholera and malaria. Some infectious diseases, such as influenza, spread so easily that all societies are affected, regardless of affluence and standards of living.

**AIDS (acquired immunodeficiency syndrome):** A disease caused by the human immunodeficiency virus (HIV) that attacks the human immune system and makes the person vulnerable to lethal infections.

**allele:** Alternate forms of a gene.

**amniocentesis:** Determining genetic abnormalities in a fetus by sampling and testing amniotic fluid in the uterus surrounding the fetus.

**anatomy:** The study of body structures, plant or animal.

**blood groups:** Human blood can be categorized or "typed" into various groups, A, B, and O being the most common. Donors and recipients for blood transfusions must be compatible. If not, the recipient will develop antibodies against the donor's blood and the donated blood cells will clump together. Death can result.

**carrier:** A person who is genetically heterozygous (has two different gene alleles for a genetic characteristic) with one normal and one potentially harmful allele. The potentially harmful allele can be passed on to a descendant, although the carrier himself/herself will not display any sign of the characteristic.

**chemotherapy:** Using specific chemical compounds (drugs) to treat specific diseases.

**chorionic villus sampling (CVS):** Detecting genetic and congenital defects in a fetus by sampling and analyzing the placenta.

**chronic, degenerative disease:** Chronic diseases, such as cancer and heart disease, are associated with older persons who live in the developed, wealthier nations where the human life span has been extended.

**CT (computerized tomography):** Cross-sectional images of the body from many angles captured by X rays; the data are collected by computers and images are constructed from the data.

**DNA (deoxyribonucleic acid):** A nucleic acid molecule carrying genetic information that directs the synthesis of proteins. Capable of self-replication, a DNA molecule is structured as a double-stranded helix.

**drug resistance:** Microorganisms that mutate and evolve to the point that they are no longer vulnerable to antibiotic drugs.

**epidemiological transition:** A change over time in the pattern of predominant illness in a culture, from infectious disease to chronic and degenerative disease.

**epidemiology:** A branch of medicine that studies epidemics, how diseases start and from where, how they are transmitted, and how to stop them.

**ether:** A chemical compound that induces unconsciousness or insensibility in those who breathe it as a vapor. Used as a surgical anesthetic to prevent pain.

**eugenics:** A movement advocating the selective breeding of organisms, most notably human beings, in hopes of creating a superior species.

**genome:** The genetic material of an organism; the complete set of genes.

**germ theory of disease:** The theory that disease is caused by microorganisms.

**heterozygotes:** Individuals with a normal phenotype (physical, physiological traits) but who have two different gene alleles—one normal and one recessive and potentially harmful.

**hirudin:** A chemical that prevents coagulation of blood, discovered in the saliva of leeches.

**HIV (human immunodeficiency virus):** The virus that causes AIDS.

**Human Genome Project:** A cooperative effort of scientists to map and sequence the DNA of the human genome.

**insect vector:** Insects such as mosquitoes or ticks that carry disease-causing microorganisms.

**insulin:** A hormone that promotes the uptake of glucose acquired from food by body cells and other metabolic functions. Individuals with the disease diabetes lack sufficient levels of insulin or have cells that do not use insulin properly.

**Koch's postulates:** Four criteria developed by Robert Koch to determine the cause of an infectious disease.

**lysozymes:** Enzymes found in human tears, saliva, and perspiration that can destroy the cell walls of invading bacteria.

**major histocompatibility complex (MCH):** A large set of antigens (substances that trigger immune response) on the surface of cells that may lead to the rejection of transplanted tissues and organs.

**morbidity:** Levels of disease or accidents in a population.

**mortality:** Number of deaths in a population.

**MRI (magnetic resonance imaging):** Magnets align nuclei in the hydrogen molecules of water found in tissues, then pulses of radio waves are sent through the nuclei. The hydrogen nuclei are knocked out of alignment, and as they move back into alignment, they give out faint radio waves that are collected by computers. This constructs an image of soft tissues in the body.

**neuron:** A nerve cell

**oral contraceptives:** Pills taken by mouth that suppress ovulation in women and, in so doing, prevent pregnancy.

**pasteurization:** Raising food products (milk, cheese) to high temperatures to kill microorganisms in the food that might cause spoilage or disease in humans. This technique was developed by Louis Pasteur.

**PCR (polymerase chain reaction):** A laboratory technique developed to amplify DNA chains, which are then used in addition to tests to identify the organism from which the DNA originally came. The PCR technique makes DNA fingerprinting possible as well as the identification of organisms that cause human disease.

**pedigree:** The genetic history of a family and each individual in that family.

**phenylketonuria:** A genetic metabolic disorder. By testing the newborn for this disorder, treatment can begin immediately and prevent damage to the infant.

**salicylate:** A chemical compound that occurs naturally in certain plants, such as willows, that reduces pain and fever. Aspirin was created from salicylic acid, a form of salicylate.

**trepanation:** Ancient Neolithic people (and some contemporary primitive people) bored holes in a patient's skull to relieve pain and perhaps to allow the escape of evil spirits.

**vaccination:** Introduction of dead or inactivated infectious material into a person to confer immunity. Early smallpox vaccinations involved introduction of cowpox material.

**variolation:** An early method of vaccination by introducing infected material into a healthy person to produce immunity.

# Chronology

**8000**
In the Neolithic era (New Stone Age), holes are drilled into a patient's skull to relieve pain and perhaps allow evil spirits to escape.

**2700–2600**
Imhotep practices medicine in Egypt, and Chinese emperor Huangdi is credited for practicing acupuncture and other forms of Chinese medicine.

**1000**
In Babylon, *The Treatise of Medical Diagnosis and Prognosis* is published on clay tablets. It describes three thousand illnesses.

**750**
Eye surgery to remove cataracts on the lens is performed by Susrutu, a Hindu surgeon in India.

**400**
Called "the Father of Medicine," Greek physician Hippocrates (460–370 B.C.) teaches that illness is caused by imbalances in body "humors" and calls for careful observation of the patient to determine the cause of illness.

**A.D.**

**129–216**
Galen, a Greek physician, writes three books, one of which is *On the Movement of the Heart and Lungs*. He travels to Rome and practices medicine there as well as in his home of Pergamon in Asia Minor. His teachings influence Western medicine for over one thousand years.

**ca. 1000**
Avicenna (980–1037), a Persian physician also known as Ibn Sina, writes many works on medicine, including the *Canon of Medicine*.

**1346–1353**
An epidemic of the plague, called the Black Death, devastates Asia and Europe and kills millions.

**1543**

Andreas Vesalius publishes *De Corporis Human (The Fabric of the Human Body)*, a profusely illustrated book of human anatomy. Vesalius had conducted extensive anatomical dissections on human bodies, and his published findings proved wrong many of the Greek physician Galen's teachings about anatomy. Vesalius is considered "the Father of Modern Anatomy."

**1628**

English physician William Harvey describes the circulation of blood through the human body in his book *Anatomical Study of the Motion of the Heart and Blood in Animals*.

**1683**

Antoni van Leeuwenhoek observes and describes bacteria using a microscope.

**1720**

Smallpox inoculation from infected material from smallpox pustules is introduced into England by Mary Wortley Montagu.

**1753**

Scottish surgeon James Lind suspects diet as the reason why sailors on long sea voyages suffer from diseases such as scurvy. He feeds oranges and lemons to one group of sailors, and they are cured of scurvy.

**1761**

Italian physician Giovanni Morgagni establishes the science of pathology when he publishes *De Sedibus et Causis Morborum (On the Seat and Causes of Disease)*, in which he describes findings from autopsies and analyzes the course of disease that led to death.

**1798**

English physician Edward Jenner begins to vaccinate individuals against the smallpox disease by infecting them with a much less serious disease, cowpox.

**1816**

French physician René Laënnec invents the stethoscope and in 1835 publishes *A Treatis of Diseases of the Chest and Mediate Auscultation*.

**1818**

British physician James Blundell successfully performs the first blood transfusion on a woman who is hemorrhaging after giving birth. She receives several ounces of her husband's blood.

**1842**
American physician Crawford Long performs surgery on a patient using ether as an anesthesia.

**1846**
American dentist William Morton anesthetizes a patient using ether and performs surgery on the unconscious patient's jaw.

**1847**
Austrian physician Ignaz Semmelweis reduces the number of postchildbirth deaths in women after instituting a practice of hand washing with a chlorine solution. Mortality drops dramatically.

**1854**
John Snow, a British physician, discovers during an epidemic that cholera is transmitted by a contaminated water supply.

**1857**
French scientist Louis Pasteur introduces the "germ theory of disease" and demonstrates that bacteria cause specific diseases in plants and humans.

**1858**
German pathologist Rudolf Virchow asserts that cells are formed from other cells.

**1865**
English surgeon Joseph Lister develops the germ theory of disease introduced by Louis Pasteur. He cleanses wounds, his hands, and surgical instruments with an antiseptic solution, and deaths from infection drop immediately.

**1866**
Austrian monk Gregor Mendel conducts extensive experiments on heredity in garden peas. He discovers patterns and mathematical laws governing inheritance.

**1895**
German physicist Wilhelm Röntgen discovers X rays while conducting experiments in his laboratory.

**1897**
Mosquitoes are identified as the carriers of a parasite that causes malaria.

**1899**
Aspirin is introduced by the Bayer Company in Germany.

**1900**
Mosquitoes are identified as the carriers of a parasite that causes yellow fever.

**1901**
Austrian physician Karl Landsteiner discovers the four major blood groups in humans: A, B, O, and AB.

**1902**
Human hormones are isolated and identified by British physiologists William Maddock Bayliss and Ernest Starling.

**1903**
Dutch physiologist Willem Einthoven invents the electrocardiograph (ECG), which can record electrical impulses of the heart.

**1906**
German surgeon Eduard Zirm successfully transplants a cornea from the eye of one person to another. British physician Frederick G. Hopkins identifies substances necessary for the body to properly use proteins; the substances are called vitamins.

**1909**
The body louse and the rat flea are discovered to be carriers of the microorganism that causes typhus.

**1912**
American neurosurgeon Harvey Cushing discovers the role of the pituitary gland in controlling human growth.

**1921**
Canadian scientists Frederick Banting and Charles Best discover and isolate insulin as a treatment for diabetes. They experiment with insulin and save the life of a dying diabetic patient.

**1924**
German psychiatrist Hans Berger invents the electroencephalogram (EEG) to measure brain waves.

**1928**
Scottish physician Alexander Fleming discovers that a mold in the laboratory kills bacteria. Penicillin is later produced from the mold.

**1931**
German engineer Ernst Ruska designs the electron microscope that is up to 1 million times stronger than light microscopes. Viruses are visible for the first time.

**1944**
The first open-heart surgery is performed by American physician Alfred Blalock.

**1949**
French physician Henri Laborit first notices that a class of drugs that includes chlorpromazine are useful in calming mentally ill patients. He initiates the use of chemotherapy to treat the mentally ill.

**1953**
The DNA structure is accurately modeled for the first time by James Watson and Francis Crick. The model is based on crucial information in X-ray diffraction photos made by Rosalind Franklin.

**1954**
American physician Jonas Salk develops a vaccine for polio.

**1960**
Oral contraceptives ("the Pill") are approved by the U.S. Food and Drug Administration (FDA).

**1967**
British engineer Godfrey N. Hounsfield develops the computerized axial tomography (CAT) scanner; this medical imaging tool creates multiple cross-section X rays of the body's internal organs; CAT scanners become available in hospitals in 1972. Christiaan Barnard, a South African surgeon, successfully transplants a human heart into an ill person.

**1973**
Herbert Boyer and Stanley Cohen invent a technique to clone DNA, making possible the production of synthetic hormones, including insulin for diabetic patients.

**1974**
American physician Raymond Damadian patents his invention, the magnetic resonance imaging (MRI) device, which can be used to view internal soft tissues.

**1979**
Smallpox is eradicated from the world. A few laboratories retain samples of the virus.

**1986**
American scientist Kary Mullis develops the polymerase chain re-

action (PCR) technique for amplifying DNA. PCR makes possible identification of the DNA in emerging diseases and for identifying DNA left at crime scenes.

## 1995
American physician David Ho and colleagues demonstrate that, contrary to conventional medical wisdom, HIV (the virus that causes AIDS), replicates rapidly immediately after infecting a person's body. Ho's discovery leads to a major change in the way patients are treated, extending the lives of thousands of AIDS sufferers.

## 2003
Scientists announce that the human genome has been 99.9 percent mapped.

# For Further Research

**Books and Periodicals**

Hervé Bazin, *The Eradication of Smallpox*. San Diego, CA: Academic, 2000.

William Bulloch, *The History of Bacteriology*. Oxford, UK: Oxford University Press, 1938.

C.N.B. Camac, comp., *Classics of Medicine and Surgery*. New York: Dover, 1909.

Neil A. Campbell, Jane B. Reece, and Lawrence G. Mitchell, *Biology*. 5th ed. Menlo Park, CA: Benjamin/Cummings, 1999.

Logan Clendening, comp., *Source Book of Medical History*. New York: Dover, 1942.

M.H. Armstrong Davidson, *The Evolution of Anaesthesia*. Baltimore: Williams & Wilkins, 1965.

Clifford Dobell, *Antony van Leeuwenhoek and His "Little Animals."* New York: Dover, 1932.

Martin Duke, *The Development of Medical Techniques and Treatments: From Leeches to Heart Surgery*. Madison, CT: International Universities Press, 1991.

Graham Farmelo, "The Discovery of X-Rays," *Scientific American*, November 1995.

Richard B. Fisher, *Edward Jenner: 1749–1823*. London: André Deutsch, 1991.

Meyer Friedman and Gerald W. Friedland, *Medicine's 10 Greatest Discoveries*. New Haven, CT: Yale University Press, 1998.

John R. Green, *Medical History for Students*. Springfield, IL: Charles C. Thomas, 1968.

Gladys L. Hobby, *Penicillin: Meeting the Challenge*. New Haven, CT: Yale University Press, 1985.

Dominique Hoizey and Marie-Joseph Hoizey, *A History of Chinese Medicine*. Trans. Paul Bailey. Edinburgh, Scotland: Edinburgh University Press, 1993.

Robert P. Hudson, *Disease and Its Control: The Shaping of Modern Thought.* Westport, CT: Greenwood, 1983.

Brian Inglis, *A History of Medicine.* Cleveland: World, 1965.

Bettyann Holtzmann Kevles, *Naked to the Bone: Medical Imaging in the Twentieth Century.* New Brunswick, NJ: Rutgers University Press, 1997.

James Le Fanu, *The Rise and Fall of Modern Medicine.* New York: Carroll & Graf, 1999.

Steven Lehrer, *Explorers of the Body.* Garden City, NY: Doubleday, 1979.

Irvine Loudon, *Western Medicine: An Illustrated History.* Oxford, UK: Oxford University Press, 1997.

Ralph H. Major, *History of Medicine.* Springfield, IL: Charles C. Thomas, 1954.

Roberto Margotta, *The History of Medicine.* New York: Smithmark, 1996.

Lara V. Marks, *Sexual Chemistry: A History of the Contraceptive Pill.* New Haven, CT: Yale University Press, 2001.

Maoshing Ni, *The Yellow Emperor's Classic of Medicine.* Boston: Shambhala, 1995.

Sherwin B. Nuland, *Doctors: the Biography of Medicine.* New York: Alfred A. Knopf, 1988.

C.D. O'Malley, *Andreas Vesalius of Brussels, 1514–1564.* Berkeley and Los Angeles: University of California Press, 1964.

Park, Davis & Company, *Great Moments in Medicine.* Detroit: Northwood Institute Press, 1966.

Roy Porter, "The Rise and Fall of the Age of Miracles," *History Today,* November 1996.

Roy Porter, ed., *Cambridge Illustrated History of Medicine.* Cambridge, UK: Cambridge University Press, 1996.

Stanley Joel Reiser, *Medicine and the Reign of Technology.* Cambridge, UK: Cambridge University Press, 1978.

Philip Rhodes, *An Outline History of Medicine.* London: Butterworths, 1985.

Charlotte Roberts and Keith Manchester, *The Archaeology of Disease.* 2nd ed. Ithaca, NY: Cornell University Press, 1995.

Charles E. Rosenberg, *Explaining Epidemics*. Cambridge, UK: Cambridge University Press 1992.

John Bertrand de Cusance Morant Saunders and Charles D. O'Malley, *The Illustrations from the Works of Andreas Vesalius of Brussels*. New York: Dover, 1950.

John Galbraith Simmons, *Doctors and Discoveries: Lives That Created Today's Medicine*. Boston: Houghton Mifflin, 2002.

Theodore L. Sourkes, *Nobel Prize Winners in Medicine and Physiology, 1901–1965*. London: Abelard-Schuman, 1966.

Farokh Erach Udwadia, *Man and Medicine: A History*. Oxford, UK: Oxford University Press, 2000.

Gerhard Venzmer, *Five Thousand Years of Medicine*. New York: Taplinger, 1968.

James D. Watson, *The Double Helix*. New York: Atheneum, 1968.

Andrew Wear, ed., *Medicine in Society: Historical Essays*. Cambridge, UK: Cambridge University Press, 1992.

**Websites**

American Experience: The Pill, www.pbs.org/wgbh/amex/pill. Based on a Public Broadcasting Service television program, this site covers the social aspects of the introduction of contraceptives, including interviews with individual women.

History of Medicine, www.medhelpnet.com/medhist1.html. This site is a chronological presentation of major medical innovations, beginning in 8000 B.C. with trepanning and ending in 1995 with information about a new blood substitute.

History of the Health Sciences Section, Medical Library Association, www.mlahss.org/histlink.htm. This website offers an extensive list of links to sites on the history of medicine, including the history of specific diseases, biographies of persons in medicine, the history of childbirth, the history of dentistry, and medical practices in specific time periods such as the U.S. Civil War. This is a comprehensive site and includes a link to "How to Write a Medical History Paper."

Medicine Through Time, www.bbc.co.uk/education/medicine. This is an interactive website on the history of medicine from prehistoric to modern times. It includes live chats with visitors to the site, fantasy chats with Louis Pasteur and Robert Koch, and a gory story from the history of medicine.

National Institutes of Health, Resources on Bioethics, www.nih. gov/sigs/bioethics/index.html. This site contains links to many sites on the topic of ethics in medicine and genetics.

Red-Gold: The Story of Blood, www.pbs.org/wnet/redgold. Basic information, history, and innovations having to do with human blood are provided by the site.

What You Need to Know About Inventors, http://inventors.about. com/library/inventors/blmedical.htm. This site offers links to short articles on a variety of topics in medical history.

# Index